Upper Crust

Editor: Ryma Bouzid
Illustrations: Alice Licata
Design: Delphine Delastre

English Edition
Editorial Director: Kate Mascaro
Editor: Helen Adedotun
Editorial Coordination and Proofreading: Penelope Isaac
Translation from the French by Kate Robinson (pages 9–199 and interviews) and Ansley Evans (recipes)
Copyediting: Carey Jones
Typesetting: Alice Leroy
Production: Christelle Lemonnier and Louisa Morard
Color Separation: IGS, L'Isle-d'Espagnac
Printed in China by Toppan Leefung

Originally published in French as *Encyclopédie du Pain Maison*
© Flammarion, S.A., Paris, 2019

English-language edition
© Flammarion, S.A., Paris, 2021

editions.flammarion.com

21 22 23 3 2 1

ISBN: 978-2-08-151707-3

Legal Deposit: 09/2021

MARIE-LAURE FRÉCHET

Photography by **Valérie Lhomme** • Photo Styling by **Bérengère Abraham**

Upper Crust
HOMEMADE BREAD
THE **FRENCH** WAY

Flammarion

CONTENTS

RECIPES

Why Make Your Own Bread?

Making bread is an age-old craft. The ultimate everyday food, and symbolic in many respects, bread has been so mistreated by our modern ways and recast as a technological, even industrial product, that it has become suspect. Gluten, the extraordinary and misunderstood network that gives bread its structure, seems to have become public enemy number one.

Yet bread is but a reflection of the living world—generous like the grains that comprise it, and full of tremendous energy like the fermentation that transforms those grains.

To make superior bread is to roll up your sleeves and rediscover the flavor and quality of a product now crafted only by artisans driven by a love for what they do. If you're lucky, there's an artisanal bakery in your neighborhood. Let's be honest: you'll have a hard time matching the artisan baker's expertise, acquired through years of experience. But it's not a competition; making bread is not an arduous undertaking. This book is a lesson in making your own bread—homemade bread, or *pain de ménage* as the French used to say—just as you would bake a cake or cook dinner at home: a treat for yourself and those around you. This is "amateur" bread in the etymological sense of the word—made by a "devotee" or an "admirer."

MAKING YOUR OWN BREAD

"How do you make country bread in the city?" muses Roland Feuillas, standing at the foot of his mill in the small village of Cucugnan, in Corbières in southern France. Joking aside, this baker, for whom bread is a way of life more than a profession, teaches us that there is more to bread than recipes. Of course, this book includes recipes, and no doubt you'll be tempted to make the classic breads that have forged the reputation of France's baking tradition, as well as other breads found around the world. The recipes will help you to gradually master essential methods and techniques. You will also discover what bread has to teach you: baking is a lesson in humility. With each new batch, the baker stands before the oven and assesses their work under the unpredictable influence of nature: flour quality, the weather, and, of course, activity in the yeast and bacteria added to the dough. "Cooking takes instinct, *pâtisserie* takes precision, and baking takes sensitivity," says Alex Croquet, a Lille-based baker passionate about levain, or sourdough, fermentation. Over time, you too will learn to use your observation, experience, and senses to make bread that suits you, rather than bread that adheres to an arbitrary standard. You'll learn to free yourself (a little) from the scale, the timer, and the thermometer, to trust your own judgement, and perhaps even come up with something new. After all, there's no one good way to make bread, but many ways to make good bread.

MAKING GOOD BREAD

"Bread is generous," wrote Lionel Poilâne, thirty years ago, in his *Guide de l'Amateur du Pain* (Bread Lover's Guide). Irritated by the "normalization" he felt he was often forced into, this Parisian baker initiated a return to rustic, artisan bread in the 1980s, and rejected the tyranny of pseudo-tradition and cardinal rules when it came to baking. He encouraged people to simply smell bread to learn how to recognize a good loaf.

Good bread is made with good ingredients—especially good flour, which should be organic at the very least, milled to preserve nutritional quality, and free of additives of any kind. Bread made using sourdough fermentation has a wider range of flavors, is easier to digest, and has a longer shelf life. This is the method we recommend, and you'll discover that it isn't any more complicated than using baker's yeast—in fact, quite the opposite.

The recipes in this book were all created in a home kitchen, with an ordinary oven. So don't blame your oven (though a good one is priceless) if you're unsatisfied with your initial attempts. A bread that you consider a failure, but that is made with carefully chosen ingredients and according to good bread-making principles, will always be better than most bread you'll find in stores.

SHARING YOUR BREAD

Good bread should be shared at the table, to be eaten with a simple dish or a grand feast. But it should also be shared with a community of amateur bakers—and why not professionals? Social networks are a good tool to create a network of "bread buddies" who will be excited to share recipes and tips. A taste for good bread is an acquired trait. Not only will you inform your friends and family of the virtues of properly made bread, but you'll probably make them want to adopt their own sourdough starter.

"ADVICE FOR GOOD HOUSEWIVES"

Antoine Augustin Parmentier is renowned for being a vocal promoter of the potato, but it is a lesser-known fact that this pharmacist, agronomist, and nutritionist was very interested in bread. He wrote some twenty or so books and articles on grains, flour, and bread making. In 1777, he published *Avis aux Bonnes Ménagères des Villes et des Campagnes* (Advice for Good Urban and Rural Housewives). Baker's yeast had just become available in France, but he encouraged homemakers to continue making bread using sourdough starter, or *levain*, which he described as "extremely nourishing and of a digestibility far more beneficial to health." He also provided advice on how to choose a good flour, refresh the starter, and properly knead the dough. Three centuries later, his recommendations can still be followed almost to the letter.

BREAD BASICS

—

Bread:
Past and Present
—

Flour, salt, and water: the age-old recipe for bread. But over time, this recipe and the ingredients themselves have changed. White bread has not always been the norm—far from it. Ironically, we're now (re)discovering that it's also not the best kind of bread to eat.

PREHISTORY: THE DISCOVERY OF GRAIN

Homo erectus began to master fire around 700,000 BCE by maintaining natural hearth fires, although much older traces have been found that indicate our ancestors ate a diet of cooked foods. In Europe, Neanderthals domesticated fire 135,000 years ago. Around 35,000 BCE, *Homo sapiens sapiens* adapted fire for multiple uses, including cooking, which led to the invention of the first ovens. Grain—emmer wheat, barley, or sorghum—was harvested when plants spontaneously released their seeds. During the Neolithic period, humans began storing grain, which enabled them to eat a porridge of stone-ground wild grains all year long. Millet and sorghum porridges, which are still consumed in parts of Africa today, hark back to agriculture's emergence in the Middle East around 8,000 BCE.

Einkorn, emmer wheat, and barley were domesticated and gradually began to be cultivated throughout the Mediterranean basin. Hybridization of several different grasses led to the emergence of common or bread wheat (*Triticum aestivum*) around 6,000 BCE.

ANTIQUITY: THE BIRTH OF BREAD

The Egyptians discovered leavened bread around 3,000 BCE, most likely aided by the fertile water of the Nile and its nutrient-rich silt. They perfected milling techniques such as using millstones and sifting flour through papyrus, and baked bread in earthenware pots. Bread was sacred to the Egyptians: it was sent with the pharaoh into his tomb and fed the laborers who constructed the Pyramids.

The Greeks imported bread-making techniques from Egypt. The poor and slaves had to make do with unleavened barley bread known as *maza*, while a fermented bread made with mead, honey, or fruit was served at feasts.

Baking flourished under the Romans and became a profession, with the first bakers' guild formed in 168 BCE. Bread broke out of the domestic sphere and the first bakeries, owned by freed slaves, opened in Rome, where a large variety of bread could be found, including a rye bread eaten with oysters (*panis ostrarium*). The expression *"panem et circenses"* ("bread and circuses"), coined by the poet Juvenal, conveys the importance of bread in maintaining social harmony.

The Celts also began making bread, and the people of Gaul, in what is now France, who cultivated rye, barley, oats, and wheat, made a lighter bread by adding foam they skimmed off beer.

After the birth of Jesus in Bethlehem (which means "house of bread" in Hebrew), bread became the sacred symbol of Christianity.

MIDDLE AGES: BREAD AND POWER

In what is now present-day France, bread became a staple food dominated by feudal power. Mills and ovens belonged to lords, and serfs were obliged to pay a tax known as a *droit de banalité* to use them. Bread making, which had hitherto taken place mainly in the home, turned into a profession. *Talmeliers* (those who sifted or "bolted" flours) controlled flour production until King Philippe Augustus allowed them to have their own ovens, at which time they became *panetiers*, then, in 1250, *boulengers* (from the French *boule:* the rounds of bread they made), when the *droit de banalité* was abolished. Bakers were united in a guild, and were closely supervised by an officer of the crown known as the *Grand Panetier*.

Most importantly, bread became an economic indicator susceptible to periods of scarcity. While the nobility and clergy enjoyed many kinds of sophisticated breads, the poor subsisted on black bread. In times of famine, it became a survival loaf mixed with straw, clay, acorns, or ferns.

THE FRENCH REVOLUTION: BETTER BREAD FOR ALL

In 1775, the Flour War broke out in France, marked by a wave of riots following increases in the price of grain and bread. In 1789, starving people stormed the Bastille, convinced that wheat was stored there. The revolutionaries abolished the guild system and imposed the *pain de l'Égalité* ("equality bread"): the same loaf for everyone, rich and poor, made of wheat and rye mixed with bran. The agronomists of the Enlightenment contributed to technological improvements in bread making during this period. Several books focused on how to make bread, particularly the work of pharmacist and agronomist Antoine Augustin Parmentier.

In 1790, the salt tax known as the *gabelle* was abolished, which encouraged the use of salt in baking, and the emergence of breweries reinitiated the use of brewer's yeast in bread making.

THE NINETEENTH CENTURY: BREAD MAKING MEETS TECHNOLOGY

In 1837, Austrian businessman August Zang established a bakery in Paris and introduced the Viennese technique of bread making using yeast-leavened dough. In 1857, Louis Pasteur explained the principle of fermentation and identified the strain of yeast responsible—*Saccharomyces cerevisiae*—paving the way for cultivation. In 1872, Baron Fould-Springer created the first yeast production factory, followed by Lesaffre, currently the world leader. Despite the appearance of the first mechanical kneading machines, the baker's trade remained incredibly difficult. The baker's assistant (the *geindre*, from the French word for "groan" or "lament") was often covered in flour dust and relied on physical strength.

TWENTIETH CENTURY: FROM WAR BREAD TO INDUSTRIAL BREAD

During World War I, flour and bread were rationed in France. "Luxury" or "fancy" breads were forbidden and a gray "national loaf" was imposed. Bread was never formally rationed in the United Kingdom; instead a Wheat Commission was formed to ensure an adequate bread supply, known as War Bread, and avoid the need for rationing. In the trenches, the Germans were given *Kriegskartoffelbrot* (known as K.K. bread): a war bread made from potatoes. A decree permitting the reintroduction of white bread was passed on March 27, 1919.

During World War II, bread was not rationed in the United States, but Americans were encouraged to self-ration in order to maintain food supplies at home and on the front. At this time, the French also consumed black bread. In the 1950s, a new "intensified" kneading technique, which resulted in a white dough, responded to demands from consumers fed up with shortages—but only for a time. Industrialized grain production, flour milling, and eventually the bread-making profession itself gradually lowered the quality of French bread to the extent that, in 1993, a decree was announced establishing guidelines for "traditional French bread."

In 1998, a law was passed in France to regulate the use of the official terms *boulangerie* (bakery) and *boulanger* (baker), henceforth reserved for professionals who, "using selected ingredients, personally knead, proof, shape, and bake their loaves on the premises where they are sold to the end consumer; products cannot be frozen or deep frozen at any stage of production or sale."

THE TWENTY-FIRST CENTURY: WHAT'S IN STORE FOR BREAD?

A return to artisan bread making began thirty years ago in Europe and the United States. *Paysans boulangers*—farm-to-loaf bakers who grow, harvest, and mill their own grain in addition to making bread—reintroduced nutritious heritage grains and levain-based fermentation to bread making. But instead of being nostalgic for the "bread of yore," which, over the centuries, has never attained the quality of our modern bread, we can (and must) envision a new bread that defies standardization—healthier, more flavorful bread that is more respectful of the biodiversity it should represent.

FROM FLATBREAD TO LOAF

The earliest breads were flat: first, because the grains used were low in gluten, and second, because heat must be contained in order for bread to rise during baking. It wasn't until the invention of ovens and other systems allowing bread to be baked in a container, such as a clay vessel, that leavening could take place. Finally, controlled fermentation made it possible to obtain loftier breads. However, flatbreads such as tortillas, pitas, and *chapati* are still found throughout the world today.

Bread and Nutrition

Bread has long been considered a staple food and a symbol of human life and labor. During times of famine, the people demanded bread, and bread was distributed to mollify the masses. Bread also embodies spiritual traditions.

In France, in the early twentieth century, the average person consumed over 2 lb. (almost 1 kg) of bread each day. Originally a staple of the French diet, bread was gradually relegated to play a secondary role at meals, except breakfast, where it still holds its own against cornflakes and other industrial cereals. By the 1920s, Americans had already acquired a taste for factory-made bread, which many ate at their midday meal. The most popular brand was Wonder Bread, which became an emblem of the American culinary landscape for generations. US consumption of white bread has since fallen in favor of whole-grain varieties, tortillas, and flatbreads, and European pastries have gained a place at the table. However, Americans still consume far less bread than Europeans: the average annual bread consumption per capita in Europe is between 95 and 211 lb. (43–96 kg) compared to 37 lb. (17 kg) in the United States.

Over the last twenty years, bread has become suspect from a nutritional standpoint. As bread becomes a product of technological processes (and less natural as a result) and a host of "anti" movements against gluten, carbs, and other food emerge, is there anything good to be said about bread?

BREAD AND GLYCEMIC INDEX

Bread is roughly half complex carbohydrates, which are the human metabolism's main source of energy. Digesting them is a several-stage process: enzymes must break down (or hydrolyze) molecules to form smaller-sized carbohydrates—mono- or di-saccharides—that can be assimilated by the intestines. Consuming complex carbohydrates tends to result in a less significant increase in blood sugar and insulin secretion than ingesting simple carbohydrates like glucose or sucrose (table sugar). Glycemic index (GI) measures a food's capacity to increase blood sugar levels, giving us the notion of fast- and slow-burning sugars. A GI of less than 55 is considered low, 55 to 70 moderate, and over 70 high. The higher a food's glycemic index, the more it increases blood sugar. This measurement is especially important for those living with diabetes. It varies by bread type: an ordinary baguette has a GI of 95 (its starch is considered a fast-burning sugar), white sandwich bread a GI of 70, light whole wheat bread a GI of 65, and dark (or 100 percent) whole wheat bread a GI of 49 (slow-burning sugar). There is a clear correlation between a food's glycemic index and the feeling of satiety it produces: ounce for ounce, a slice of whole wheat bread at breakfast will keep you feeling full longer than a slice of baguette.

BREAD AND NUTRIENTS

In addition to carbohydrates, bread contains vegetable proteins (about 8 percent) and mineral salts. While it generally contains little fat, this may vary with the addition of olive oil, butter, nuts, or milk (for example, in enriched breads like *pain de mie* or *pain viennois*).

Vitamin content, mainly B and E vitamins, varies by bread type. White bread, made with highly refined flour, has a vitamin content two to three times lower than that of whole wheat bread. The nearly intact kernel (or berry) of whole grains, before the germ and outer layer (called bran) are removed, contains a high concentration of vitamins, minerals, and fiber. Each grain (wheat, rye, spelt, etc.) has different nutritional qualities.

Like any food, bread cannot be considered for its nutrients alone, since not all of them are bioavailable, meaning the body cannot immediately absorb them: they interact with each other (but also with nutrients present in other foods) within a "food matrix" whose physicochemical properties enable or prevent absorption of nutrients by the body via the digestive tract. So it's difficult to say that consuming a certain quantity of bread has specific health effects. Bread consumption should instead be considered from a qualitative perspective that includes ingredients and bread-making technique, and within the context of a balanced diet.

IS PHYTIC ACID AN ANTI-NUTRIENT?

Phytic acid, also known as myo-inositol hexakisphosphate, is a phosphorylated molecule naturally present in the bran layer of many cereals and legumes. It merges through biochemical fusion with minerals and trace elements present in chewed food to form insoluble salts called phytates. Phytic acid has been identified as a potential inhibitor of iron and zinc bioavailability, but certain biological mechanisms reduce this effect: long fermentation with levain cultures activates enzymes present in grain (called phytases) that break down phytic acid, while a portion of phytic acid is also destroyed during germination.

BREAD AND CALORIES

Bread provides an average of 250 calories per 3½ oz. (100 g), with whole wheat bread at around 240 calories and white bread at around 255 calories. The calorie is a unit of measure that expresses the quantity of heat released by a food during combustion. It was long thought that all calories are equal, and that once the body consumes enough to meet its energy needs, anything extra is unnecessary and leads to excess weight gain.

Recent studies have shown, however, that this is not the case; a "fat" calorie does not provoke the same metabolic response as a "sugar" calorie. In other words, all calories are not equal within the calorie's matrix environment; for example, slow- and fast-burning sugars with the same caloric value do not produce the same physiological effect.

Nevertheless, when considering bread consumption, it is necessary to take into account an individual's total daily calorie intake, which varies from person to person, and their physical activity. Finally, remember that what you put on your bread (butter, jam, cheese, charcuterie, etc.) can definitely tip the scales.

BREAD AND FIBER

Bread is a source of dietary fiber, which is not digested in the stomach and small intestine, but ferments, more or less, in the colon and contributes to regulating digestive transit. By slowing digestion, fiber also contributes to a feeling of satiety. In addition, by providing a substrate for the intestinal microbiota, fiber supports the immune system and helps in the prevention of certain metabolic diseases like diabetes and obesity.

The amount of fiber in bread varies depending on how refined the flour is. The more of the whole grain a flour contains, the higher the amount of fiber it has. So, while 3½ oz. (100 g) of whole wheat bread contains on average ¼ oz. (7 g) of fiber, the same quantity of baguette contains only about ⅒ oz. (2.8 g).

Any products applied to grains before or after harvesting build up on and in the bran layer, so it's best to consume organic varieties of whole wheat breads, which are rich in bran.

BREAD AND GLUTEN

Demonizing bread because it contains gluten is like condemning wine for containing alcohol or pastries for containing sugar. Gluten is a fundamental component of bread that supports leavening through fermentation. In recent years, there has been an increase in cases of celiac disease, as well as digestive problems in the general population unaffected by the disease (known as non-celiac gluten sensitivity). Studies are underway to determine if gluten is the only culprit, and, in fact, the study that launched the "No-Glu" movement, published in 2011 by Australian researcher Peter Gibson, has been disputed. Of particular interest for researchers is the role of FODMAPs—fermentable oligosaccharides, di-saccharides, monosaccharides, and polyols—which are poorly absorbed by the intestine.

Based on current research into the reasons why bread produced under these modern conditions can be difficult to digest, here's what we know for sure:

- Modern wheat varieties are not "richer" in gluten. On the whole, their protein levels are stable. However, they have undergone a gradual selection process to develop wheat with high levels of glutenin that can withstand mechanical kneading. To ensure a totally controlled bread-making process, unhampered by environmental factors such as weather conditions, industrial millers may add "dough improvers" to flour, including gluten or ascorbic acid, which strengthen the gluten network.

- A long, oxidizing mechanical kneading process considerably strengthens the gluten network.

- Modern baking relies heavily on fermentation using industrially cultured yeast rather than levain. Yet the acidification produced by levain cultures helps initiate gluten breakdown.

- Modern breads tend to have a thin crust and little to no chew, but mastication is key to triggering salivation, which initiates pre-digestion.

It is not so much gluten itself that causes problems, but the overstrengthening of gluten through excessive processing, which can make it more difficult to digest. More digestible bread is made using long fermentation with levain and additive-free wheat milled from heritage grains, without excessive kneading.

 GOOD TO KNOW

- **Celiac disease** is a chronic intestinal autoimmune disease that affects about 1 percent of the population. For sufferers of the disease, ingesting gluten triggers an abnormal immune reaction in the small intestine causing inflammation that damages the intestinal lining; this hinders the absorption of nutrients and can lead to significant malnutrition.

- **Wheat allergy** affects about 0.1 percent of the population. Symptoms range from eczema to anaphylactic shock.

- Intestinal issues linked to **gluten sensitivity** resemble those of irritable bowel syndrome (IBS). Gluten's role in these problems has yet to be formally established.

BREAD AND ADDITIVES

In France, there are no laws or regulatory guidelines governing the ingredients that may be used in bread. A review of bread-making practices undertaken in 1977 simply states that different types of bread are made by baking a fermented dough composed of bread-making grains and authorized raw materials, and according to a specific recipe for each type of bread. French law only stipulates regulation for "traditional French" bread, which allows the use of four natural additives and a processing aid. Additives are subject to European regulations, and millers often add them directly to flour. The situation is a little less clear in the US, where the FDA definition of bread is far less restrictive, although Standards of Identity exist for individual product groups. Wheat bread, for example, must be made from 100 percent whole wheat flour. The agency defines white bread as a bakery product produced by baking a "mixed yeast-leavened dough that contains refined wheat flour, yeast (any of its commercial forms) and hydrating or moistening ingredients such as water, whole eggs, milk, and liquid sweeteners." Authorized additional ingredients include shortening, lecithin, emulsifiers, dough strengtheners and conditioners, redox agents, etc.

In France, fourteen additives are permitted in ordinary bread, and about a hundred are allowed in specialty breads. Some of these additives, like E471—a texturing agent derived from food-grade fats—may contain products of animal origin. Coloring agents are forbidden. For fresh-baked and unpackaged bread sold directly to the consumer, there is no legal obligation in many countries to provide a complete list of ingredients; only the most common allergens, such as eggs, milk, and gluten, must be indicated. Most additives are not considered allergens, but they have not been ruled out as possible triggers of certain inflammatory diseases and intestinal disorders.

Be cautious when buying industrial gluten-free bread: some varieties get their pleasant texture from the use of many additives, thickeners, and emulsifiers.

 GOOD TO KNOW

An additive is a natural or artificial substance—a colorant, sweetener, preservative, antioxidant, or thickener—added to a food to achieve a particular change in its properties. Additives have an effect on the final product and are therefore considered ingredients. Processing aids, such as enzymes that catalyze chemical reactions in bread, are also an added substance, but serve only to assist in the production process and usually disappear upon cooking; as a result, they are not included in the list of ingredients.

The Grain Makes the Bread: From Cereal Grains to Flour

Imagine our diet without bread, pasta, and rice—or beer, whisky, and rum, for that matter. Without grains, we would die of hunger. Half of all calories consumed by humans come from about fifteen kinds of grain that are among the most cultivated plants in the world, with corn topping the list, followed by wheat, rice, and barley. But only a quarter of grain production is consumed in food form; more than a third is reserved for livestock farming, and the rest is used for industrial purposes, mostly in the form of starch. As we increasingly pay attention to what's on our plates and to the balance of animal- and plant-derived food sources, we should really consider the role of grains, which have been a staple of the human diet for over ten thousand years.

Formerly known as Gramineae, members of the Poaceae family (grasses and cereals) evolved on Earth following the mass extinction event that wiped out the dinosaurs and the forests where they lived twenty-three million years ago. Vast steppes and prairies subsequently developed and the first grasses appeared; with a root system that allowed them to survive periods of drought and reemerge when the rains came, they were particularly resilient and provided food for an entirely new herbivore fauna. It would be another few millennia before our hunter-gatherer ancestors made the connection between highly volatile grass seeds and the plant life cycle, and then came to understand that they could give nature a helping hand. The first farmers began to identify the best grain varieties and domesticated ancient wheat (emmer and einkorn) and barley, notably in Mesopotamia, in the region known as the Fertile Crescent—the cradle of modern agriculture. Grain-based recipes appeared, first in the form of gruel, then flatbreads which prefigured bread, and a fermented barley juice that closely resembled beer. With the exception of equatorial regions, which were unsuited for grasses, grains spread and were adapted around the world: wheat in Europe, rice in Asia, corn in the Americas, and millet and sorghum in Africa.

A LESSON IN BOTANY

Botanically speaking, grains are fruits; in other words, seeds rich in proteins and starch enveloped in a fiber-rich outer skin called bran. The seed's cell walls are fused with this skin, which, unlike a nut's chemically inactive shell, contains a layer of aleurone: a protein-rich nutrient that enables the seed to germinate. At this stage, the grain still contains the micronutrient-rich germ and is considered a "whole grain."

Grains may then be refined, using abrasive milling techniques on whole grains or by sifting flours. Grains are considered partially refined when a small portion of their bran and germ has been removed. When they are highly refined, all that remains is the endosperm, which mainly provides energy at the expense of nutrients contained in the other parts of the grain. Grains can be puffed (corn and rice), split, rolled, hulled (to make groats), or ground into flour.

THE MAKEUP OF GRAINS

Most grains are similar in chemical composition, although they may have their own specificities. The endosperm, which comprises 84 percent of the kernel, is mostly made of starch, which breaks down easily when it comes into contact with saliva or is cooked, making it digestible. Some grains also contain the polymer gluten, primarily composed of proteins stored in the endosperm, which generates a viscoelastic network upon contact with water. This network traps CO_2 produced during fermentation, which causes bread to rise—this is the principle behind bread making, or *panification* in French. Some grains contain more gluten than others and will result in bread with more rise.

WHAT IS GLUTEN?

Jacopo Beccari, a professor at Italy's University of Bologna, discovered gluten in 1745. He massaged a ball of wheat dough under a stream of water, and when the starch washed away, he was left with a sticky, elastic substance—gluten, from the Latin *glutinum*, for "glue." Gluten is a polymer composed mainly of storage proteins (gliadins and glutenins in wheat) located in the endosperm. It may also contain fats (5 to 7 percent), starch (5 to 10 percent), and water (5 to 8 percent). But the substance known as gluten does not exist as such inside the kernel—it is only when water is added during kneading that gluten forms, through the combination of its component parts, gliadin and glutenin. The bonds created by this combination form a viscoelastic network. Gliadins give bread its extensibility, viscosity, and plasticity; glutenins give it resistance and elasticity. During fermentation, the action of yeast and bacteria releases CO_2, which is then trapped within the strands of the gluten network, causing bread to rise. The strength of this molecular bond depends on many factors: genetics, the type of seed, how the wheat was cultivated, the nature of the flour (composition and milling), the intensity of kneading, and the type of fermentation and cooking method, with effects on the bread that range from the speed at which it cools to the length of its shelf life.

Bread-making grains

Common wheat (*Triticum aestivum*)

The result of crossbreeding an emmer wheat and an Aegilops (a grass in the Poaceae family), this is the most commonly produced grain in the world, used mostly for bread flour. In France, it is cultivated in the Paris Basin, Upper and Central France, Poitou-Charentes, and Burgundy. It derives its French name, *blé tendre* (literally "tender wheat"), from the white, crumbly starch enveloping the seed, as opposed to durum wheat (*blé dur*), which contains a yellow, glassy substance used to make semolina and pasta. Common wheat is also called *froment* in French, from the Latin *frumentum*, meaning "cereal," "grain," or "wheat." Over a hundred varieties are cultivated in France. Rich in gluten, common wheat is the best flour for making bread.

There are six categories of wheat grown in the US, but they fall into two main groups, hard and soft wheat, defined by their protein content. Hard wheat should not be confused with durum wheat, which has the highest protein content of all. Hard wheat flours are most often used in yeasted and levain-raised breads, while soft flours are generally reserved for chemically leavened baked goods such as muffins, cakes, and cookies. Hard wheat is mostly ground in the northern Great Plains, while soft wheat is grown in the Carolinas and the western states.

Spelt (*Triticum spelta*)

Also known as Gallic wheat, spelt in France is mostly grown in the Paris Basin and Burgundy. Although less popular in the US, recent demand for ancient grains has spurred cultivation of the crop, especially in western states like Washington and Montana. Spelt is a "hulled" grain, which means it needs to be dehulled before milling. It is a low-yield crop, which explains why it has been more or less abandoned in favor of common wheat.

Khorasan wheat or Kamut (*Triticum turanicum*)

This relative of durum wheat is cultivated in the region of Khorasan, located between Iran and Afghanistan, from which its name derives. It is also sold under the brand name Kamut, following its importation to the US in the 1950s. Although still a marginal crop, Khorasan wheat has caught the eye of consumers and farmers, and in 2016 there were 70,000 acres of land planted with Khorasan wheat in Montana and the Canadian provinces of Alberta and Saskatchewan.

Einkorn (*Triticum monococcum*)

In French, einkorn is inaccurately referred to as *petit épeautre* ("little spelt"), though spelt has little in common with this relative of common wheat. It was one of the first grains to be domesticated by humans, but its cultivation was gradually abandoned in France in the Middle Ages, and today it is rare. The protected geographical indication (*Indication Géographique Protégée*) *Petit Épeautre de Haute-Provence* was created in France to protect it. Einkorn is among the ancient grains gaining popularity in the US and the UK, and domestic production is centered on small organic farms. Although einkorn has a low gluten content, it can still be used to make bread and produces a dense, low-rise loaf with many nutritional benefits.

Rye (*Secale cereale L.*)

A member of the grass family, rye is closely related to the genus *Triticum*. Rustic and very resilient, it tolerates poor and acidic soils. The Ségala, a region in central France, was named for this grain (*seigle*), which used to be the only crop grown in the region. The US and Canada are leading rye producers, and the hearty grain is cultivated throughout the countries. Despite a rather low gluten content, rye can be used to make bread. It contains mucilage: a substance that expands in water and becomes viscous, which reduces the cohesive power of gluten in bread dough. This is why rye is often mixed with wheat flour.

Barley (*Hordeum vulgare*)

Among the oldest cultivated grains, barley is the third most commonly produced grain in France. It is also one of the most widely grown arable crops in the UK, after wheat. Used in brewing and distilling, it can be consumed pearled (polished and without the germ) or hulled (stripped of its outer skin, with the germ and bran intact), as well as rolled. When it has been germinated and roasted, it becomes malt. Though barley is rarely used to make bread on its own, it can be blended with wheat flour.

Oats (*Avena sativa L.*)

Most commonly consumed in North America and the UK, in the form of rolled oats or porridge, oats are cultivated elsewhere mainly as fodder for livestock. They can be used as a bread inclusion (mixed into a dough before baking) or topping, and a non-dairy milk can also be extracted from oats. Canada is the world's largest exporter of oats.

COMMON WHEAT

SPELT

EINKORN

RYE

HERITAGE AND LANDRACE WHEAT

The term "heritage" or "ancient" grain has no official definition. Many people think that heritage wheat has not undergone selective breeding, but all wheat is the result of crossbreeding undertaken by humans in order to produce plant varieties that meet certain expectations at a given time in history. In the past, farmers cultivated and named wheat varieties as they wished. The term *blé de pays*, or landrace, refers to a grouping of similar regional wheat varieties under a generic name, such as Blanc de Flandre, Hâtif de la Saône, or Bladette de Bordeaux. In France, these wheat varieties were gradually replaced by others imported from Spain and Russia, and the first hybrids developed by Henry de Vilmorin in the late nineteenth century.

To put these varieties in order, a catalog was established in France in 1933, accompanied by authorizations to produce and market grain varieties. Similar seed certification programs were developed in the US between 1915 and 1930. Wheat was selected according to yield and technological criteria, including regularity and quality, at the expense of biodiversity and adaptation to the local environment. As a result, the number of varieties of French wheat fell from 562 to 40 in 1945. Since then, the number has climbed to 250 with the development of new hybrid varieties. Currently, ten varieties of bread-making grains are grown on 50 percent of land cultivated with wheat, with Rubisko leading. Five seed companies share the French wheat market, and a handful of corporations control the global seed market today. In the last fifteen years or so, however, farmers have once again begun to grow varieties like Rouge de Bordeaux, Barbu du Roussillon, and Blé Meunier d'Apt, which existed before the catalog was created and are not included in it. A similar ancient grain movement has begun in the US and UK. According to French law, which has some of the strictest legislation in the world regarding seed sales, these wheat varieties cannot be sold or exchanged, except for research purposes: on April 25, 2018, the members of the European Parliament authorized this practice, taking effect in 2021.

GOOD TO KNOW

A wheat landrace is a mix of genetically diverse varieties adapted to their environment, unlike purely commercial varieties. The farmer can let natural selection play out or guide the process by selecting individual plants. Landraces were very common in most regions of France and the US until the 1950s, when they were replaced by more homogenous and productive varieties produced by large seed companies. Today, they are valued for their qualities that make them suitable for organic farming.

Gluten-free grains

Cereals that contain gluten are known as *"panifiable"* in French, which roughly translates to "suitable for bread making," while gluten-free cereals are called *"non-panifiable."* But in fact, corn-based flatbreads—such as arepa, tortilla, and *taloa*—and "gluten-free breads" use gluten-free flour, challenging the French terminology. It's more accurate to simply call them gluten-free. Rice, corn, teff, sorghum, millet, and fonio flour can be used alone or combined with other flours. Let's take a closer look at two of them.

Rice (*Oryza sativa* and *Oryza glaberrima*)
There are over eight thousand varieties of rice, divided into two major subspecies: indica—a light, long-grain, non-sticky rice—and japonica—a round, stickier rice with a higher starch content. Nearly 90 percent of the world's rice is grown in Asia. France cultivates forty-two thousand acres of rice, mainly in the Camargue region on the Mediterranean Sea. Rice cultivation in the United States is concentrated in California and the south, and annual production is roughly 10 million tons. Rice kernels have a hard hull that must be removed. Polishing the grains removes the multiple external layers to obtain white rice—the most commonly consumed form. The grain can also be parboiled using steam and pressure, which makes it easier to cook. Rice flour is one of the main ingredients in gluten-free bread.

Corn (*Zea mays*)
Corn exists in myriad varieties and has many uses. In the United States, more than ninety million acres of land are planted with corn. While the crop is grown in almost all fifty states, production is concentrated in the Heartland region. However, most of it is used as livestock feed, and 10 to 20 percent is exported to other countries. Corn was imported to Europe from Mexico by Christopher Columbus, and in France it is most often used in the form of cornstarch. *Farine de gaude* is a toasted corn flour and a specialty of the Bresse region. Nixtamalized corn flour, called *masa harina*, is most commonly used in Mexico, Central America, and South America. Nixtamalization is the process of cooking corn in a lime bath before milling, which softens the kernel, adds calcium, and preserves proteins and vitamins, in addition to enhancing flavor.

GOOD TO KNOW

Buckwheat, like quinoa, is not really a cereal. It belongs to the Polygonaceae family, along with sorrel and rhubarb. The angular seeds are dark in color, which is why the plant is called *blé noir* ("black wheat") in French. Imported during the Crusades and popularized by Anne de Bretagne, it was sown in the western region of Brittany in the fifteenth century. Buckwheat was a common crop in colonial America, grown on farms for livestock feed and flour.

In France, an IGP has existed for *blé noir tradition Bretagne* ("traditional Breton buckwheat") since 2000. A growing interest in gluten-free alternatives in the United States has led to renewed interest in buckwheat and the revival of more flavorful heritage varieties. Perhaps most commonly recognized as an ingredient in pancakes, buckwheat can also be bought as groats or kasha (dry-roasted), and is the main ingredient in soba noodles. In bread, it is used in combination with other flours and contributes a distinctive nutty flavor.

MAKING GLUTEN-FREE BREAD

During the standard bread-making process, strands of the gluten network trap carbon dioxide produced during fermentation. When there is no gluten present, the carbon dioxide bubbles escape, which means the bread won't rise. To make gluten-free bread, something else has to trap the gas. In this case, bakers rely on dough viscosity to trap CO_2, either by using flours that become naturally viscous when in contact with liquid, or by using natural emulsifiers like carob powder (made from the seed of the carob tree), guar gum (made from the seeds of the legume *Cyamopsis tetragonoloba*), or mucilage-rich psyllium. These plant-derived substances are comprised of polysaccharides, which expand when in contact with water and acquire a viscous, sometimes sticky consistency similar to gelatin.

FLOUR

Flour is the main ingredient in bread. The French word for flour, *farine*, is derived from the Latin *farina*, from *far* or *farris* meaning "cultivated wheat" or "spelt." The English word "flour" is derived from the Old French *flour* or *flor* from the Latin *flos*, meaning "blossom," or "the best part" of something. Both "*farine*" and "flour" have become generic terms for a white powder obtained by grinding grain. Without a modifier, they usually refer to wheat flour, which we'll discuss below, but there are many different types of flour.

Wheat kernels have three parts: bran, endosperm, and germ. Bran contains several layers of outer seed coats (the pericarp), an inner seed coat, and a vitamin- and mineral-rich aleurone layer. Ever since humans began consuming cereals, they have been searching for ways to eliminate the undigestible outer layer, made of cellulose. The first mills, driven by animals, water, or wind, could not achieve this separation, and flour had to be sifted to remove as much bran as possible.

Industrial extraction

In the 1880s, a Hungarian process ushered in the development of industrial milling based on a system of cast-iron cylinders, or rollers, that crush grain without abrading it, and a bolting system (sieve). The technique separates the flour—ground from the friable endosperm—from the germ and the bran, known as middlings. But nutrient-rich elements are lost as a result. To obtain a more or less whole flour, a portion of the bran must be added back into this white flour—a highly questionable practice. Bran is difficult to digest and contains phytic acid, which disrupts the bioavailability of nutrients. In addition to this, residue from crop treatments builds up in bran. There is debate as to whether adding the inner seed coat to flour provides any nutritional value, since naturally occurring enzymes that support nutrient bioavailability are not released during industrial extraction. The germ—a by-product rich in fat and therefore more sensitive to spoilage—is removed for use in other industrial applications.

Stone-ground flour

The best way to preserve a grain's nutritional properties is to grind it between two millstones, which smooths the grain and splits the inner seed coat. Using this ancient technique, the most nutritional parts of the grain (including the germ) can be extracted and thoroughly combined, while separating out the bran. The result is a light whole wheat flour, similar to French T80 (see below), with more nutritional value. Brothers André and Pierre Astrié developed a grain mill based on this technique that allows organic farmers and farm-to-loaf bakers to grind their own flour.

Flour types

Flour contains minerals originally present in the bran; when incinerated at 1650°F (900°C), all that remains is an ashy mineral residue. The higher the ash content (*taux de blutage*), represented by the letter T, the higher the number assigned to the flour; the lower the ash content, the lower the number. For example, incinerating 100 g of type 55 flour (T55) produces about 0.55 g of mineral ash.

There are six categories of French flour based on ash content. While American and British flour differs in protein and gluten content, the following chart suggests near equivalents. Some bakers will combine different foreign flours to mimic those available in France.

Type 45 (*farine de gruau*): **Cake and pastry flour**
>> pastry, pizza

Type 55 (*farine de gruau*): **All-purpose flour**
>> many uses, including pastry, pizza, breads

Type 65 (*farine blanche*): **Bread flour**
>> white breads

Type 80 (*farine bise* or *semi-complète*): **White whole wheat flour**
>> country breads

Type 110 (*farine complète*): **Light whole wheat flour**
>> whole wheat breads

Types 150–180 (*farine "intégrale"*): **Dark/100 percent whole wheat flours**
>> bran breads

White flour—such as cake, all-purpose, or bread flour—is flour that has been stripped of nutrients, which are mostly contained in the wheat germ and bran; the whiter the flour is, the more nutrients it has lost, reducing its function to a mere source of energy.

In contrast, whole wheat flour is rich in minerals and vitamins (essential B and E vitamins), but is harder to digest because of the higher fiber content—hence the importance of making bread with a method based on long fermentation.

Italy has another classification system to categorize flour. Italian 00 flour, used in pizza, is equivalent to a T35 or T40 flour. Some American brands make an Italian-style flour appropriate for pizza and flatbreads.

GOOD TO KNOW

Gruau, from the Middle Dutch *groot*, meaning "great" or "thick," originally referred to hulled ground wheat. By extension, the word has come to refer in French to the finest part of the grain or the highest-quality flour. The English word "groat" refers to hulled whole grains that are often prepared by soaking and simmering to make soups, porridges, or stews. Groats can also be milled into flour at home, but they have a very short shelf life due to the presence of an intact germ.

Wheat strength

Individual varieties within a single flour type may present different bread-making qualities, depending on their specific protein content, particularly gluten. In general, cake and all-purpose flours contain between 8 and 12 percent gluten. The higher the gluten content, the stronger a flour is said to be (*farine de force* in French), meaning the gluten network that forms during kneading will more or less resist deformation. This resistance to deformation is determined using a Chopin Alveograph: a device that measures the force required to blow and burst a bubble of dough. Gluten strength is expressed as a value between 100 and 300. Flour with a value below 100 is considered unsuitable for bread making, while flour with a value over 250 becomes difficult to shape, and is reserved for spongy breads like sandwich breads or brioche. In France, flour strength is rarely indicated on packages intended for home use, although some US brands include this information. Commercial flours generally have a strength between 180 and 220. Although there is no direct correlation between flour type and gluten strength, flours T45 to T65 are usually stronger than whole wheat flours.

ADDITIVES AND PROCESSING AIDS

There may be more to your flour than first meets the eye. Since the 1950s in France—and even earlier in the United States—traditional baking, which relies on natural fermentation of dough obtained through a simple blend of water and flour, has evolved toward a technology-supported process that uses flour containing dough improvers. These are additives and processing aids used to improve the appearance of bread and, more importantly, to facilitate the baker's work. Most bread flour contains some additives. In the US, enrichment with B vitamins and minerals niacin, thiamin, iron, and riboflavin has been required in bread flours and all-purpose flours in most states since the 1940s. Only the ingredients in "traditional French" bread, and hence the flour used in this type of bread, are strictly regulated. In France, the Label Rouge ("Red Label") quality certification stipulates additional conditions regarding wheat selection and production, which must be controlled from wheat to flour. In the UK, the Red Tractor certification program ensures home-grown wheat meets the requirements of millers and food safety standards. A similar program exists in Scotland, where 1% of the UK wheat crop is grown. Few regulations exist in the US, aside from voluntary USDA certification programs, but the Whole Grains Council has developed a Whole Grain Stamp program to distinguish products containing 8 g (about ⅓ oz.) or more of whole grain ingredients per serving.

About one hundred additives, often added directly to flour by millers, are authorized for use in ordinary bread in France. Ready-to-use premixes and concentrates, as they are known in the industry, may contain all the ingredients necessary to make bread on a large scale.

WHEAT FLOUR

RYE FLOUR

KHORASAN/KAMUT FLOUR

SPELT FLOUR

RICE FLOUR

BUCKWHEAT FLOUR

CORN FLOUR

CHICKPEA FLOUR

LEAVENING BREAD

Scientists call it serendipity—in other words, a fortuitous scientific discovery made during a search for something entirely different. That's how the world's most wonderful culinary development—bread—was invented. For thousands of years, humans subsisted on grain mash, then a pancake-like flatbread cooked on a hot stone. The story goes that one day, towards the end of the Neolithic period, a young woman was kneading dough for one of these flatbreads on the banks of the Nile when she was called to other chores, leaving it at the bottom of a pot. When she returned, the dough had taken on a pleasing round shape, no doubt with a little help from the hot, humid climate. When baked, it turned out to be delicious and easy to digest. We may never be able to verify the story, but the technique certainly spread. A thousand years later, the Greeks improved upon the recipe using grape must, while the tribes of Gaul added the foam from their beer to make lighter bread. These recipes all started with the same natural phenomenon: fermentation.

It wouldn't be until the seventeenth century that anyone understood what was really at work. A Dutch fabric merchant, Antoni Van Leeuwenhoek, developed a simple microscope to count the threads in his cloth. He took a liking to the exercise and began to use his microscope to observe the microorganisms he called *levende Dierkens* ("small living animals"). They were not animals, in fact, but included single-cell fungi—yeast. The Dutchman was right about one thing, though: they were indeed living organisms. Like all living things, yeast breathe and feed. Their diet consists of carbohydrates, present in grains. As they break down these carbohydrates, yeast release carbon dioxide—they also produce alcohol—which inflates the environment around them, causing liquids to bubble and dough to expand. This of course has practical applications for brewing and baking. But in their natural state, these wild yeasts trigger spontaneous fermentation. It takes experience, attention to weather conditions, and quality flour to obtain a more or less predictable result—

and that's the miracle of levain. First housewives, and then bakers, when bread making became a profession, learned to save a bit of kneaded, leavened bread dough from the previous day to transfer to a new batch of dough, where the yeast would find a nourishing environment in which to multiply. The baker's art lies in understanding a levain's temperament and creating the best conditions to support its full potential. In addition to wild yeasts, levain cultures are home to a wide range of bacteria that trigger lactic and acetic fermentation and contribute flavor and nutritional qualities to bread.

Humans are never happy with what they can't control—especially nature. With the help of science, they sought to domesticate wild yeasts. Adding brewer's yeast in tandem with levain has been practiced since at least the sixteenth century. In 1770, compressed brewer's yeast was sold to bakers as a tool for simplifying the bread-making process. But it was still an experimental process. To gain control over fermentation (and production), brewers and distillers in Lille turned to Louis Pasteur for help. In 1857, the chemist identified the role of bacteria and yeast, and demonstrated that a specific microorganism is responsible for each type of fermentation. He then isolated *Saccharomyces cerevisiae* (literally "beer fungus that uses sugar") or brewer's yeast. Baker's yeast was developed using certain strains of brewer's yeast. To render it more stable (and achieve a longer shelf life), baker's yeast was pressed using an Austrian method that removed much of its water. In 1871, Baron Max de Springer, an Austro-Hungarian immigrant, established the first yeast factory in France, and the Viennese method of baking with yeast sprang up in counterpoint to the French levain method. Yeast manufacturing began to develop in France, and the Lesaffre company was founded in 1873 near Lille (the company is still a leading yeast producer). In 1868, Austro-Hungarian immigrants Charles and Maximilian Fleischmann brought the method to the United States, where they developed the country's first commercially produced yeast in the form of a compressed cake.

While cubes of fresh yeast are a common sight in domestic European kitchens, American bakers are more familiar with packets of active dry or instant yeast. Both resulted from the development of an entire industry, one that began a relentless process of selecting yeast strains for vigor or aroma, for brewing or winemaking, and in the food industry as a flavor enhancer—and most of all, for baking. The more yeast you use, the faster you can go: you can even have a hot baguette in two hours. As a result, few bakers still make bread with levain. But that approach ignores the extraordinary nutritional value of levain and its biological wealth—for each levain is unique. In 1992, 164 countries signed the Convention on Biological Diversity, which states that "conservation of biological diversity is a common concern of humankind." Though few conservation efforts have focused specifically on microorganisms and the microscopic world, continuing to make bread using levain contributes to the preservation of biological diversity.

FERMENTATION: LIFE WITHOUT AIR

The word fermentation comes from the Latin fervor, which means "bubbling" or "boiling." "The consequence of life without air," according to Louis Pasteur, is the process of anaerobic decomposition of organic substances by microorganisms, during which ethanol (alcoholic fermentation) and/or lactate or lactic acid (lactic fermentation) is produced from the breakdown of carbon compounds such as glucose. The microorganisms at work include lactic and acetic bacteria, yeasts, and molds.

Fermentation was observed happening naturally for thousands of years until the nineteenth century when humans began to control it. These days, fermentation can be spontaneous or controlled, and offers several benefits for food: it aids in preservation by protecting from pathogens, makes food easier to digest, and confers sensory properties by changing the color, texture, and flavor of foods.

LEVAIN

Levain is a fermented blend of flour and water that is regularly fed (with more flour and water) to obtain a *levain-chef* (master levain), at which point bread making can begin. The *levain-chef* can be made with a bit of dough taken from the previous batch of bread, or started from scratch. Before it can be used to make bread, the *levain-chef* is refreshed to obtain the *levain tout point*, meaning it has reached maximum fermentation (see Techniques p. 131). This may sound a lot like sourdough starter, and levain is similar to sourdough starter in many ways; the main difference lies in the fact that levain does not always impart the distinctive sour flavors associated with sourdough cultures. In this book, we will follow French tradition and refer to a culture of fermented flour and water as levain.

Levain is a living medium that is home to a wide variety of microorganisms, mainly lactic bacteria and yeasts that are naturally present in flour, the air, and what is known as house microbiota (the baker's indoor environment). One hundred grams of flour (about ⅔ cup) contains one million yeast cells and ten million bacteria cells.

These microorganisms live in symbiosis. Although they compete for food, they work together to create a bioprotective effect against pathogenic flora and spoilage flora by secreting alcohol (yeast) and acetic acid (bacteria), which lowers the pH of the levain. This action gives rise to "spontaneous" fermentation, meaning it doesn't need seeding, like baker's yeast does, for example.

Yeast and lactic bacteria also produce aromatic compounds including alcohols, aldehydes, diacetyl, acetoin, and esters.

Yeast

Yeasts are eukaryotic, single-celled fungi, which means their chromosomes are concentrated in a cell nucleus. In the presence of oxygen, they breathe and reproduce by budding. Yeast feed on the sugars contained in grain—glucose and fructose to be precise—and as they break down these sugars, they release carbon dioxide (CO_2), which causes bread to rise. In the absence of oxygen, they transform sugar into alcohol. The yeasts in levain are considered "wild" because they are naturally present in the environment. More than a dozen species of yeast have been identified in levain cultures made with wheat and rye.

Bacteria

Bacteria are eukaryotic, single-celled organisms composed of a single circular chromosome contained in the cytoplasm. They reproduce by cell division. In levain, lactic bacteria in particular play a role in fermentation. As they break down sugars, bacteria produce lactate, acetate, and ethanol, which influence the taste, texture, and shelf life of bread; they also produce CO_2. Around fifty species of lactic bacteria have been identified in levain.

LEVAIN BREAD: BEWARE OF IMITATIONS

Levain is considered "natural" when it is naturally seeded with ferments—yeast and bacteria—present in the air and flour. French law regulates use of the term *pain au levain* to mean bread made on-site (kneaded, shaped, and baked on the same premises) and following the French tradition (no freezing during preparation; no additives; a baked dough made of wheat bread flour, water, and kitchen salt; fermented with yeast and levain), with a maximum pH of 4.3, and a crumb with an acetic acid content of at least 900 mg/kg. An addition of 0.2 percent yeast relative to flour weight is allowed (2 g/1 kg).

Commercial and industrial bread-making processes typically employ a single strain of yeast, *Saccharomyces cerevisiae*, selected for its fermentation strength. To compensate for the lack of flavor imparted using this method, industrial bakers will sometimes resort to adding inactive levain cultures whose ferments have been destroyed in baking. They also use "starters," which are concentrates of one or several strains of lactic bacteria and/or yeasts (not to be confused with home-grown sourdough starters). These living microorganisms are selected from among the flora in natural levain cultures and stabilized using processes that guarantee their survival. *Levain fermentescible* (dried levain starter, available in France) is a mixture of yeast and dehydrated, inactive levain—baking with it is essentially like using baker's yeast.

Levain lovers

Levain has produced some stars, like San Francisco sourdough, which has been part of the city's cultural heritage since French expats founded Boudin Bakery in 1849. *Lactobacillus sanfranciscensis*, a strain of lactic bacteria, was named after the city, and is found in levain cultures around Europe. Levain even has its collectors, like the Belgian Puratos Group, which manufactures industrial bread-making supplies. The company created a library where more than seven hundred strains of wild yeast and fifteen hundred lactic bacteria collected from levain cultures around the world are held and catalogued. And then there are those people who keep their levain for decades—and even give it a name.

In reality, levain, like all living organisms, undergoes changes. You can think of it like a city, where the population increases or decreases, and welcomes new residents. What makes levain so precious is that it takes several days to create and several months to become truly active.

GOOD TO KNOW

It is entirely possible to make a levain without gluten by using a gluten-free flour like rice or buckwheat; follow the same technique as you would to make a classic, wheat-based levain.

COMMERCIAL YEAST/BAKER'S YEAST

As stated above, commercial or baker's yeast is the result of a single strain, *Saccharomyces cerevisiae*, which was domesticated and selected for its capacity to adapt, long shelf life, and suitability for bread making. There are ten billion living cells in 1 g of yeast.

Commercial yeast production uses a substrate of beet or sugarcane molasses, a syrupy by-product of the sugar industry, supplemented with water, air, and nutrient salts. The yeast is obtained through a series of fermentations of increasingly larger culture size in order to grow the biomass—in other words, the quantity of cells created to obtain a sufficient volume of yeast. The yeast is then separated from the fermented liquid using centrifugal pumps called separators to achieve what's called a cream yeast. At this stage, yeast can be commercialized for industrial baking, among other uses. It can also be pressed to remove some of the water and obtain fresh or cake yeast, easily available in mainland Europe and the United Kingdom, or dried to make active dry yeast or instant yeast (95 percent dry material), the most commonly found and used yeasts in the US.

Brewing and winemaking employ several strains of yeast, which influence the flavor of the final product in different ways. This diversity does not exist in commercial baking; bakers who want access to a larger variety of yeasts and their attendant flavors must seed their doughs with levain.

Yeast-leavened bread

The use of commercial yeast led to the development of several bread-making techniques (see Techniques p. 137). The first is a poolish, which probably derives its name from the Polish bakers who invented it.

The poolish method was adopted by Austrian bakers in the nineteenth century, hence the terms *méthode viennoise* ("Viennese method") and *pain viennois* ("Vienna bread"), used to describe the first yeast-leavened breads. In fact, these words still appear on the facades of some older bakeries in France. The method involves making a pre-ferment using yeast and a portion of the total flour and water called for in the recipe, which is then added to the remaining flour, water, and salt.

The *levain-levure* ("levain-yeast") or *pâte fermentée* technique is similar to levain, but uses only commercial yeast. It calls for incorporating pre-fermented dough into a new batch of dough.

Finally, the most commonly used technique is the straight dough method, which requires no pre-fermented cultures: all the ingredients are simply kneaded together at once. This has been the most commonly used method in baking since the 1920s, because it is the simplest, fastest, and most predictable.

 GOOD TO KNOW

Yeast quantity and fermentation time are directly correlated. The more yeast you use, the faster fermentation will be. Controlling for temperature, we can write the following equation:

$(y \times t) \div n = x$

y: the percentage of fresh yeast in relation to the weight of flour indicated in the recipe

t: the fermentation time indicated in the recipe

n: the desired fermentation time

x: the percentage of fresh yeast needed to increase or decrease the fermentation time

Remember that temperature influences fermentation: the higher the temperature, the faster fermentation progresses, and vice versa.

OTHER LEAVENING AGENTS

Although in theory baking uses live ferments, the baking industry also relies heavily on leavening agents. In some cases, chemistry trumps biology. These chemical agents release carbon dioxide to catalyze leavening, and because they are so fast-acting, the dough must be put into the oven as soon as they have been added.

Baking powder

Baking powder is composed of a mild alkali (usually baking soda, also known as bicarbonate of soda), a mild acid (such as cream of tartar or tartaric acid), and a stabilizing agent (like cornstarch). When the acid and alkali come into contact with moisture, they react to produce carbon dioxide. This is known as an acid-base reaction. Double-acting baking powders (found in the US) also react a second time when exposed to the heat of the oven. Baking powder is mainly used in cake, cookie, and pastry making.

Baking soda

Baking soda, or bicarbonate of soda, is an alkaline salt that produces carbon dioxide when in contact with an acid (an acid-base reaction). For example, baking soda (an alkali) is combined with buttermilk (an acid) to make soda bread.

Water
——

Water is a crucial ingredient in any bread recipe, whether it is used directly as is, or indirectly as milk or another liquid. It unites all the other ingredients. It plays a hydrating role, and also interacts chemically with salt, yeast, and the starch in flour. The amount of water in a recipe is determined by the amount of flour. In French, the amount of water needed for the dough to come together is called *eau de coulage* and varies according to dough hydration, which is calculated by the type of flour and the type of bread you want to make. When water evaporates, bread goes stale. Strictly speaking, however, bread doesn't dry out; instead, the starch in bread loses humidity through a phenomenon called retrogradation.

Properties

Water is a chemical compound—H_2O—composed of two hydrogen atoms and one oxygen atom.

A solvent
Water's molecular composition means that its molecules interact with similar molecules. Put another way, water dissolves certain substances that share its molecular makeup, like starch, salt, or sugar, without changing their chemical structure, or that of the water itself.

A suitable environment
Water supports enzyme reactions that transform the starch in flour into compound sugars (maltose) and simple sugars (glucose). Water also creates an environment conducive to yeast growth and activity.

A boost for gluten
Gluten cannot exist without water. The gluten network forms when proteins in flour (see p. 28) are moistened and combined during kneading. These proteins agglutinate (clump together), relax, and lengthen when hydrated. The more water that is added to a recipe, the more the gluten

network can be strengthened (up to a point—it all depends on the flour's absorption capacity and the baker's experience in working with a very moist, sticky, and elastic dough).

Remember that hard water (see below) will produce a firmer, less sticky dough—requiring a slightly slower fermentation process—and a somewhat tighter crumb.

An adjustable variable

The baker can control the quantity of water (see Water p. 123) and the temperature of that water (see Desired Dough Temperature p. 125) to influence fermentation and leavening.

Choosing the right water

If you're going to spend time carefully selecting flour, it's only logical that you would take the same care choosing water, which is second only to flour in terms of quantity in a bread recipe. Most bread is made with tap water, which is treated to be safe for drinking. It is not, however, free from trace levels of nitrates or pesticides, which vary in quantity from city to city; it also contains chlorine (between 0.1 and 0.4 mg per liter, or up to 4 parts per million, in Europe and the US).

Natural mineral and well water are drawn from groundwater tables deep below the Earth's surface, where they are protected from human pollution. They are both naturally suited for drinking, and natural mineral water is considered to have healthful properties by virtue of its stable levels of minerals and trace elements. Water is referred to as hard or soft depending on the amount of mineral salts present (especially lime).

Pure water can be defined as fresh water that contains only the H_2O molecule and is free from any other matter such as impurities or mineral salts. It can be obtained through boiling, distilling, deionization, and reverse osmosis, but it does not exist in nature. This kind of water is suitable for drinking but is bland in flavor.

Water can also be energized, a principle based on the concept of water memory, which suggests that water retains the properties of the substances with which it has come into contact, even when these are no longer present. Magnetic fields and vibrations are also purported to modify its properties. Water that has been energized—using a vortex, for example—would then supposedly play a more significant role in hydrating and oxygenating cells.

Amateur bakers who don't live near a natural source of clean drinking water might be tempted to opt for bottled water to be sure they are using safe water that will support the growth of the yeast and bacteria that are vital to fermentation. But bottled water has several major disadvantages.

First, it's about thirty to forty times more expensive than tap water. More importantly, the production, packaging, transportation, and even recycling of bottled water all take a heavy toll on the environment. For all practical purposes, we suggest you use tap water purified using a water filter or water purification system. Or you can leave tap water to sit in an open container; chlorine, often added to tap water, is highly volatile and evaporates naturally. The one instance when bottled water might be preferable is when you're starting and feeding your levain, to create the best conditions for growth.

GOOD TO KNOW

Eau de coulage doesn't have to be water; depending on the recipe, it can be easily replaced by any other liquid, such as beer, wine, fruit or vegetable juice, or broth.

FULL STEAM AHEAD!

Water in the form of steam also contributes to a successful loaf of bread. When putting dough in the oven, creating a *coup de buée* ("blast of steam") will imitate the steam injection provided by professional bread-baking ovens (see Adding Steam p. 182). This addition of steam plays a crucial role during baking. The presence of a thin layer of moisture slows crust formation, which enables the dough to expand more easily and contributes to a thinner, more crackly crust. It also gives bread a glossy appearance and improves the way scoring marks open during baking.

Salt

Salt is almost always used in baking. Even though it is a minor component in most recipes, it plays a vital role in the bread-making process and in the flavor of the finished product. Before the French Revolution, bread was lightly salted, or not salted at all, but after the fall of the Ancien Régime, salt taxes like the *gabelle* were abolished, leading to a more widespread use of salt.

Salt-free bread can still be found, however: for example, *pane sciocco* is a Tuscan specialty said to have been created during a salt embargo in seventeenth-century Florence.

Properties

Salt is an ionic chemical compound formed by sodium (Na+) and chloride (Cl−) ions which are easily pulled apart in water and bond with other components in the dough.

A tool for bread making
During kneading, salt improves dough's plasticity by creating ionic bonds, supporting the development of bonds between proteins and contributing to a more stable and resistant gluten network. Salt is hygroscopic (it retains water), which prevents dough from drying out and acts as an antioxidant to slow the process of bleaching.

A fermentation regulator
Salt tends to dehydrate yeast and retard its activity; this is why the two should not come into contact until later in the kneading process. Salt also extends fermentation time, which encourages flavor development, and it regulates the formation of carbon dioxide, resulting in a more regular crumb.

A boost during baking
Salt improves crust color and contributes to a thinner, crunchier crust.

A flavor enhancer

Salt doesn't add flavor to bread; instead it enhances the flavors already present in grains, as well as the flavors that develop during the fermentation process.

A preservative—or not

Salt's hygroscopic nature has two effects on baked bread: in a dry environment, it slows the staling process and prevents the crust from hardening, extending shelf life. However, in a moist environment, salt makes crusts go soft and bread turn stale faster.

Choosing the right salt

Try to use unrefined sea salt or other unrefined salt. In addition to sodium chloride, salt contains magnesium and many other trace elements. This is true of French Guérande and Noirmoutier sea salt, for example. Similar unrefined sea salts are increasingly available from small producers in the US and UK. On the other hand, refined salt has been purified and bleached using a chemical process that also extends its shelf life. The refining process destroys any minerals present, except for sodium chloride. Additives and anti-caking agents are also added, as well as iodine and fluoride, which are both antiseptics and may inhibit fermentation activity.

Use fine salt that will dissolve well in dough, or dissolve it in the *eau de coulage*. It is important to be very precise when weighing salt, both to ensure flavor and a successful bread-making process; this is why salt is indicated in grams, not teaspoons, even for home bakers.

TOO MUCH SALT

Until the early 1950s, bread was only lightly salted, at a ratio of about 1 percent of flour weight. Modern baking techniques have led to increased salt to compensate for them: salt counteracts intensive mechanical kneading and counteracts the lack of flavor that results from using refined flour and shorter fermentation times. Perversely, salt inhibits fermentation, which necessitates using more yeast. Currently, we consume more salt than our bodies need to function. The World Health Organization recommends that individuals consume no more than 5 g of salt per day to reduce the risk of cardiovascular diseases. The FDA recommends that Americans limit their sodium intake to less than 2,300 mg per day, which is equal to about 1 tsp of salt. In 2002, the French Agency for Food, Environmental, and Occupational Health & Safety (ANSES) published a recommendation to reduce the amount of salt in bread, which accounts for 30 percent of French citizens' daily salt intake. The agency suggests using 18 g of salt per 1 kg of flour, or roughly 1.8 percent based on flour weight. The UK's Real Bread organization encourages bakers to aim for a maximum of 0.85 percent of salt in their bread (0.85 g per 100 g), in accordance with a 2024 salt reduction target set by Public Health England.

Sugar

Sugar is not as vital to baking as it is to cake, cookies, and pastry making, and is only used in certain kinds of bread. But sugar—or sugars, to be more precise—are naturally present in flour. Moisture and the mechanical action of kneading trigger an enzyme reaction that breaks down the starch (a polysaccharide) in flour into simple sugars, glucose and fructose, which then undergo various chemical reactions that can be strengthened by the addition of other sweeteners, like table sugar or honey.

Properties

A texturizing agent
Sugar diminishes the ability of protein naturally present in flour to absorb water and, by extension, retards the formation of the gluten network; as a result, a sweet dough is less elastic and easier to work with.

A fermentation trigger
Yeasts subsist on glucose and fructose alone, using these sugars to activate fermentation and produce CO_2. So when we add sugar to dough, we stimulate this activity. But when we add too much, sugar's hygroscopic power reduces the amount of available water in the dough necessary for the yeast to multiply.

A crust activator
When exposed to heat, sugars caramelize and improve crust color. They also play a role in the Maillard reaction (see p. 76). Adding milk, which contains lactose, another sugar, also plays a role in these reactions.

A flavor enhancer
Sugar tempers flavors, especially acidity.

A preservative
Sugar retains water, so a sweet bread tends to be soft and keeps longer.

Choosing the right sugar

Any kind of sugar can be added to bread dough—white granulated sugar, refined or raw cane sugar, molasses, or even honey. However, they do not all have the same sweetening power, so stick with what is indicated in the recipe.

HONEY

Honey has a distinctive flavor and is 1.3 times sweeter than white sugar. So for every 1¾ oz. (50 g) of sugar, substitute 1¼ oz. (30 g) of honey (basically, divide the quantity of sugar by 1.66). Honey also contains about 18 percent water, so you'll have to reduce the total amount of water in the recipe if you want to use honey in place of sugar. For example, if you substitute 1¾ oz. (50 g) of honey for white sugar, subtract ⅓ oz. (10 g) of water from the ingredients.

GOOD TO KNOW

Avoid sugar substitutes—they are not all heat stable. Furthermore, since they tend to be exceedingly sweet, they are used in such small quantities that their effect on dough is limited to flavor; they play no role in developing color or texture.

Fats, Eggs, and Milk

Butter, milk, and eggs are usually associated more with pastry than bread. But they are undeniably satisfying, which explains why they are found in "enriched" breads, usually some variation on the brioche. While not as rich in fat and sugar as *viennoiserie* (sweet, yeast-leavened baked goods), these specialty breads make use of the transformational properties of these indulgent ingredients.

FATS

Fats are most often used in Vienna breads, which call for the addition of butter, and Italian breads like ciabatta or focaccia, which contain olive oil.

Properties

A source of flavor
Fats, particularly butter and olive oil, contribute their own distinct flavors. They also bring out other flavors already present in dough.

A texturizing agent
Fat influences the formation of the gluten network. Dough made using a solid fat will be easier to shape and result in a silkier crumb. Fat also influences crust structure, contributing to a thinner, less crumbly final result.

A preservative
Fat retains water and slows the retrogradation of starch, the phenomenon that causes bread to go stale, resulting in bread with a longer shelf life.

Choosing the right fat

Butter
In France, butter contains about 82 percent fat (closer to 80 percent in the US; between 80 and 83 percent in the UK). Look for high-fat European-style or cultured butters if possible, now produced in the US by both small

creameries and large brands, and available in many supermarkets and online. For most of the recipes in this book, you should use a high-quality unsalted butter. If all you have is salted butter in a recipe that calls for unsalted butter, reduce the total salt called for in the recipe. Butter at room temperature is more easily incorporated into the dough. For vegans, cocoa butter and coconut oil make good butter substitutes.

Oil

Oil is 100 percent fat. If substituting oil for butter, remember that because oil is also a liquid, you will need to adjust the quantity of water called for in the recipe accordingly or risk creating a dough that is difficult to work with. Oil is more commonly found in savory breads, notably in Italian breads, which often call for olive oil.

BUTTER TYPES
The recipes in this book generally require unsalted butter, though a few call for *beurre demi-sel* or *beurre salé* (see below).

- **Beurre cru**, raw or unpasteurized butter, is made exclusively with raw cream that has not undergone thermal pasteurization. Raw butter is available in some areas of the US, but sale across state lines is forbidden.
- **Beurre extra-fin** is butter made from pasteurized cream that has not been frozen or deep-frozen.
- **Beurre fine** is butter also made from pasteurized cream, but unlike *extra-fin* butter, up to 30 percent may be frozen or deep-frozen.
- **Beurre concentré**, or concentrated butter, contains a minimum of 99.8 percent milkfat.
- **Beurre demi-sel** (semi-salted butter) in France contains 0.5 to 3 g of salt per 100 g of product. According to the National Dairy Council, American salted butters generally contain 1.6 to 1.7 percent salt, but each company determines how much salt to use in its product. For the recipes in this book, American salted butter can be used in place of French *beurre demi-sel*.
- **Beurre salé**, or salted butter, in France contains more than 3 percent salt.
- **Beurre de tourage** is called dry butter because it contains less water and more butterfat than other butters: 84 percent. It is ideal for making *viennoiseries*.
- **Beurre tartinable**, or spreadable butter, is made with added emulsifiers to keep it soft when cold.
- **Margarine** contains 80 percent fat, mostly plant-based, with 3 percent added milkfat.

 GOOD TO KNOW
To avoid hindering the formation of a dough's gluten network, fats are added during the second stage of kneading.

MILK

Milk contributes moisture, fat, and sugar to dough. Whole milk in France contains nearly 90 percent water, about 3.5 percent fat (3.25 percent in the US; 3.5 percent in the UK), and 5 percent sugar in the form of lactose.

Properties

A texturizing agent
Although milk mainly provides moisture to a dough, because of its fat content it also contributes to a fluffier bread.
A crust activator
When exposed to heat, lactose caramelizes and colors the crust.
A preservative
Milk retards the drying process and improves shelf life.

Choosing the right milk

Cow's milk is the most commonly used variety in baking. Choose whole (rather than low-fat or skim), organic, pasteurized milk whenever possible, unless specified otherwise. You can also use powdered milk, which is shelf-stable and easier to store.

Plant-based milks can also be used in place of animal milks, but beware: some have a strong flavor.

Buttermilk—*lait ribot*, *babeurre*, or *petit lait* in French—was originally a by-product of butter making. Now, fermented buttermilk is cultured by adding lactic acid bacteria to milk. It is also used to make soda bread (see recipe p. 319).

VIENNA BREAD

Vienna bread, the precursor to *viennoiserie*, was imported to France in the nineteenth century by the Austrian businessman August Zang. This milk bread was made using a poolish (see p. 137), milk, brewer's yeast, and *farine de gruau*, a finely ground, highly refined flour used in enriched breads. The Austrians developed a way to stabilize yeast by compressing it, building on Louis Pasteur's research into fermentation. They also invented Viennese steam ovens, which inject steam during baking to produce a shiny crust.

EGGS

Rarely used in bread making, eggs are mostly used to achieve a specific texture in specialty breads.

Properties

Eggs are roughly half water, 32 percent fat, and 16 percent protein.

An emulsifier

Egg yolks contain lecithin, which acts as a binder: it stabilizes emulsions and helps to evenly disperse fat. Egg proteins have surface-active properties that help aerate dough and contribute to the formation of holes in the crumb, called *alvéolage*.

A texturizing agent

The fat in eggs makes for a softer crumb and improves volume.

Crust action

Used as a wash, eggs add color and shine to crust (through the Maillard reaction).

Crumb action

Yellow and red pigments contained in the egg yolk, called xanthophylls, add color to the crumb.

Choosing the right eggs

In the US, eggs are categorized according to one of three consumer grades established by the USDA. Only eggs that have been officially graded by the USDA are eligible to bear the USDA stamp.
- USDA Grade AA – The freshest and highest-quality eggs
- USDA Grade A – Very high-quality eggs
- USDA Grade B – These eggs are usually used for baking or to make egg products, depending on the number of defects

Egg cartons can be found with many labels: cage-free, pasture-raised, organic, etc., which may suggest the chickens from which the eggs came did not live on factory farms. Other labels, like natural, farm-fresh, and pasteurized have no relevance to animal welfare and are more about marketing.

European eggs, including UK eggs, are stamped with a code beginning with a number that indicates how the hens were raised:
- 0 for organic hens;
- 1 for free-range hens;
- 2 for floor-raised hens;
- 3 for cage- or battery-raised hens.

 GOOD TO KNOW

Eggs in the recipes refer to hens' eggs with an average weight of 2 oz. (55–57 g) in its shell: 1 oz. (30 g) for the white and ¾ oz. (20 g) for the yolk. These are classed as "large" eggs in the USA and Canada and "medium" in the UK.

Special Ingredients
—

You can add all kinds of ingredients to bread, and that's what makes "specialty" or "fancy" breads so full of possibility. However, there are specific ways and means of adding these "inclusions." The texture and the density of whatever is being added shouldn't impede the rising process. As a general rule, choose small foods or chop solid foods into pieces beforehand.

The kind of dough should also be considered: a stiff dough, for example, is more suited to the addition of solid ingredients than a wet dough.

SEEDS VS. GRAINS

When it comes to bread inclusions, oleaginous (oil-containing) seeds like poppy, pumpkin, sunflower, flax, and sesame are different from grains (wheat, rye, millet, quinoa, etc.). Small in size and tender, oleaginous seeds can be added directly to the dough. Grains are very hard and must be soaked before using, which also makes them easier to digest. They can also be cooked as a pilaf.

Method
1. Place the grains in a bowl.
2. Cover with boiling water; stir to mix well.
3. Cover the bowl tightly with plastic wrap.
4. Refrigerate for at least 12 hours, until all (or most of) the water has been absorbed by the grains.
5. Drain off any excess water before adding the grains to the dough.

SPROUTED GRAINS

Any whole grain can be sprouted (and then added to bread), as long as sanitary growing conditions are maintained. Choose sprouting seeds available in health food shops and use a seed sprouter to protect the germination process from risk of contamination by pathogenic bacteria or molds. Sprouted grains can be kept for several days in the refrigerator.

Method

1. Place the grains in the seed sprouter tray and cover with filtered or bottled water.
2. The following day, drain off the water. Keep the seeds moist by rinsing them twice a day, in the morning and evening, until the germ emerges. If necessary, use your fingers to untangle the germs.

ESSENE BREAD

The Essenes were members of a Jewish community of ascetics who lived in Palestine, on the shores of the Dead Sea, over two thousand years ago. They encouraged a life lived in harmony with nature, and they ate a diet of mostly bread and raw fruits and vegetables. Essene bread was a thin cake made of grains that were sprouted, then crushed and ground, before being laid out to dry in the sun on rocks.

To make your own, press sprouted grains (you can crush them lightly) into pastry rings on a baking sheet lined with parchment paper. Dry in a convection oven at 176°F (80°C).

NUTS AND NUT BUTTERS

Walnuts, hazelnuts, almonds, and other nuts all marry well with bread. Choose blanched (without skin) and unsalted varieties. To bring out their flavor, you can also lightly toast them in the oven or a dry skillet. Avoid using the dregs from bags forgotten at the back of the cupboard, as nuts go rancid quickly and will ruin the taste of bread. Chop larger pieces with a knife or in a food processor.

Hazelnut, pistachio, and peanut butters, and even tahini (sesame paste), make excellent bread inclusions. Nut butters contribute flavor and their high fat content makes for a softer crumb.

HERBS, SPICES, AND POWDERS

Herbs, spices, and powders are very easy to add to bread dough; used in minute quantities, they have little impact on the structure of the dough or its ability to rise.

Powdered spices and powders in general (cocoa, matcha, etc.) should be mixed directly into the flour. How much you use depends on dough volume and the intensity of flavor or color you wish to achieve. Spices, both whole and ground, can be toasted to bring out their flavor (let them cool well before adding them to dough). Avoid spice blends, which often contain salt. Whole spices, like caraway or fenugreek, should be added during the second phase of kneading.

Fresh herbs are typically better in bread than dried ones, and should be finely chopped to prevent oxidization.

 GOOD TO KNOW

Both European and American law forbid the use of food coloring in bread baking. From this standpoint, activated charcoal, considered an additive (E153), is not legally authorized for use in bread, even though it is entirely edible. Turmeric, matcha, and fruit and vegetable juices can be used as natural colorants.

FRUIT AND VEGETABLES

Fruit and vegetables make a tempting addition to your bread. However, because of their high water content, any fruit or vegetables used must be cooked before they can go into the dough. Whatever method you decide to use, the goal is to remove as much water as possible to avoid dough saturation.

Depending on the fruit or vegetable, you might roast, poach, grill, or steam it. Cut fruit and vegetables into cubes before adding them to dough, or consider using small pieces of candied or dried fruit.

CHEESE

Cheese works really well with bread, and not just as a topping or decorative finish. However, it's important to consider the texture of the cheese before adding it to dough.

Coarsely shred hard and semi-hard cheeses like Emmental, Mimolette, Cheddar, and Pecorino. If shredded too fine, these cheeses risk melting into the dough.

Soft cheeses like fresh goat or blue cheeses tend to blend with the dough and will impart flavor to the bread. These creamy cheeses will also enrich the dough, bringing it closer to a brioche-style bread.

MEAT AND FISH

For food safety, storage, and textural reasons, meat and fish must be cooked, salted, or smoked before being added to bread. Bacon bits, small cubes of ham or chorizo, and pork scratchings/cracklings all make good inclusions. Seafood options might include smoked salmon, bottarga, or bonito flakes. Eat any bread containing meat or fish quickly; it doesn't keep well.

From Crust to Crumb

—

Bread is evaluated according to several criteria: crust, crumb, color, and flavor, as well as other sensory properties like odor and mouthfeel. Each bread has its own personality. Obviously a rustic *tourte de meule* won't have the same crust as a delicate *pain de mie*. To the question "What makes a good bread?" there is only one answer: "Trust your senses." You should touch, smell, taste, look at, and even listen to bread. The question, "What makes a beautiful bread?" becomes meaningless if you consider each of these criteria, rather than limiting yourself to visual appearance alone.

CRUST

"The crust on a loaf of French bread is a marvel, first off, because of the almost panoramic impression it gives, as though one had the Alps, the Taurus range, or even the Andean Cordillera right in the palm of the hand," writes the poet Francis Ponge in *The Nature of Things*. Thick or thin, soft or crunchy, crust is an invitation to break bread. It captures the eye, whets the appetite, and suggests the flavors to come. It also reveals much about the fermentation process in the way it splits cleanly along *grignes*, cuts made during scoring that open up into sharp, crunchy ridges that bakers call *oreilles* or "ears."

Texture

At temperatures above 212°F (100°C), water evaporates from the surface of bread and triggers the drying process. Heat and moisture trigger several chemical reactions that impact crust texture, color, and flavor.

Color

When exposed to heat, starch molecules break down into dextrin, which produces a reddish color. At temperatures above 320°F (160°C), residual sugars begin to caramelize. At temperatures above 347°F (175°C), the Maillard reaction (see p. 76) triggers the development of melanonids, which contain brown pigments. These reactions are heavily influenced by temperature and moisture levels. In contrast, bread baked at a low temperature using steam will remain white.

Flavor

The reactions described above produce characteristic flavors: dextrinization imparts a biscuit-like flavor; caramelization creates grilled or toasted notes that may verge on bitter; and the Maillard reaction also produces complex flavors.

What a professional baker looks for in a crust:

- a well-proportioned shape;
- loft (amount of rise);
- scoring (ideally open);
- crust thickness;
- shine;
- a blistered surface.

GOOD TO KNOW

The Maillard reaction is a chemical reaction that was discovered and described by French chemist Louis-Camille Maillard in 1911. It occurs when sugars and the amino acids in proteins are heated together, producing a browning effect and releasing powerful flavors similar to what the Japanese call *umami*.

CRUMB

The crumb lies hidden under the crust, only revealing itself when the loaf is sliced open. It's the professional's reward for a job well done and the Holy Grail for amateurs who finally achieve regular holes. Technically, the crumb is a sort of mousse congealed by the gelatinization of starch, which traps water; this explains why fresh bread is so supple. Over time, the starch crystallizes (retrogradation), and the bread dries out and hardens.

Texture

Between 158°F (70°C) and 208°F (98°C), gluten coagulates into the crumb's final structure. The crumb remains white because it never reaches a temperature greater than 212°F (100°C). The texture of the crumb depends on the hydration level of the dough, fermentation, and the type of flour used. Low hydration produces a bread with a tight crumb, like *pain de brié*, a Norman specialty that is beaten during kneading. Breads rich in gluten are more elastic and will more easily trap CO_2 bubbles to create beautiful holes, like those found in a baguette or ciabatta. Rye and einkorn flours tend to absorb water and will result in a dense, creamy crumb.

Color

Crumb color depends in part on the type of grain used. Bread made with einkorn will have a lovely golden crumb, while rye imparts a dark beige color. The type of flour—and its ratio of whole grains—also plays a role. In the past, *pain bis*, a grayish-brown bread, and *pain noir*, black bread, were made with flour rich in bran. The term *pain noir* is still used to describe German rye bread. *Pain blanc*, or white bread, made with highly refined flour and a symbol of quality in the post-war years, is less popular today in artisan baking. Very white bread may also be the result of oxidization from over-kneading; the excess oxygen introduced into the dough destroys carotenoids (orange pigments) that are naturally present in flour.

Flavor

Grains express their characteristic flavors through the crumb: the roundness of wheat, the nuttiness of einkorn, and the spiciness of rye. Fermentation also contributes its own flavors. A "yeasty" taste is characteristic of very yeasty breads. Bread made with levain develops a vast palette of flavors due to the wealth of bacteria present and the multiplication of lactic and acetic acids. Watch out for "false notes," which are not naturally present in bread: chlorine (from tap water or chemicals in flour); a levain flavor from inactive levain; and toasty flavors from dough improvers.

What a professional baker looks for in a crumb:
- intensity of color;
- size, depth, and evenness of holes;
- shine;
- moisture;
- elasticity;
- acidity.

GOOD TO KNOW

The smell of warm bread immediately whets the appetite; in fact, studies have shown that it actually activates salivation. This is due to aromatic compounds that form as a result of the Maillard reaction, notably 6-acetyl-2,3,4,5-tetrahydropyridine—an unwieldly name for molecules that could very well contribute to better well-being. Researchers have demonstrated that the aroma of freshly baked bread triggers feelings of happiness and contentment.

LISTEN TO BREAD!

Sound is a key element in fully experiencing bread. As soon as it comes out of the oven and the cooling phase—*ressuage* in French—begins, you can hear the bread "sing," as bakers say: a series of quiet crackling sounds caused by air escaping through the crust.

You can also judge the crustiness of bread by listening as the knife slices through it, and when you chew it. Think of the sound a fresh baguette makes when you bite into the crusty end.

Breads of France

Baguette, *pain de campagne*, *tourte de meule*—French bakeries often serve a dozen different kinds of bread, defined by many different criteria, including weight, shape, and the use of a specific flour, ingredients, or technique.

Bread in France is governed by:
- regulatory standards (organic bread, *pain maison* [bread made on-site], bread made with levain, traditional French bread);
- common and agreed-upon commercial use (for example, the difference between baguettes and *flûtes*);
- law ("wood-fired" bread must be baked in a wood-fired stone deck oven).

There are no official regulations regarding the price and weight of bread in France, other than that it must conform to what is indicated on the label—which must include the name of the bread, the weight if less than 7 oz. (200 g), and price.

Finally, a store can only call itself a bakery if bread is made entirely on-site and has not been frozen or deep frozen at any time during the bread-making process.

 GOOD TO KNOW
- *Flûtes* are thicker and heavier than baguettes (14 oz./400 g).
- *Ficelles* are thinner and lighter than baguettes (4½ oz./125 g).

TRADITIONAL FRENCH BREAD

It was on the initiative of the bakers themselves that the appellation *pain de tradition française* (traditional French bread) was established by decree no. 93-1074, passed in 1993. Known as the "bread decree," it was developed to safeguard the unique characteristics of the French bread-making tradition in response to the increasing use of additives (following harmonization of European regulations).

The ingredients in traditional French bread are specified in article two of the decree, which also stipulates that the bread cannot have been frozen at any stage. The decree states that traditional French bread must be made with wheat flour, salt, and water, and fermented with baker's yeast or levain. The addition of three dough improvers is allowed: relative to the total weight of flour used, a maximum of 2 percent fava bean flour, 0.5 percent soy flour, and 0.3 percent malted wheat flour. Eventually the list was expanded to include gluten (because it's naturally present in flour); fungal amylases, which are processing aids that disappear during baking and are not considered additives; and "inactive yeast for salt reduction," which is yeast that has been rendered inactive by heat and helps relax the gluten network. The decree does not officially define "traditional French" flour, a name used by millers to refer to a blend of wheat flours and authorized additives and processing aids.

The addition of seeds and fruit to French bread does not comply with regulations but is sometimes tolerated. The "bread decree" also establishes a definition for *pain maison*, which must be kneaded, shaped, and baked where it is sold (or on a defined sales circuit, in the case of an itinerant baker), and must be made with levain. Baker's yeast may be added at a ratio of no more than 0.2 percent of the total flour weight (for example, 1 g for 500 g of flour).

 GOOD TO KNOW

- Fava bean flour acts as a bleaching agent by causing dough to turn white through oxidation. It also strengthens the gluten network.
- Soy flour has the same properties as fava bean flour, but it also relaxes dough.
- Malted wheat flour promotes fermentation and gives color to the crust during baking.

BAGUETTE

The baguette symbolizes French bread, and the French consume ten billion each year. No one really knows when it was created, but it's at least a century old—the first use of the word "baguette" in reference to bread appeared in 1920.

The baguette wasn't created for aesthetic reasons, but for two practical ones. In the late nineteenth century, standard breads weighing 4½ lb. (2 kg) and measuring a little over 2½ ft. (70 cm) were taxed. By changing the size of the bread, bakers avoided the tax. Then, in March 1919, a law was passed prohibiting "the employment of workers to make bread and pastry between ten o'clock at night and four o'clock in the morning." In response, bakers invented new, less time-consuming shapes that they would be able to sell to customers in the morning. The baguette remained a specialty, even luxury, bread until the 1950s.

Neither the weight nor the shape of an ordinary baguette is regulated. The dictionary of the Académie Française describes a "long, thin bread weighing 250 grams." Traditionally there are five *grignes* (the slashes made on dough to allow CO_2 to escape during baking) on a baguette. Only the "Label Rouge" appellation has specifications, established in 2002: Label Rouge flour no. 32.89, drinking water, salt, no more than 1.5 percent yeast, five *grignes*, a length of 23 to 25½ in. (60 to 65 cm), a width of 2 to 2⅓ in. (5 to 6 cm), and a weight of 8¾ to 10½ oz. (250 to 300 g).

Each year, two French contests attempt to crown the best baguette. The Confédération Nationale de la Boulangerie and Boulangerie-Pâtisserie Française organize a national competition to determine the best traditional French baguette. The Grand Prix de la Baguette de la Ville de Paris (Best Baguette in Paris Competition) has been held each year since 1994, on the initiative of Jacques Chirac, the City of Paris, and the Chambre Professionnelle des Artisans Boulanger-Pâtissiers. A list of the ten best artisan bakers in the capital is established, by order of merit. First place receives a medal, €4,000 in prize money (about $4,700, or £3,400), and becomes the official supplier to the Elysée, the French presidential residence, sending fifteen baguettes each morning for a year.

CLASSIC FRENCH BREADS

The following breads contribute to the diversity of the French baking tradition. While they each have common names, none of them is subject to any official regulations.

Pain de campagne

In his book *The Taste of Bread,* chemist and bread expert Raymond Calvel writes, "Country-style bread epitomizes the dominant aspects of the countryside and the supposed virtues that are attributed to it: naturalness, simplicity, and a rustic wholesomeness." He notes with regret that these "overly dusted" breads are rarely worthy of their name. No strict recipe exists for *pain de campagne*, and bakers generally use a blend of whole wheat and rye flours. To prevent the crumb from going too white, avoid excessive kneading and use a method with long fermentation to develop flavor (poolish, *pâte fermentée*, levain, etc.). See recipe p. 250.

Tourte

In pastry making, the word *tourte* refers to a covered tart, while in baking a *tourte* is a round, low-rise bread, often made with rye flour. The term "*de meule*" refers to the use of stone-ground flour. See recipe p. 206.

Bâtard

As its name suggests, this bread has a "bastard" form, something between a baguette and a round bread. It weighs about 1 lb. (450 g) and has an elongated, stout, torpedo-like shape.

Pain bis

This name, rarely used today, refers to a bread made with T80 "*bise*" flour.

Pain complet

A bread made using "*complète*" (T110) or "*intégrale*" flour (T150), equivalent to whole wheat and dark whole wheat (100 percent whole wheat) flours, respectively. In Germany, *vollkornbrot* is made with whole rye flour and whole grains.

Pain de son

This "bran bread" made with wheat flour and added bran, the external layer of the wheat kernel, is rich in fiber (see Bread and Nutrition p. 21).

Pain de méteil

Méteil originally referred to a natural combination of wheat and rye (or other grains) cultivated together in the same field. This method of farming is no longer practiced today, and *pain de méteil* is made using a blend (usually 50/50) of rye and wheat flours.

Pain de mie

This white, often square bread has a soft crumb and is used to make croque monsieur, club sandwiches, toast, and canapés. In the US, it is often known as a Pullman loaf, after an American railway car company that served the bread on its trains. See recipe p. 222.

Pain viennois

This lightly enriched, indulgent bread usually appears shaped like a baguette. The name—Vienna bread—derives from the Viennese style of bread making. See recipe p. 294.

SPECIALTY BREADS

French baking tradition customarily uses the term *pain spéciaux* ("specialty bread") to refer to breads that are not commonly consumed. This is, however, a vague and outdated definition; considering the diversity on offer today, it's difficult to label any bread as either ordinary or special.

REGIONAL BREADS

Fifty years ago, France had a rich heritage of regional breads, as diverse as the country's wine and cheese traditions. In the 1980s, the baker Lionel Poilâne began the fascinating task of collecting and cataloging these breads, which had fallen victim to modern bread making. Only about a dozen remain today. They vary by shape, the way they are kneaded, and the flour used; some used to be made with landrace (local variety) wheat.

Faluche Upper France

This small, tender crustless bread is made with white flour, and has short baking and rising times. It also goes by the name *flamique* or *flamiche*, and used to serve as a quick meal for laborers and a snack for children. The word *faluche*, the black velvet cap traditionally worn by students in Lille, is derived from the bread. See recipe p. 234.

Boulot Upper France

This white, yeasty bread is usually sold pre-sliced and is used for making open-faced sandwiches.

Tabatière Picardy

To make this variation on the *boule*, a quarter of the dough is spread and folded up over the top. This type of bread is also found in the Jura region.

Pain régence Oise

Composed of five balls of dough, this bread was one of the first to be made with brewer's yeast, in the seventeenth century, and was considered a luxury bread.

Pain brié Normandy

This very white, compact, low-hydration *pain de mie* was historically kneaded by beating the dough with a stick called a *brie*. It is scored with lovely open *grignes*. See recipe p. 236.

Pain plié de Morlaix Brittany

This round of white bread is shaped so that a sort of "cap" crowns the loaf.

Pain chapeau Brittany

This large *boule* is topped with a smaller one, and then poked (with a finger) in the center of the bread. The English cottage loaf has a similar shape.

Fouée Touraine

A flat round of dough baked in a very hot oven to make it "puff." The name is derived from the woodstove in which it is cooked (*fou* is Old French for "fire"). It's easy to make by flattening a small piece of dough and baking it in a hot pan on high heat for a few minutes.

Couronne bordelaise Gironde

This bread crown is composed of six to nine balls of dough connected by a disk of dough cut and folded back from the center to form a "collar." Proofing is done in a crown-shaped banneton.

Tordu Southwest France

This long bread is rolled into a twisted shape. It may also be made by braiding two pieces of bread together.

Portemanteau de Toulouse Upper Garonne

To make this uniquely shaped bread, the dough is first stretched, then the ends flattened and twisted along a third of its length. Proofing is done in a linen cloth with the dough seam-side up so that the twists are on top during baking.

Michettes de Provence Provence

To make these small, elongated breads split down the center, the dough is first rolled out in a rectangle. A mixture of water and oil is applied to one half and the other half is dusted with flour. The dough is then folded in half. After proofing for 30 minutes, the dough is cut into rectangles using a pastry ruler and placed sliced edge down so they open during baking.

Fougasse Provence

This oval-shaped bread begins as an olive-oil-based dough that is rolled out and scored on each side to resemble a palm frond. It was originally intended to allow the baker to make sure that the oven was at the right temperature before baking other breads. See recipe p. 238.

Pain de Beaucaire Languedoc

This bread is made with the same technique used for *michettes* de Provence, but on a larger scale. A cleft down the middle divides the bread in two.

Main de Nice Southeast France
This bread of Italian extraction, shaped like a four-pointed croissant, was immortalized by the photographer Robert Doisneau in a photograph showing Picasso with two mains de Nice next to his plate. The firm crumb is similar to that of *pain brié*.

Coupiette Corsica
This bread is shaped into two easily detachable lobes.

Couronne lyonnaise Auvergne-Rhône-Alpes
This round loaf has a hole in the center made using an elbow or the palm of the hand, which is then enlarged using thumbs and hands.

Auvergnat Auvergne
This *boule* is topped with another circular piece of dough.

Pain vaudois Savoy
This Swiss bread is shaped like a ball and scored to form a cross in the center. Sometimes another ball is placed in the center of the cross.

Pain cordon Burgundy
This oblong bread is topped with a rope of dough that causes the loaf to split during baking. The rope is placed at the bottom of the banneton, before the main dough.

Sübrot Alsace
This uniquely shaped bread demands all the baker's expertise. The dough is divided into two rectangles that are rolled out and greased, then layered on top of one another and cut into diamond shapes. The name means "penny bread."

Bretzel Alsace
This small bread is braided into a classic pretzel shape and scalded in boiling water before being baked in the oven. It is usually sprinkled with salt, but sweet versions also exist. See recipe p. 243.

REGIONAL BREADS

FALUCHE

BOULOT

TABATIÈRE

PAIN PLIÉ
DE MORLAIX

PAIN
RÉGENCE

PAIN BRIÉ

BAGUETTE

BRETZEL

PAIN CORDON

SÜBROT

PAIN CHAPEAU

FOUÉE

PAIN VAUDOIS

COURONNE
BORDELAISE

AUVERGNAT

COURONNE
LYONNAISE

TORDU

MICHETTES
DE PROVENCE

FOUGASSE

MAIN DE NICE

PORTEMANTEAU
DE TOULOUSE

PAIN DE BEAUCAIRE

COUPIETTE

Breads of the World

——

Bread is made all over the world, and each kind has its own distinctive flavor, form, or characteristics based on local tradition, culture, or resources. While this is by no means an exhaustive list (there are hundreds, perhaps thousands of breads in all corners of the globe), this general overview by continent offers a look at the immense variety of breads—and shapes, and ingredients, and preparations—found worldwide.

WHITE AND BLACK BREADS OF EUROPE

Generally speaking, European bread preferences fall into two regions. To the west of an imaginary border stretching from Brussels to Zagreb, people prefer white, well-risen breads made with wheat flour, from Belgian *pisolets* to Italian focaccia and encompassing the entire French repertory. Wrapped *pain de mie*-style breads dominate in the United Kingdom, and are used for toast and sandwiches. Small artisanal bakeries produce traditional loaves and local specialties. *Broa de milho*, made with half wheat flour and half corn flour, has a yellow crumb and is eaten in Portugal, where bread is consumed in large quantities, as it is in Spain, notably in bars in the form of *bocadillos* or *montaditos* served with tapas and other dishes.

To the east of this imaginary border line and all the way to Russia, there exists a tradition of black bread like German pumpernickel and *vollkornbrot*, and Swedish *knäckebröd*, made with rye flour. These breads are often rich in grains and seeds and flavored with spices like caraway, coriander, and cumin.

FLATBREADS, FROM THE MIDDLE EAST TO INDIA

Flatbreads from the region that encompasses what was once the Fertile Crescent, the birthplace of agriculture, resemble the first breads ever made. The Egyptian *baladi*, the pita, and the naan are all variations on these flat, round breads. Turkey is the largest consumer of bread in the world, and the country boasts a wide variety that includes *ekmek*, *simit*, *pide*, and *bôrek*. In India, flatbreads cooked in a tandoori oven or fried are eaten with every meal. They include *chapati*, *paratha*, *papadam*, and *roti*.

STEAMED BREADS OF EAST ASIA

East Asian breads are distinctive for their fluffy crumb and nearly absent crust, both of which are a result of steam cooking. One example is the Chinese mantou, also called *bao*, which comes in filled or plain versions. The Korean *jjinppang* is a small steamed bun filled with red bean paste. A very puffy *pain de mie* called *shokupan* is popular in Japan.

FLATBREADS OF NORTHERN AND SUB-SAHARAN AFRICA

There still exists in Northern Africa a tradition of making homemade bread and cooking it in the village or neighborhood oven. These breads are often made with semolina, like Moroccan *tarfarnout* or Algerian *matlouh*. In sub-Saharan Africa, local grains are used to make bread or flatbreads: teff for Ethiopian *injera*; sorghum or corn for *ablo*, a small steamed bread from Western African; fermented corn for *kenkey* in Ghana.

AMERICAN BREADS

North America is often associated with the sandwich bread or Pullman loaf, a very white, oversized *pain de mie*. But it's also the home of San Francisco sourdough and Southern cornbread. Indigenous peoples in the American Southwest make fry bread (thin rounds of dough fried in oil) or pueblo bread (a moist, puffy bread enriched with lard or butter). In Central and South America, corn is a staple, and the breads, like tortillas (Mexico, Honduras, Guatemala, Nicaragua, and Costa Rica) or arepas (Venezuela) reflect that. The Brazilian *pão de queijo* and the Colombian *pan de queso* are soft rolls made with cheese and (gluten-free) tapioca flour.

AUSTRALIAN BUSH BREAD

Australia, a land of immigrants, has imported bread from around the world. However, Aboriginal Australians crushed wild seeds into flour that was then mixed with water. The dough was baked in the ashes of the camp fire to make bush bread. Settlers from other parts of the world adapted this into a typical Australian bread suited to rustic bush life: known as damper, this slightly enriched soda bread is made with baking powder or baking soda.

BAGELS AND BURGERS: FROM EUROPE TO AMERICA

Jewish immigrants from Eastern Europe brought both the bagel and the burger across the Atlantic, where they became staples of North American cuisine. The bagel was supposedly invented by a Jewish baker from Vienna. The story goes that he developed a small bread shaped like a stirrup (*beugel* in Austrian German) as a gift for the king of Poland, Jean III Sobieski, who, with the help of his soldiers, fought off the Ottomans during the Battle of Vienna in 1683. The *beugel* entered Polish cuisine and became, inexplicably, a traditional gift given to new mothers. Eventually it traveled east, all the way to Russia. The burger, or hamburger, was created in Hamburg, Germany, where salted beef was mixed with onions and breadcrumbs to extend shelf life. In the nineteenth century, this ground beef dish was served aboard the ships that transported Eastern European migrants from Hamburg to New York. Americans took a liking to it and came up with the idea to eat it in a bun.

 GOOD TO KNOW

One of the most prestigious and popular literary conferences in the United States, the Middlebury Bread Loaf Writers, Conference, was created in Vermont in 1926. It derives its name from Bread Loaf Mountain. Renowned writers including Robert Frost, Carson McCullers, Norman Mailer, Toni Morrison, and John Irving have all participated.

Sandwiches
and More

By the Middle Ages, nobles were using bread as a support for meat, called a *tranchoir*. In the countryside, people ate *trempes*: milk, soup, or wine poured over a slice of thick bread. Putting something on or in bread is the best invention since bread itself!

SANDWICH

The sandwich is the answer to turning a hunk of bread into a complete meal; billions are sold worldwide every year. The invention of the sandwich is attributed to Englishman John Montagu, Earl of Sandwich (a city in southeast England near Dover), and the same man for whom an archipelago of eleven islands off the coast of South America was named. The story goes that in the 1760s, this inveterate card player ordered a servant to bring him bread topped with cold meat so he wouldn't have to interrupt the game he was playing. Two and half centuries later, his biographer revised the story, maintaining that the minister actually spent his time working at his desk.

In 1762, the historian Edward Gibbon described in his journal the sandwiches eaten at the evening meal in his London club. Nineteenth-century American cookbooks mention smoked tongue or lobster sandwiches. In 1928, the American engineer Otto Frederick Rohwedder invented the first machine for slicing bread. In France, the widespread use of the word "sandwich" is a recent phenomenon. The writer Honoré Balzac used it to describe a snack eaten by the bourgeoisie. With the advent of paid vacations, the sandwich became a staple of picnics and the holiday exodus, before becoming a common lunch option for office workers.

Many variations on the sandwich are found around the world, from the Vietnamese *banh mi* to the Italian panini, from the Turkish *döner kebab* to the American hot dog and grilled Reuben. The chic club sandwich is standard fare at the fanciest brasseries and on room service menus at luxury hotels.

OPEN-FACED SANDWICH

The French call it a *tartine*, and as the name implies, the open-face sandwich wears its filling spread across a single slice of bread. Appropriate at every meal, from breakfast to snack time, it also makes for a savory hors d'oeuvre in the form of canapés. The baker Lionel Poilâne made the *tartine* a classic brasserie dish.

In Spain, *tartines* are known as *tostas*; in Italy, crostini and bruschetta; and in Denmark, *smörbröd*.

CASSE-CROÛTE

The expression *casse-croûte* (literally "breaking crust") dates from the late nineteenth century, and refers to a simple meal of bread eaten by laborers and farmers. Long associated with the laboring professions, certain people in France—night workers, for example—are entitled to an *"indemnité casse-croûte,"* or meal allowance.

BRIQUET

Coal miners were allowed a break to eat their *casse-croûte*, which consisted of cheese or charcuterie between two slices of bread. The name *briquet* supposedly derives from the sandwich's resemblance to a brick, or perhaps from the English word "break." Upon returning home in the evening, the miner would give the leftovers to his children. The bread, which had the flavor and odor of the mine pit, was called *pain d'alouette*, literally "lark's bread."

PAN BAGNAT

Literally *pain baigné* or *pain mouillé*, meaning "soaked bread" in Occitan, *pan bagnat* is a specialty of Nice. Originally it was a meal eaten by the poor: stale bread softened with water or tomato juice. It is topped with the same ingredients used in a salade niçoise, as well as a boiled egg, the only cooked ingredient tolerated by the Commune libre du pan bagnat, an organization that defends the appellation. See recipe p. 366.

CANAPÉS

Most likely inspired by Russian *zakousi*, canapés (small pieces of bread or pastry topped with savory food, often eaten as hors d'oeuvres) are named for their cushion-like shape (*canapé* means sofa in French). Canapés were de rigueur at cocktail hour in the 1970s and 1980s, before industrial savory snacks proliferated.

CROQUE MONSIEUR

This hot ham-and-cheese sandwich supposedly appeared for the first time on the menu of a Parisian café in 1910. The grilled cheese is the American version, and cheese toasties—or Welsh rarebit—are what you'll find in the UK. See recipes pp. 352 and 363.

MOUILLETTES

These strips of bread, sometimes buttered and toasted, are the constant companion of the soft-boiled egg. Some chefs give them a gourmet touch by topping them with truffle or foie gras.

JAMBON-BEURRE

The emblematic French *casse-croûte*, the *jambon-beurre*, or ham-and-butter sandwich, was made popular by the laborers who worked in Paris's central market, Les Halles, carrying heavy loads within the belly of the city. But it wasn't until the 1950s that bakers began making it with the easier-to-transport baguette. This sandwich is now the most commonly consumed variety in France: one in two sandwiches sold is a *jambon-beurre*, and a total of 1.2 billion were eaten in 2017—and this despite the fact that in the last ten years, burger sales have been steadily gaining on the sandwich (and ultimately exceeding it). It's also called "the Parisian." To make one, you need a good baguette, real butter, and a fine *jambon blanc de Paris*.

Glossary of Bread Baking Terms

Alveoli The holes in the crumb formed by air pockets.

Autolyse This is a stage of rest, after the flour and water have been gently mixed together, and before the remaining ingredients are added.

Baguette peel or **baguette transfer peel (*paline*)** A thin wood board used to transfer baguettes to the oven.

***Baiser du boulanger* (baker's kiss)** The mark made when two breads join during baking.

Baker's kiss See *Baiser du boulanger.*

Baker's peel A beveled-edge piece of flat wood or aluminum with a handle used to transfer large loaves and pizzas to the oven.

Baker's yeast/commercial yeast (*levure de boulangerie*) A concentration of various strains of *Saccharomyces cerevisiae* used to ferment bread dough, available as fresh, active dry, or instant yeast.

Baking stone/pizza stone (*pierre à pain*) A porous, refractory stone used to bake pizzas and hearth breads.

Banneton A proofing basket, sometimes lined with linen, in which dough is proofed.

Bassinage The addition of water during kneading bread dough.

Batch (*fournée*) The amount of bread that can be baked at one time in an oven.

Bench scraper (*coupe-pâte*) A rigid, straight-edged tool used to divide dough.

Boulage The process of shaping a round of dough, or *boule.*

Boulangerie The French word for a bakery selling mainly breads, especially traditional French breads like baguettes and *pain de campagne*. Although a *boulangerie* may sell pastries, it is not a specialized pastry shop (which is called a *pâtisserie*). In France, the term *"boulangerie"* is regulated by law and can only be used by establishments that make their own bread.

Bowl scraper (*corne*) A handle-free piece of flexible plastic with one curved edge and one straight edge used to remove dough from bowls, fingers, and just about anywhere else.

Bulk fermentation (*pointage*) The first phase of rest after kneading and the first step in fermentation; also called "first rise."

Chew (*mâche*) A term used to describe the pleasant texture of the crumb in levain-based bread.

Cooling (*ressuage*) The phase just after bread is removed from the oven when water is allowed to evaporate outward through the crust.

Corne See Bowl scraper.

***Couche* (proofing cloth)** A piece of linen used to proof breads such as baguettes.

Croûte See Crust.

Crumb (*mie*) The soft part of a leavened bread located within the crust. An open crumb has plenty of alveoli while a closed crumb is more dense.

Crust (*croûte*) The exterior part of bread that hardens during baking.

Dust (*fleurer*) To lightly cover with flour.

Ear (*oreille*) A ridge on a bread's crust that forms where score marks are made prior to baking.

Elasticity The dough's ability to return to its original shape after being stretched or otherwise deformed.

Enriched dough A dough contain enriching ingredients such as eggs and butter.

Extensibility The dough's capacity to stretch, extend, or elongate under the influence of force, stress, or pressure. A certain degree of extensibility is necessary for dough to be shaped and to expand as gas pressure builds during fermentation.

Fleurer See Dust.

Folding (*plier*) The act of stretching and folding a portion of the dough back over itself during bulk fermentation in order to strengthen the gluten network.

Fournil The premises in France where the oven (*four*) is located and where the baker (*boulanger*) kneads the dough. It is part of the boulangerie (see above). Unlike *"boulangerie,"* the word *"fournil"* is not regulated by law in France.

Frasage Mixing ingredients together before kneading.

Grigne See Scoring mark.

Kneading The process by which a baker builds up the dough's strength and structure.

Kneading trough (*pétrin*) A basin used to knead bread in eighteenth- to twentieth-century France.

Lame A curved razor blade set into a handle; used by bakers to score rustic loaves before baking.

Levain Culture of a microbial ecosystem obtained through spontaneous fermentation of a combination of water and flour.

Levain-chef or **chef** The mother levain from which a refreshed levain is made to create a *levain tout point*.

Levain tout point Levain that has reached its optimum level of fermentation and is ready to be added to dough.

Levure See Yeast.

Mâche See Chew.

Mie See Crumb.

Oreille See Ear.

Oven spring The increase in dough volume that occurs just after a loaf is transferred to the oven. The more oven spring, the airier the crumb.

Pain de ménage (homemade bread) Bread that is mixed, kneaded, and fermented at home, and then baked in a home oven.

Pain de mie (Pullman loaf) Also called "sandwich loaf." A loaf baked in a long rectangular pan with straight sides and a lid, known as a Pullman loaf pan or *pain de mie* pan.

Panifiable Used in France to describe flour that contains gluten and is therefore suitable for bread making.

Panifier To make bread.

Pâte fermentée Literally "fermented dough," this preferment was traditionally made by reserving a portion of mixed bread dough overnight. A *pâte fermentée* can also be prepared separately the day before baking.

Pâton A piece of fermented dough that is shaped into bread.

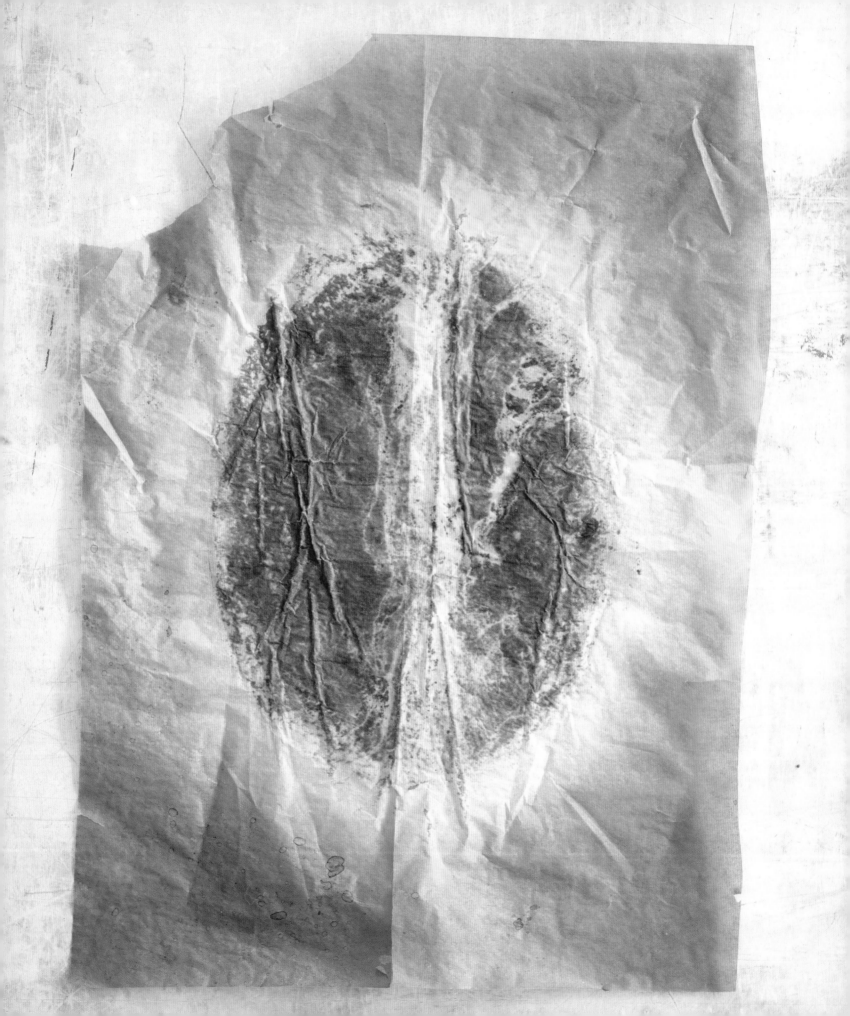

Peel See Baker's peel.

Pétrin See Kneading trough.

Pétrissage The act of kneading, or working dough.

Pointage See Bulk fermentation.

Poolish A yeast-based pre-ferment.

Proofing (*apprêt*) Second resting phase after shaping bread (also called "second rise"); the final stage in fermentation.

Proofing basket See Banneton.

Proofing cloth See *Couche*.

Pullman loaf See *Pain de mie*.

Quignon A large crust or chunk of bread, usually one that has already been cut into.

Refresh (*rafraîchir*) The act of feeding levain with equal parts water and flour.

Ressuage See Cooling.

Rest (*détente*) Inactive time between dividing dough and shaping it; it allows the gluten to relax and makes the dough easier to handle.

Retarding/Retarded proof A method of slowing down the rising process by chilling the dough, to increase flavor.

Retrogradation The process by which the bread becomes stale.

Scoring mark (*grigne*) A cut made by the baker on the bread—usually with a lame—before transferring it to the oven.

Seam (*clé*) The place where the bread has been folded or rolled toward the center during shaping.

Smoothing (*lissage*) The change in dough's appearance during kneading, from shaggy and rough to smooth and elastic.

Sole **(floor)** The bottom part of the oven on which bread is baked in professional bakeries. Also used to refer to the underside of a loaf of bread in French. Using a bread stone is the best way to replicate the effect of the sole when baking at home.

Yeast (*levure*) A single-celled fungus capable of triggering fermentation.

French Expressions Involving Bread

Avoir du blé, se faire du blé (lit. to have/to make wheat): To have/to make money

Avoir du pain sur la planche (lit. to have a loaf on the breadboard): To have a lot to do

Avoir la gueule enfarinée (lit. to have a flour-covered face): To be full of excess optimism

Bon comme du bon pain (lit. as good as good bread): To be generous or kind

Bonne pâte (lit. good dough): A simple and generous person

Ça ne mange pas de pain (lit. it doesn't consume any bread): It can't do any harm; there's nothing to lose

Être dans la panade (lit. to be in bread soup): To be in a very difficult situation

Être dans le pétrin (lit. to be in the kneading trough): To be in a mess/fix

Faire passer le goût du pain à quelqu'un (lit. to take the taste of bread away from someone): To wipe the smile off someone's face; to kill someone

Long comme un jour sans pain (lit. as long as a day without bread): Exceedingly long and boring; as long as a month of Sundays

Manger son pain blanc (lit. to eat one's bread white): To enjoy something while it lasts

Mettre la main à la pâte (lit. to put one's hands in the dough): To help out

Ne pas manger de ce pain-là (lit. don't eat that bread): Stay out of a doubtful situation; have nothing to do with something

Ne pas pouvoir être au four et au moulin (lit. you can't be at the oven and at the mill): You can't be everywhere/do everything at once

Pour une bouchée de pain (lit. for a mouthful of bread): For a pittance/next to nothing

Rouler dans la farine (lit. to roll in the flour): To fool or cheat someone

Se prendre un pain (lit. to get a loaf of bread): To take a punch

TECHNIQUES

Getting Started

—

Bread making requires a bit of organization. Following a few simple rules will make the process easier.

THE BEST PLACE TO MAKE BREAD

The kitchen is obviously the most practical place to make bread, since you will have everything you need on hand. Clear enough space on your counter to set up your stand mixer and a large wood board for shaping.

If you don't have a large kitchen, you can also set up your workspace in a utility room, a laundry room, a sunroom, or any other room where your equipment fits.

STORAGE

Set aside a large drawer or cupboard shelf to store your bread-making tools (proofing basket/banneton, bowl scraper, bench scraper, etc.). If this isn't possible, you can keep everything in a large bin with a lid. A large plastic container with an airtight lid is also a good place to put opened bags of flour. Large glass jars work as well—just don't forget to label them. Store flour in a dry, relatively cool place.

LEAVENING BREAD

It is usually recommended that you place dough in a warm area during bulk fermentation (first rise) and proofing (second rise).

Professional bakers use a specialized container called a proofing cabinet or proof box, which you can approximate at home. Identify the warmest room in your house, or find a draft-free space near a radiator, and put your dough there when it's rising. You can also place rising dough in a turned-off oven along with a bowl of hot water. Finally, if you're crafty, the Internet is full of suggestions for building your own proof box.

CLEANING UP

Remember, where there's bread, there's flour, and flour is highly volatile. It forms a fine white film on floors and countertops that is best removed with a broom and a dry cloth. Levain and bread dough are pretty sticky, so rinse your bowl and equipment immediately after use. If you're in a hurry, leave them to soak after removing any excess dough with a bowl scraper. Use a small dish brush to clean your equipment instead of an abrasive sponge. To clean the wood board where you shape your dough, scrape away any residue with a bench scraper (rather than a sponge) and brush away any remaining flour with a dish towel.

INTRUDERS IN MY FLOUR

You like high-quality flour? Well, so do bugs. Weevils are small black insects, $\frac{1}{16}$–$\frac{1}{8}$ in. (2–4 mm) long, with an elongated snout. They tend to proliferate in open packets of flour, the backs of cupboards, and the bottoms of bannetons. So clean your work and storage spaces well, store open bags of flour in an airtight container in a cool place, and regularly put your bannetons in a hot oven or in the freezer for several minutes. Throw out any flour that has become noticeably infested.

Grain or flour mites are small grayish-brown moths that proliferate rapidly in dry goods. Avoid them with the same precautions you take for weevils. If you notice an infestation, you can use a pheromone trap.

Equipment

Here's some good news: bread making doesn't require a lot of equipment. In fact, you probably already have the basics in your kitchen. For a very small investment you could treat yourself to a few tools used by professional bakers—but there's no need to go overboard, especially if you're just starting out. Soon enough you'll have your favorite bowl scraper and banneton. Here's a list of tools and equipment by order of importance.

Oven
Most home ovens on the market today will do just fine. Ideally, you want an oven that heats to 500°F (260°C/Gas Mark 10).

Scale
Choose the simplest digital scale you can find. A small precision scale that can measure to the nearest hundredth is also useful to have around when weighing yeast or salt, which both demand exact measurements.

Electric mixer
Although not essential, an electric mixer makes it easier to knead high-hydration doughs. Stand mixers are best (see Kneading with a Mixer p. 144).

Mixing bowl
A mixing bowl is useful if you knead by hand. You can also use it for bulk fermentation. If you don't have a banneton (see below), you can also proof your dough in the mixing bowl, covered with a towel.

Bowl scraper
A plastic or silicone bowl scraper/dough scraper is useful to remove dough from the stand mixer, mixing bowl, or work surface, and for removing dough stuck to your fingers. Choose one that is flexible and not too large.

Bench scraper

Unlike a dough scraper, a bench scraper is rigid and has a straight edge that is used for dividing dough. You can also use it to scrape excess dough from your work surface.

Bannetons

Bannetons are typically made of cane or rattan (avoid plastic), and may be lined with linen. They are used to proof shaped breads and are available in a variety of shapes and sizes.

Baking stone/pizza stone

A baking stone (also known as a pizza stone) is a slab made of stone, clay, or other heatproof material on which a bread can be placed in the oven to imitate the environment of a professional deck oven. The stone accumulates heat, which is transferred to the bread as it bakes directly on the stone. Choose a stone that isn't too thick; otherwise it will be difficult to manipulate and require more time to preheat. Choose a stone at least ½ inch (1.2 cm) thick, as thinner stones may crack. Be sure the stone is adapted to the size of your oven; there should be at least 2 inches (5 cm) of clearance on all sides to allow heat to circulate.

Lame

A lame (pronounced "lahm") is a sharp razor used for scoring. Fitted onto a support (which makes it easier to handle), it is called a *grignette* or *incisette* in French. You can also use a box cutter. If you have neither, a very sharp, straight-edged knife will do just fine.

Bread peel

A bread peel is used to transfer bread to the oven. If you don't have one, a thin board about 8 in. (20 cm) wide will work (smooth the edges with fine sandpaper). If you make baguettes, a baguette peel or *paline*, a narrow board about 12 in. (30 cm) long and 4 in. (10 cm) wide, is very useful.

Fine-mesh sieve

A sieve is practical for dusting your workspace and bread evenly with flour. A flour sifter or sugar duster works as well.

Large, airtight rectangular or square container made of glass or plastic

This is used to leaven your dough, so choose one adapted to your batch size. If you are using cold fermentation, you'll find that a square container is easier to store in the refrigerator than a round one.

Towels

Towels are useful for covering dough, lining a mixing bowl if you don't have a banneton, and for proofing baguettes and ciabatta. Choose clean towels, ideally made of linen—try flea markets and antique stores. And of course you'll need ordinary dish towels for (constantly) wiping your hands.

Small brush with soft, flexible bristles

This brush is helpful for delicately sweeping excess flour from shaped dough. You should also have a small, short-handled brush for sweeping your workspace and baking stone.

Metal wire or wood cooling rack

Bread is cooled on a rack to let the steam escape (a process called *ressuage* in French).

Loaf pan

A loaf pan is essential for making *pain de mie*, spelt bread, and *vollkornbrot*-style (rye) bread. Find a pan that corresponds to your dough volume.

Timer

A timer will help you keep track of proofing and baking times.

Instant-read thermometer

Though not essential, a probe or instant-read thermometer enables you to verify the temperature of water before it goes into dough, or dough at the end of kneading. An infrared thermometer or oven thermometer is useful for verifying oven temperature.

Dough docker

Although not necessary (a fork will work in a pinch), a dough docker—a kind of spiked rolling pin—is practical for pricking *faluche*, matzo, and Swedish *knäckebröd*.

PLASTIC IS NOT FANTASTIC

Dough is covered during rising times to avoid a "crust" from forming on the surface, which would retard leavening. The easy solution is to cover it with plastic wrap—which ultimately ends up in the trash. To be more eco-conscious, opt for a container with a sealable lid. Some stand mixers have lids for their bowl; universal silicone lids are also available. Otherwise use reusable (e.g. beeswax) wraps or elasticated bowl covers.

Timing

People often say that making bread is time-consuming. That's not exactly true. In all, you'll spend hardly more than an hour getting hands-on with the dough. However, the whole process takes place over a long period of time, although actual total time will vary, depending on the fermentation method you choose and rising times. In a way, time is a necessary ingredient for successful bread making. With this in mind, program the active stages (mixing, shaping, etc.) in whichever way fits in best with your schedule. You will find them easier and faster to complete as you gain experience and master the basics. Early batches can be rather epic events—don't give up!

Remember that while making bread with levain takes more time, it also offers the most flexibility, which means levain-based bread making is actually quite compatible with an active lifestyle.

BREAD TIMELINE

Main steps

Refreshing your levain: Creates a robust *levain*. (See p. 130.)
Kneading: Combines ingredients and activates the gluten network. (See p. 143.)
Folding: Strengthens the dough through a series of folds. (See p. 154.)
Bulk fermentation: First rise. (See p. 153.)
Shaping: Gives the bread its final form. (See p. 158.)
Proofing: Second rise. (See p. 166.)
Scoring: Slashing the dough to allow the bread to rise well during baking. (See p. 171.)
Baking: Baking your bread on a baking stone or baking sheet or in a Dutch oven. (See p. 181.)
Cooling: An important final step. (See p. 191.)

LEVAIN-LEAVENED BREAD (FOR ONE LOAF): 24 HOURS

If you refresh your levain at noon, you'll have bread for lunch the next day.

You can also refresh your levain late in the evening, before you go to bed, and bake your bread for dinner the next day.

If you want bread for breakfast, you'll have to get up early (three hours before baking).

The indicated times are theoretical and depend on several factors: how active your levain is, the dough temperature (see p. 125), the temperature in the proofing area, your refrigerator temperature, etc.

Cold bulk fermentation or cold proofing (in the refrigerator) allows you to make your dough "wait" longer and push back the time at which you intend to bake your bread. Your levain won't hold it against you either if you wait an hour or two longer.

Create your own timeline according to the variable factors indicated above and your own schedule.

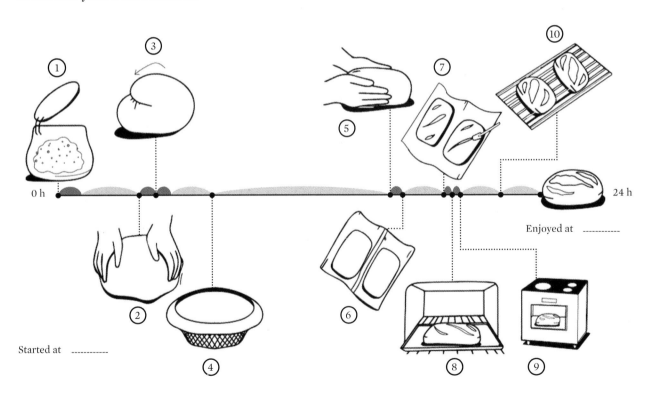

Started at _____

Enjoyed at _____

1. **Refresh levain** | 🌑 10 min | 🌗 5 h to 8 h
2. **Mise en place and knead** | 🌑 20 min
3. **Folds** | 🌑 10 min | 🌗 1 h 20 min to 2 h
4. **Cold bulk fermentation** | 🌗 14 h (between 8 h and 20 h)
5. **Shape** | 🌑 10 min
6. **Proof and preheat oven** | 🌗 1 h to 2 h
7. **Score** | 🌑 5 min
8. **Transfer to oven** | 🌑 5 min
9. **Bake** | 🌑 40 min
10. **Cool** | 🌗 1 h

🌑 **Active**

🌗 **Rest**

YEAST-LEAVENED BREAD (FOR ONE LOAF): 5 HOURS

If you want bread at lunch, get up relatively early and start the process in the morning.

If you want bread at dinner, start around lunchtime.

If you want bread ready for breakfast, make it the day before—unless you're an insomniac.

Unlike levain-based fermentation, which is subject to all kinds of unpredictable factors, yeast fermentation is relatively predictable and reproducible. However, it demands stricter adherence to rising times.

It's difficult to leave the kitchen very often or for very long when making bread using yeast. So stay attentive to your dough and watch for signs that it's ready—otherwise you risk over-proofing it.

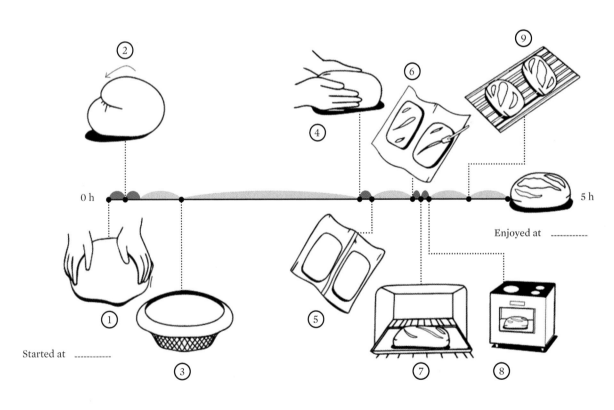

Started at _____

Enjoyed at _____

1. **Mise en place and knead** | 🌑 20 min
2. **Folds** | 🌑 10 min
3. **Bulk fermentation** | 🌓 1 h 20 (up to 2 h)
4. **Shape** | 🌑 10 min
5. **Proof and preheat oven** | 🌓 1 h (up to 2 h)

6. **Score** | 🌑 5 min
7. **Transfer to oven** | 🌑 5 min
8. **Bake** | 🌓 40 min
9. **Cool** | 🌓 1 h

🌑 **Active**

🌓 **Rest**

Measuring Ingredients

Baking is often compared to pastry making, the epitome of precision. While pastry does indeed rely on recipes that call for precise measurements and reproducible techniques, baking isn't exactly an improvised affair. Ingredients are determined according to percentage-based formulas and, more than mastery of techniques, bread making requires skill and experience to measure flour, water, and yeast and/or levain in a way that encourages good fermentation.

FLOUR

The quantity of flour called for in a recipe determines the percentage of other ingredients.

Recipes for homemade bread usually start with 4¼ cups (500 g) flour to obtain a 2-pound (1 kg) loaf, or 3¼ cups (375 g) to obtain a 1¾-pound (800 g) loaf. You probably won't be able to easily bake a loaf any bigger than that in a home oven (or bake two loaves at once), and it's difficult to control rising times between batches. If you go any smaller, the amount of dough may not be sufficient to support effective fermentation.

WATER

The next factor to consider is hydration: the percentage of water or liquid in a recipe, calculated based on flour weight, not total dough weight. The higher a bread's hydration, the lighter the crumb and the more holes it has (in theory). But dough with high hydration can also be difficult to work with. With this in mind, don't think of it as adding water to a recipe, but as adjusting the quantity of water depending on flour and bread type (ciabatta, for example, is a high-hydration dough). An average hydration of 65 percent is suitable for bread flour (T65). Flours higher in whole grain content and made with heritage grains can tolerate a hydration of 75 percent.

Hydration will also depend on environmental factors like temperature, humidity, and altitude, and levain hydration (in other words, whether you use stiff or liquid levain).

In practice, this means that to obtain 65 percent hydration for 2 pounds (1 kg) of flour, you'll add 30 oz. (650 g) of water, and for 4½ cups (500 g) of flour, you'll add 11½ oz. (325 g) water.

SALT

Health organizations in France and elsewhere have issued recommended allowances for salt use in bread making. The French ANSES currently advises using 18 g of salt per kg of flour and is expected to reduce that amount to 16 g. You can adjust the amount of salt to suit your taste, but remember that salt plays an important role in the bread-making process (see p. 55).

LEVAIN

Levain is generally added at a ratio of 30 percent of the flour weight (1½ cups/150 g for 4½ cups/500 g flour). Keep in mind that the more bubbles a cup of active levain contains, the less it weighs. Measuring by volume may mean using more or less levain depending on where it is on the fermentation curve; measuring levain by weight is a more reliable method. You'll probably want to use a little more levain if the ambient temperature is cool, and a little less in summer when it's warmer. The amount you use will also depend on whether your levain has reached maximum fermentation, known as *levain tout point* (see p. 131). If a recipe calls for adding a few grams of yeast, the amount of levain will usually be reduced.

YEAST

The quantity of yeast in a recipe is also calculated based on flour weight. In France, where fresh yeast/cake yeast is easily available in 42 g cubes, the recommendation is half of a cube (21 g)—or one packet of active dry yeast (7 to 9 g)—for 4½ cups (500 g) of flour. In reality, these proportions are rather high and you'll adjust them according to the type of fermentation you use; for example, adding just a few grams of yeast in a poolish.

BAKER'S PERCENTAGE OR BAKER'S MATH

Also known as the rule of proportions, this formula makes it possible to determine a proportional quantity of an ingredient based on three other variables, *a*, *b*, and *c*.

$$d = \frac{b \times c}{a}$$

You'll find this formula useful when you want to increase or decrease batch weights to make a larger or smaller loaf.

Example: One loaf calls for 4½ cups (500 g) of flour (*a*) and 12.5 oz. (350 g) water (*b*). What is the weight of water needed for 6¼ cups (750 g) of flour (*c*)? Answer: *(b × c) ÷ a* or (350 × 750) ÷ 500 = 525 g

GOOD TO KNOW

Some recipes are expressed in percentages rather than weight, especially those found in professional manuals or large-scale baking. In this case, flour is always represented as 100 percent.

DESIRED DOUGH TEMPERATURE

Desired dough temperature (DDT) is an essential factor in professional baking. The temperature of the water and flour as well as the surrounding temperature all influence the mixing and kneading process and fermentation.

The desired dough temperature can be calculated by adding together the temperature of the water, the temperature of the flour, and the surrounding temperature. Water temperature is usually the only variable that can be adjusted.

$$T° \text{ of water} = \text{desired dough } T° - (T° \text{ of flour} + \text{room } T°)$$

The desired dough temperature is around 136°F (58°C), which after kneading will result in a dough with a temperature of 75°F (24°C).

At home, you can use an instant-read thermometer to determine with precision if your dough falls within this range. If you don't want to get into all the calculations, remember that if you're working in a warm room, use cool (but not icy) water, and if you're working in a cool room, use warm water.

As a general rule, kitchens are around 68°F (20°C), except during heat waves, so you can usually work with room-temperature water. The exceptions are when making certain yeast-based recipes, which call for warm water or liquid, and rye bread, which calls for hot water.

MAKE THE RECIPE YOUR OWN

Don't be afraid to modify recipes as you progress, but only change one parameter at a time. Keep a record of your batches—there's nothing more annoying than scraps of paper that are easily lost. And don't be afraid to make notes in this book.

Fermentation

Levain fermentation:
Starting and maintaining a levain

The uninitiated often see levain as a strange and hard-to-tame beast. And yet there's nothing more natural: all it takes is flour, water, and time to create and maintain a levain.

Unlike baker's yeast, each levain is unique and home to a flora of lactic bacteria and wild yeasts (see Leavening Bread p. 41) present in the environment, which lend their own particular character to bread.

Levain-based fermentation takes time and experience. While it might seem more restrictive than yeast-based fermentation, the end result is easier-to-digest bread with more flavor.

To make levain-based bread, you need a *levain-chef*, the mother culture that, when regularly fed, or "refreshed," will provide a vigorous levain, known as a *levain tout point*, for each batch of bread. Levain is known as a pre-ferment—it activates fermentation in the bread.

Starting and maintaining a levain is not at all complicated; it just requires a little discipline and attention. As a living organism, levain is sensitive to environmental factors (water and flour quality, ambient temperature, regularity of feeding, etc.) and it will reward you for taking good care of it. Your levain will be a permanent resident in your kitchen for months and perhaps even years, so get to know it: observe, smell, and taste it. Soon you'll know just what it needs and how to feed it without relying so much on the scale.

When you first create your levain and start to feed it, you'll have to throw out the excess regularly, or its exponential growth will quickly overwhelm you. Likewise, the first few batches of bread you make will inevitably imply throwing out some levain to obtain the right quantity of *levain tout point*. But soon enough, and with a little math, you'll learn to adjust feedings to avoid having to throw out levain and waste flour as a result.

LEVAIN-CHEF

Ingredients
- 2⅓ cups (9.25 oz./265 g) organic white whole wheat (T80–T110), spelt, or rye flour
- 1¼ cups (10.5 oz./300 g) unchlorinated water (bottled or filtered), lukewarm (77°F/25°C)

Equipment
- 1 clean glass bowl or jar, rinsed with boiling water

Method

Day 1
- In the morning, combine 1 generous tbsp (10 g) of flour and 2 tsp (10 g) of lukewarm water in a glass bowl or large jar. The mixture should have the consistency of pancake batter.
- Cover with a non-airtight lid or a piece of perforated reusable plastic wrap to keep the levain in contact with the air while preventing a crust from forming. Place the container in a warm place. If the ambient temperature is too cold, the levain will have difficulty getting started. In winter, you could place the bowl or jar near a radiator.

Day 2 (+24 h)
- In the morning, add 3 tbsp (1 oz./30 g) of flour and 2 tbsp (1 oz./30 g) of water to the previous day's mixture. Stir to combine. Cover again and leave to ferment in a warm place.
- That evening *(+12 h)*, weigh out 1.75 oz. (50 g) of the mixture and throw out the remaining 1 oz. (30 g). Return the 1.75 oz. (50 g) to the jar and stir in ⅔ cup (2.5 oz./75 g) flour and ⅓ cup (2.5 oz./75 g) water.

Day 3 (+24 h)
- In the morning, weigh out 1.75 oz. (50 g) of the mixture and throw out the remaining 5.25 oz. (150 g). Stir in ⅔ cup (2.5 oz./75 g) flour and ⅓ cup (2.5 oz./75 g) water.
- That evening *(+12 h)*, weigh out 1.75 oz. (50 g) of the mixture and throw out the remaining 5.25 oz. (150 g). Stir in ⅔ cup (2.5 oz./75 g) of flour and ⅓ cup (2.5 oz./75 g) of water.

The levain will gradually begin to produce tiny bubbles and develop a nice sour odor similar to yogurt, raw sauerkraut, or pear brandy. If it gives off an unpleasant odor of rot or mold, that's a bad sign: throw it out and start over. If it has a hard time getting started, keep feeding it the same proportions of flour and water as indicated on day three for an additional day or two; if necessary you can thicken it up a bit by adding an extra tablespoon or two of flour.

LEVAIN-CHEF

The *levain-chef* is ready when it expands vigorously—a third of its volume–after each feeding.

At this point, you have a couple of options. You can:
- maintain a liquid consistency by continuing to feed it the same proportions of water and flour. This is called a liquid levain;
- choose to make a thicker levain by feeding it half the amount of water based on flour weight. This will produce a stiff levain.

If you intend to make bread on a regular basis, keep your levain in an airtight jar or container at room temperature, except during heat waves when temperatures exceed 77°F (25°C).

If you make bread once a week or less, keep your levain in an airtight jar or container in the bottom of the refrigerator, where temperatures tend to be around 43°F–45°F (6°C–7°C).

The levain will continue to grow, so don't fill your container more than two-thirds full, and make sure the lid can withstand high pressure.

GOOD TO KNOW

-Rye flour has more fermentable sugars than other flours, so you could create your levain with rye flour, or use half rye and half wheat flour. You can use a rye levain to make bread with any kind of flour.

-Some professional and amateur bakers add honey, dried fruit, or fruit juice to their levain. While any of these may help to get the levain started, they won't significantly impact subsequent activity, so are really not necessary; high-quality flour contains all the yeast and bacteria necessary for fermentation.

-If you make a lot of bread and regularly use different flours, you can create a levain for each type of flour—but you can just as easily maintain one single levain and use it with all types of flour.

LA BONNE IDÉE

If you're not ready to start your own levain or you're in a hurry, ask a friend or your local baker for a bit of their levain.

REFRESHING LEVAIN

The bacteria and yeast in levain feed on sugars present in flour, producing CO_2 that causes both levain and dough to rise. When they have consumed all the sugars, they stop producing gas and the levain falls. If the levain is deprived of water and flour for a longer period, it will become more liquid as the gluten is "digested"; it will also grow acidic. To keep the bacteria and yeast active, they must be fed regularly in a process known as "refreshing" or "feeding." See Storing Levain (p. 132) for information on the frequency of feeding.

To make refreshed liquid levain, feed the levain at a minimum ratio of 1:2 by weight. For example: if you have 1.75 oz. (50 g) of *levain-chef*, refresh with a scant ½ cup (3.5 oz./100 g) of water and ¾ cup + 2 tbsp (3.5 oz./100 g) of flour. For a stiff levain, refresh with a scant ⅓ cup (2.5 oz./70 g) of water and 1 cup + 1 tbsp (4.5 oz./130 g) of flour.

Ingredients
-*Levain-chef*
-Unchlorinated water (bottled or filtered), at room temperature
-Organic white whole wheat (T80–T110), spelt, or rye flour

Method
-Place the required amount of *levain-chef* in a large bowl. Heat the water until is it barely lukewarm and mix the levain and the water using a spoon or spatula, allowing air to penetrate well. Add the flour, and stir

to combine until the mixture resembles pancake batter. Partially cover with a lid or a sheet of perforated reusable food wrap. Leave the bowl at room temperature (68°F–70°F/20°C–21°C) for four to eight hours, or until the levain has doubled in volume and has the consistency of chocolate mousse.

REFRESHED LEVAIN

LEVAIN TOUT POINT

Bread is made with refreshed levain, not *levain-chef*. When the refreshed levain has reached peak fermentation, as described above, it is ready to be mixed into dough. At this point, it is referred to as *levain tout point*.

You can see if the levain is ripe by dropping a small amount in a glass of water. If it floats, that means it's releasing CO_2 and is very active. But you'll quickly learn to recognize the visual clues that indicate the levain is ready. Remember to always keep a portion of *levain-chef* to use for future batches.

Method
To make a liquid levain-chef *(1.75 oz./50 g)*
- If you need 5.25 oz. (150 g) of *levain tout point* to make bread, you will refresh the 1.75 oz. (50 g) of *levain-chef* with a scant ½ cup (3.5 oz./100 g) of water and ¾ cup + 2 tbsp (3.5 oz./100 g) of flour. This will give you almost 9 oz. (250 g) of *levain tout point*. You'll use 5.25 oz. (150 g) to make the bread dough and keep 1.75 oz. (50 g) for your *levain-chef*. You can add the remaining 1.75 oz. (50 g) to the batter for pancakes, crèpes, waffles, blinis, or quick breads.

- If you don't want any leftover levain for baking, you can also refresh 1.5 oz. (40 g) of *levain-chef* with ⅔ cup (3 oz./80 g) of flour and ⅓ cup (3 oz./80 g) of water (you'll throw out the remaining 10 g, roughly 1 tsp, of levain). Use 5.25 oz. (150 g) of the *levain tout point* to make the dough and keep 1.75 oz. (50 g) as your *levain-chef*.
- If you need more levain for a larger batch of bread, refresh the levain twice, at least four hours apart, to obtain the desired amount, or refresh with greater quantities of water and flour: for example, refresh 1.75 oz. (50 g) of *levain-chef* with 1 cup + 2 tbsp (5.25 oz./150 g) of flour and ⅔ cup (5.25 oz./150 g) of water. Allow for a longer resting time.
- If the levain hasn't been refreshed in a week and doesn't seem very active, refresh it twice before using.

STORING LEVAIN

Levain gets better with time, so it's important to store and maintain it correctly.

If you make bread every day, a daily feed will keep your levain in top form: like an athlete, the more it trains, the better it performs. Levain should be refreshed at peak fermentation, when it has risen to its highest point.

If you make bread once a week or less, ideally you should refresh your levain three times a week and at least once a week.

Remember: if you don't make bread often, regularly discard levain (as you did when creating it) to avoid ending up with a bucket of the stuff!

If you have to travel, don't worry: your levain can hibernate in the refrigerator for up to two weeks, especially if you are in the habit of refreshing it regularly. Or entrust it to a "levain-sitter" to care for it while you're away. Levain can also be frozen, ideally when it has reached peak fermentation. Cold destroys certain bacteria, so fermentation may take some time to activate after thawing. Don't freeze levain for more than two weeks, and use thawed levain in a recipe that also calls for yeast.

GOOD TO KNOW

- The more often you feed your levain, the less acidic it will be.
- The warmer the surrounding environment, the faster fermentation will progress, and the more often you'll have to feed your levain (in the summer, for example).
- To preserve your levain, especially if you don't refresh it often, gradually convert your liquid levain into a stiff levain. When you're ready to bake, convert it back into a liquid levain (see Refreshing Levain p. 130).
- Some recipes call for adding a small amount of baker's yeast in addition to levain to accelerate fermentation. Professional bakers in France are allowed to use 0.2 percent yeast based on flour weight in breads with the appellation "au levain."

ZERO-WASTE RECIPE

If you don't want to throw out levain, try making these crumpets: small, tender, slightly tangy biscuits.

Remember to save a bit of levain for future batches.

Ingredients
- 1 cup (7 oz./200 g) *levain tout point*
- ½ tsp fine salt
- ½ tsp baking soda
- 1 tsp sugar

Method
1. Preheat the oven to 350°F (180°C/Gas Mark 4). Generously grease a muffin pan. In a large bowl, quickly mix the levain together with the salt, baking soda, and sugar.
2. Pour the batter into the muffin pans to a height of ¾ in. (2 cm).
3. Bake for 15 minutes.

Other pre-ferments

Besides levain, there are several other pre-ferments, all of which call for baker's yeast. They rely on the same principle of incorporating active yeast into the dough, which reduces kneading and rising time (bulk fermentation), strengthens the gluten network and contributes to a more extensible dough, and makes for a more flavorful bread. They're good alternatives to the "straight dough" method, which requires a large quantity of baker's yeast; although it is faster and produces bread in a just a few hours, that bread is less flavorful.

POOLISH

This method was supposedly developed in Poland, hence its name, and imported to France by Viennese bakers. It is sometimes called the "French method."

Poolish can be thought of as a quick version of levain. It is composed of equal parts flour and water, and a dose of fresh yeast that varies according to the fermentation time: the longer the resting time, the less yeast added.

For 2 lb. (1 kg) of flour:
- 0.5 oz./15 g yeast for 3 hours of fermentation
- 0.25 oz./8 g for 6 hours of fermentation
- 0.1 oz./3 g for 8 hours of fermentation

The yeast accelerates the fermentation process, improves the texture of the dough, and results in a bread with longer shelf life.

Prepare the poolish in the evening for use the next morning, or in the morning for use in the evening.

Ingredients for 7 oz. (200 g) of poolish
- 0.05 oz./1 g fresh yeast
- Scant ½ cup (3.5 oz./100 g) unchlorinated water (bottled or filtered), at room temperature
- 1 cup (3.5 oz./100 g) organic white whole wheat (T80–T110), spelt, or rye flour

Method
1. Whisk or stir the yeast together with the water.
2. Sprinkle in the flour and mix until combined.
3. Cover with a lid or reusable plastic wrap.
4. Let sit at room temperature for about ten hours. The poolish is ready to use when it has tripled in volume and is just beginning to fall.

PÂTE FERMENTÉE (LEVAIN-YEAST)

This method consists of reserving a piece of dough from the previous batch (*pâte fermentée* means "fermented dough" in French) and incorporating it into the new batch of dough.

Pâte fermentée is used at a proportion of 15 to 30 percent based on the weight of flour in the new dough. For example: 10.5 oz. (300 g) of *pâte fermentée* for 2¼ lb. (1 kg) of flour.

Some recipes call for preparing a separate *pâte fermentée* that is then added to the new batch of dough.

AUTOLYSE

The autolyse method calls for hydrating the flour before adding the other ingredients in the recipe, in order to "relax" the gluten network, which helps to reduce kneading time.

Autolyse is useful for making breads that call for quick fermentation, like baguettes. It has little to no relevance for making slow-fermented, levain-based bread, and is most often used with very strong flours (*farine de force*) (see p. 36). Autolyse is not used with rye or einkorn flour.

Method
1. Combine the water and flour in the bowl of a stand mixer.
2. Knead for 3 to 4 minutes on speed 1.
3. Let sit 30 minutes to 1 hour.
4. Add the rest of the ingredients and continue with the recipe.

PRE-GELATINIZATION

This technique used to make Asian *pain de mie* is known as *yukone* in Japanese and *tangzhong* in Chinese. It results in a featherlight crumb similar to a brioche, but with very little egg or butter, and has a long shelf life. The process is similar to making a roux, as for a bechamel sauce, but does not use fat. Instead, heating the flour and water together creates a gelatin-like substance that helps the dough absorb water.

Make *yukone/tangzhong* using one part water and five parts liquid (water or milk). This "roux" represents one-third of the total flour weight called for in the dough.

Ingredients
- Scant ½ cup (3.5 oz./100 g) water
- 2 tbsp (0.75 oz./20 g) pastry or all-purpose flour (T45–T55)

Method
1. Combine the water and flour in a saucepan.

2. Cook over low heat, stirring constantly.

3. When the mixture thickens, and reaches 149°F (65°C), remove from heat. (Verify the temperature with a probe thermometer.)

4. Refrigerate the mixture at least 6 hours and ideally overnight.

Yeast-based fermentation

Baker's yeast, also referred to as commercial yeast, is a single strain of yeast, *Saccharomyces cerevisiae*, that is industrially grown and concentrated, then compressed to make fresh yeast or dehydrated to make instant or active dry yeast (see p. 46).

Yeast is used "straight"; in other words, incorporated directly into the dough without pre-fermentation, except when making a poolish (see p. 137).

Contrary to levain-based fermentation, which is subject to changing environmental factors, yeast-based fermentation results in faster and controlled fermentation, but at the cost of digestibility and flavor.

FRESH YEAST

In France, fresh yeast, also known as compressed, wet, or cake yeast, can be purchased in bulk from bakers. It is also available in French grocery stores in cubes of 1½ oz. (42 g), and in other European countries in cubes of 1 oz. (25 g). It is more difficult to find in the US, but is sold in 2-oz. (57-g) packets by several major brands.

Fresh yeast can be stored for two to three weeks in the refrigerator; wrap opened packets well in plastic wrap. It can also be frozen. If fresh yeast turns red or becomes sticky, throw it out.

Fresh yeast is activated when combined with liquid, preferably lukewarm to warm—77°F–86°F (25°C–30°C)—for 15 minutes. Use 10–20 g (2–5 tsp) of the liquid—water or milk—called for in the recipe; heat as needed and mix with the yeast using a spoon. You can give the yeast a boost by adding 1 tsp sugar and a little of the total flour called for in the recipe. Then let it rest for 30 minutes until the mixture begins to foam. You can also crumble the yeast directly into the flour. The amount of yeast used depends on the length of fermentation.

Maximum dose: 0.75 oz. (21 g) for 4 cups (1 lb. 2 oz./500 g) of flour.

Many of the recipes in this book call for fresh yeast. If fresh yeast is difficult to find in your area, you can use active dry or instant yeast instead, but you'll need to adjust the amount. As a general rule, if you are using active dry yeast, multiply the fresh yeast quantity in grams by 0.4. If you are using instant yeast, multiply the fresh yeast weight in grams by 0.33. Incorporate into the recipe as explained in the active dry and instant yeast sections below.

ACTIVE DRY YEAST

Active dry yeast is sold in packets of tiny granules. It's the same strain as fresh yeast, but dehydrated. Active dry yeast can be stored for several months in the cupboard unopened, and two days after it's been opened.

As with fresh yeast, active dry yeast must be reactivated in a bit of warm liquid for 15 minutes before being added to the other ingredients in the recipe. You can also add the yeast directly to the flour, but fermentation takes longer to activate.

Maximum dose: one packet, 2¼–2¾ tsp (7–9 g) for 4 cups (1 lb. 2 oz./500 g) of flour.

INSTANT YEAST

Also obtained through drying fresh yeast, instant yeast comes in the form of small slender threads or granules and also has a long shelf life.

It does not require any pre-activation and can be added directly to flour during initial mixing and kneading.

Maximum dose: 1½ tsp (5 g) for 4 cups (1 lb. 2 oz./500 g) of flour.

LEVAIN FERMENTESCIBLE

Levain fermentescible, sold mostly in France, is a mixture of dry yeast and levain that has been "killed" by heat, meaning it only adds flavor and has no impact on fermentation. *Levain fermentescible* makes bread rise as fast as yeast and is activated the same way.

Maximum dose: 0.75 oz. (20 g) for 4 cups (1 lb. 2 oz./500 g) of flour.

 GOOD TO KNOW

- Never use hot water to activate yeast! Water hotter than 122°F (50°C) will kill it.
- Fresh and dry yeast produce the same effect, so it's up to you to choose the form that best suits your needs. Remember you will need 2½–3 times less dry yeast than fresh.

KNEADING BY HAND

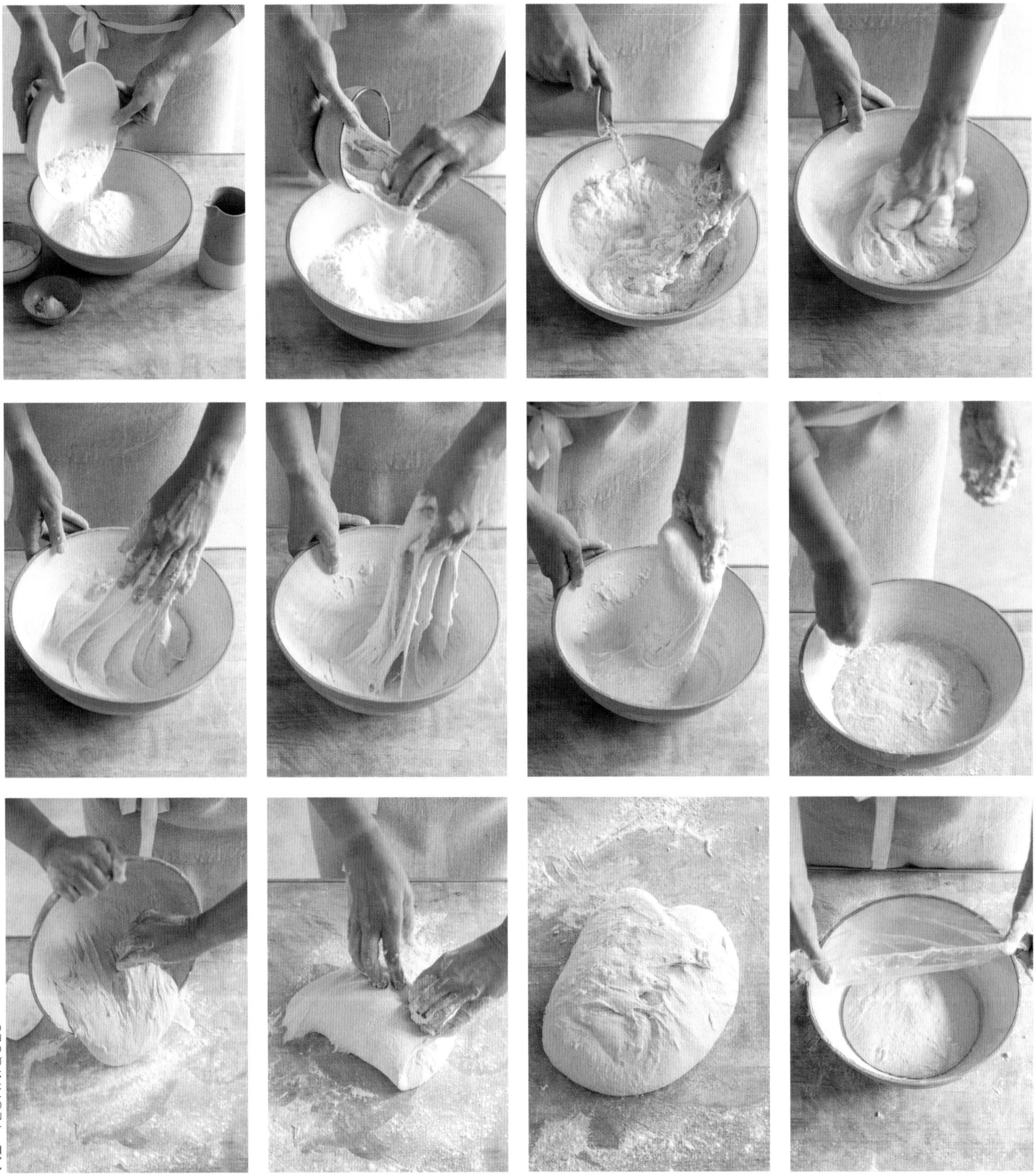

Kneading

Kneading is an important step. More than the act of combining ingredients, it activates the gluten network by hydrating flour through contact with water (or another liquid). It also incorporates air into the dough, which is necessary for the formation of holes in the finished crumb.

Whether you choose to knead by hand or machine, you'll have to get a feel for the dough to see how it changes and evaluate its texture and progression. Kneading times are given as a guide and may vary depending on the ambient temperature, the temperature of the water and flour, and even on the nature of the flour itself.

KNEADING BY HAND

Kneading by hand is an ancient, natural, and intuitive act that requires more sensitivity than strength—unless you're kneading twenty pounds of dough. Kneading by hand is always an option, especially for the home baker and when working with small quantities of dough.

Try to use one hand for the dough, at least in the beginning, and keep the other hand clean. It will hold the container, wield the bowl scraper, or do whatever else might be necessary (like reaching for that ingredient that you forgot to grab ahead of time). Avoid kneading with a spatula or bowl scraper, which aren't as flexible as your hands.

Knead on a wood surface or in a wide mixing bowl. You can also knead in a flat plastic tub like those used by professional bakers; this is a handy way to keep the kitchen clean, and you can leave your dough to rise in the tub.

Method
1. Lightly dust a counter or container with flour. Place the flour and salt in the middle of the workspace and make a well in the center.
2. Add the levain or yeast to the center of the well.

3. Gradually add the water, folding the flour towards the center in a regular, circular motion.

4. Combine the ingredients until they come together in a smooth mass (called *frasage* in French).

5. Stretch and fold the dough continuously for 5–10 minutes, giving a quarter turn at regular intervals. Try not to add flour as you do so.

6. Continue kneading until the dough becomes more elastic, smoother, and easily pulls away from the workspace or bowl (medium gluten development, see p. 151). If necessary, you can fold in any dough pieces with a bowl scraper.

7. Add any additional ingredients (dried fruit, nuts, herbs, etc.).

8. Fold the dough in on itself, giving it a quarter turn at regular intervals.

9. Shape the dough into a ball and place it in a lightly oiled or flour-dusted container.

KNEADING WITH A MIXER

Kneading with a mixer makes combining ingredients easier and saves (a little) time. It also creates heat and warms the dough, which activates fermentation more quickly. It's a better option for high-fat doughs (Vienna breads, pizza, etc.).

Mixers

Stand mixer

The stand mixer is the home kitchen appliance that comes closest to imitating professional kneading machines.

The dough hook circulates in a planetary motion, meaning it rotates on its own axis while also rotating around the bowl.

Choose a bowl according to the amount of dough that you intend to knead on a regular basis. For 2- to 4-lb. loaves (1 to 2 kg), choose a 5-quart (5-liter) bowl.

The spiral, or "pig tail," hook is best, but not all stand mixers offer this accessory. If you don't have one, the basic dough hook will work for most doughs. For low-gluten dough, use the paddle attachment.

Food processor

Food processors are equipped with two fast-spinning blades. They can be used for most doughs, but their high-speed action causes the gluten network to form very quickly, so kneading time should be reduced. They work well with low-gluten dough, but are not recommended for use with high-hydration dough (like ciabatta). A Thermomix can also be used to mix dough.

BREAD MACHINE

Bread machines knead and bake in the same appliance. While they may seem like an easy solution, they don't offer the benefits of homemade bread. You can't get a feel for the dough (figuratively or literally), make allowances for different variables (flour, ambient temperature, etc.), achieve impressive crusts, airy crumbs, or shape breads into different forms. Plus, they can't be used to make levain bread.

Bread machines are strictly for beginners. If you find one in the back of a cupboard, use the kneading cycle if you don't have a stand mixer, and the leavening cycle for yeast doughs (take out the blades first).

Ingredient order

There are several schools of thought when it comes to adding ingredients to the mixer. In reality, it doesn't make much difference in what order you add them, especially if you turn the machine on quickly. The real objective is getting the ingredients to combine well.

Yeast-based bread

Depending on the type of yeast you are using, dissolve it into all or a portion of the liquid (water or milk) called for in the recipe (instant yeast can be added directly to flour). Add to the mixer bowl, then add the flour and salt.

Levain-based bread

Add the salt to the mixer bowl, then add the water. Stir to dissolve the salt. Add the flour, followed by the levain.

Dough with added fat

Add butter and oil during the second stage of kneading, in two or three batches on low speed.

Adding other ingredients (inclusions)

Other liquid or dry ingredients (like cocoa powder) are added in the early stages of kneading. Add solid ingredients (like nuts or chopped fruit) at the end of the kneading time, on low speed.

 GOOD TO KNOW

You'll often hear it said that yeast and levain should never come into contact with salt, because it will "kill" them. In reality, salt is hygroscopic, meaning it absorbs water. So by dehydrating yeasts and bacteria, salt has a tendency to retard their activity.

Dough volume

The amount of dough you can work with at one time will depend on your stand mixer. That being said, as a general rule, avoid filling the bowl more than halfway so the dough hook can knead without difficulty. If, on the other hand, you don't have enough dough, the hook will struggle to incorporate all the ingredients; in this case, knead by hand.

Speed and time

Dough is a fragile substance that should be handled with care. There's no need to subject it to high mixing speeds and long kneading times. Remember, kneading time also depends on fermentation time. A longer fermentation time (for *pain au levain*, for example) means a shorter kneading time.

Method

1. Begin mixing the ingredients on low speed (speed 1). This is known as *frasage* and takes 3 to 5 minutes.

2. Increase to medium-low speed (speed 2) until the dough starts to look smooth, pulls away from the bowl, and wraps around the dough hook. At this point, if working with a stiff dough, you may need to turn off the mixer and free the dough from the dough hook using a bowl scraper. Continuing kneading until the gluten network has developed to a medium stage (as gauged by the windowpane test p. 150). This step takes 3 to 7 minutes.

3. If the dough is too dry or too stiff, gradually add a little water by drizzling it down the side of the bowl. If the dough is too wet, add a little flour and continue kneading. Always keep an eye on the mixer. If you're kneading stiff dough, work in short bursts to avoid damaging the motor.

4. Gather the dough into the center of the bowl, using the bowl scraper if necessary.

5. Using your hands, gently shape the dough into a loose round. Place in a lightly oiled or flour-dusted airtight container. You can also leave it in the bowl. In this case, dust the bowl lightly with flour and cover with reusable food wrap or a lid.

Levain-based bread

After kneading, levain-based dough can seem very flaccid. Resist the temptation to add flour; instead, strengthen it by creating tension through a series of folds before proceeding to bulk fermentation.

Method
1. Dust a work surface with flour.
2. Dust the walls of the bowl with flour.
3. Remove dough from the bowl using a bowl scraper and ease it onto the work surface.
4. With lightly oiled or damp hands, fold the dough in on itself.
5. Turn the dough 90 degrees (a quarter turn) and make another fold or two until the dough grows taut.
6. Place the dough seam-side down in the bulk fermentation container and let it rise.

 GOOD TO KNOW

-Only dough made with gluten-rich flours like wheat or spelt really requires kneading to develop the gluten. Low-gluten dough made with rye or einkorn, for example, won't benefit from excessive kneading, and it's quite normal for these kinds of dough to be rather sticky and clay-like in texture.

-Dough made with gluten-free flour doesn't require kneading at all—no gluten means no gluten network!

-Dough that is over-kneaded becomes shiny and viscous and may oxidize: excess oxygen destroys the orange pigments called carotenoids that are naturally present in flour, resulting in bleached bread.

FOLDING

Bassinage and *contre-frasage*

Some recipes call for *bassinage*, which means adding a small amount of water at the end of kneading. The gluten network forms more easily in dough that is not too hydrated, so adding water at the end of kneading is a way to adjust hydration, which influences the formation of holes in the crumb.

Adding flour rather than water at this stage is known as *contre-frasage*.

THE NO-KNEAD METHOD

This was probably the original method used to make bread, before we came to understand and master fermentation. Rediscovered and popularized by American baker Jim Lahey, the no-knead technique consists of simply mixing the ingredients to form a smooth, high-hydration dough with a soft, sticky texture. Fermentation time "replaces" the effect of kneading. It's easy to get good results using this method, especially if you bake the loaf in a Dutch oven.

Depending on the recipe:

1. Follow steps 1 to 4 of kneading by hand (see p. 143), but don't begin kneading. You want to combine the ingredients well, but the dough will be shaggy. Wet your hands if it's too sticky, but don't add flour.
2. Cover and let rest at least 6 hours at room temperature, or at least 12 hours in the refrigerator (bulk fermentation). The dough should double in volume.
3. Transfer the dough to a floured surface. Quickly shape it without deflating it.
4. Place the dough seam-side down on a generously floured dish towel and cover. Let proof for one hour.
5. Use the towel to transfer the dough to a Dutch oven (see method on p. 184), flipping it so the dough is seam-side up. There's no need to score the dough; the bread will open naturally.

Development of the gluten network: the windowpane test

The gluten network begins to form the moment you start kneading. The amount of time you spend kneading and the level of gluten development obtained will depend on the type of dough and fermentation. To determine your dough's strength, use the windowpane test: Break off a piece of dough and stretch it between your thumbs and first two fingers to form a thin membrane (the windowpane). The further you can stretch the membrane without breaking it, the more developed the gluten network is.

Weak development

The dough offers little resistance and tears easily. This corresponds to the first phase of kneading, *frasage*.

Medium development

The dough stretches quite easily, but tears if stretched very far.

Kneading usually stops at this stage. A subsequent series of folds will further strengthen the gluten network.

Complete development

The dough is elastic and stretches easily to form a translucent membrane.

Aim for this level of development when kneading dough for Vienna bread or pizza.

The Stages of Fermentation

—

The stages of fermentation can be divided into two phases: bulk fermentation (first rise) and proofing (second rise). The dough is shaped in between.

Depending on the result you want to achieve and the amount of time you have, you can choose direct or indirect fermentation.

Direct fermentation
The dough is kneaded, bulk fermented, and quickly shaped (3–4 hours total), and then baked after a short proofing time. The result is well-risen bread with a tight crumb, thin crust, and short shelf life, which dries out quickly and develops little flavor. This type of fermentation is used with yeast-leavened breads. It can be practical when you're short on time, but requires careful monitoring of fermentation times.

Indirect fermentation, or cold bulk fermentation
The dough is kneaded, left to bulk ferment briefly at room temperature, then placed in the refrigerator (at around 43°F/6°C), without shaping, for 8 to 18 hours (and up to 48 hours). This step, known as cold bulk fermentation, retards the fermentation process. Kneading is generally done in the afternoon, fermentation takes place overnight, and the bread is baked the next morning after shaping and proofing. The crumb is fleshy and filled with holes, and the crust is thick. Bread made this way develops complex flavors and keeps for 4 to 5 days. This method is ideal for levain bread or breads made with very little yeast. Although it requires planning, it offers more flexibility in determining the final baking time.

BULK FERMENTATION

Bulk fermentation (also known as the first rise) is resting time. At this point, the dough has not yet been divided and shaped. It needs to be reinforced with folding, which will tighten up the gluten network and reactivate fermentation. This is called "strengthening" the dough. Some recipes require the dough to be folded several times at regular intervals.

Folding

1. Moisten or lightly oil your hands.
2. Stretch the left side of the dough up and back over the rest of the dough.
3. Stretch the right side of the dough up and back over the rest of the dough.
4. Repeat on the remaining two sides.
5. Flip the dough so that the folds are on the bottom.

FLOURING

Before turning out dough, you should dust your work surface with flour to ensure the dough doesn't stick. Be sure to flour the banneton or *couche* (linen proofing cloth) that will hold your dough after shaping as well. You can also dust your peel if you're using one to transfer bread to the oven.

For dusting, it's a good idea to use a mixture of equal parts rice and wheat flour, as rice flour is less absorbent, which is useful when working with sticky dough. You can prepare this mixture ahead of time and store it in a jar.

Don't go overboard when dusting, or you may add too much flour to your dough; a light coating is enough. You can also use a fine-mesh sieve for better distribution. Dough that has been over-dusted tends to form a thin unsightly "skin" on the surface that will create folds in the crumb. If this is the case, tap the shaped dough lightly to remove excess flour (you can also use a soft-bristled flexible brush) and mist it with a bit of water if needed.

READYING YOUR DOUGH FOR SHAPING

Shaping is an important step. Not only does it give bread its pleasing form, but it also restores strength to the dough after fermentation and pulls it taut, which will support even rising during baking.

This quintessential hands-on action demands a bit of experience, as well as a gentle but firm and skillful touch, not to mention observation and practice. Success will come after a few (or many) attempts. Don't give up—your bread will be all the more beautiful for it.

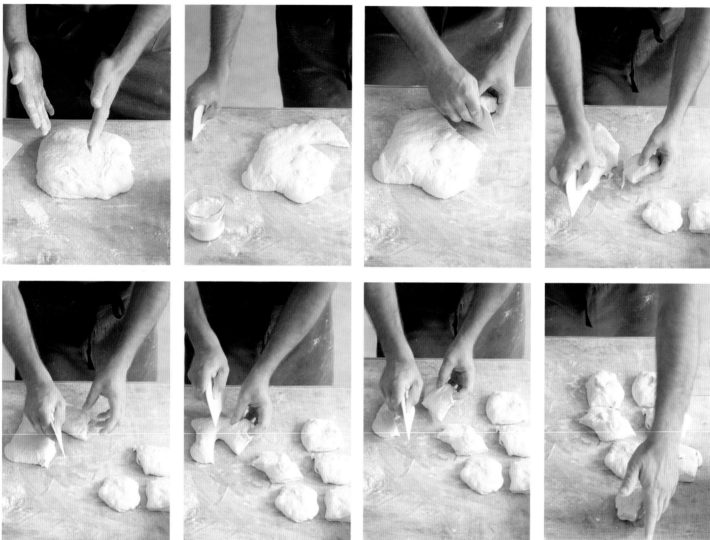

The right time

The fermentation times indicated in recipes are only guidelines. It's up to you to determine if the dough is ready to be shaped. For yeast-leavened breads, this is usually when the dough has doubled in volume. It should have risen significantly and be much smoother than it was at the beginning of bulk fermentation. The windowpane test (see p. 150) is a good way to tell if your dough has reached complete gluten development. If you perform the windowpane test and the dough still tears when you stretch it, go through the folding process and let it rest for another 30 minutes to 1 hour.

Dividing dough

If you would like to make several small loaves or baguettes, for example, you must divide the dough into pieces. To do this, use a bench scraper or the straight edge of a bowl scraper; dividing dough by hand may damage its structure.

Method
1. Dust a work surface with flour.
2. Lightly flour the walls of the bowl or container and gently slide the dough onto the work surface without tearing it.
3. Divide the dough into pieces using a bench scraper. Use a scale to weigh the pieces for extra precision.
4. Line the dough pieces up on the work surface as you go along.

Take special care with:
- sticky, high-hydration doughs (like ciabatta, for example);
- very yeasty doughs that quickly begin to rise and form a crust. To keep the dough from drying out, shape the pieces as soon as you cut them, and keep them covered.

Resting

Some dough needs to rest longer to facilitate shaping and encourage elongation. This resting time is preceded by pre-shaping.

Method

Pre-shaping a round (for a boule or miche)
1. Place the dough on a floured work surface. Bring the edges towards the center.
2. Position the dough seam-side down and roll it between your hands as you tuck the dough towards the bottom to form a nicely rounded ball.
3. Cover with a towel and let sit 15 to 30 minutes at room temperature.

Pre-shaping an elongated form (for a baguette or bâtard)
1. Gently flatten the dough using the palm of your hand.
2. Roll up lengthwise; place the dough seam-side down.
3. Cover with a dish towel and let sit 15 to 30 minutes at room temperature.

Shaping

Shaping takes place in three stages: the dough is lightly stretched, then pulled taut, then given its final form.

Shaping high-hydration dough
Resist the temptation, strong as it may be, to add flour to a very sticky or soft dough.
You have two options:
- oil the work surface and oil or wet your hands. Shape the dough and place it in a banneton dusted with fine-ground semolina or rice flour;
- place the dough in the refrigerator for 10 to 20 minutes to make it easier to shape. In this case, allow for a longer proofing time (second rise).

THE SEAM
The seam (or *clé* in French) is the term bakers use to describe the area on the dough where the edges come together during pre-shaping or shaping.
During the initial stage of fermentation (bulk fermentation), the dough is placed seam-side down, which makes it easier to create tension. To proof in a banneton or other container, the dough is placed seam-side up, then turned out onto a peel or baking stone seam-side down for scoring and baking. If you want the dough to open naturally during baking, don't score it.

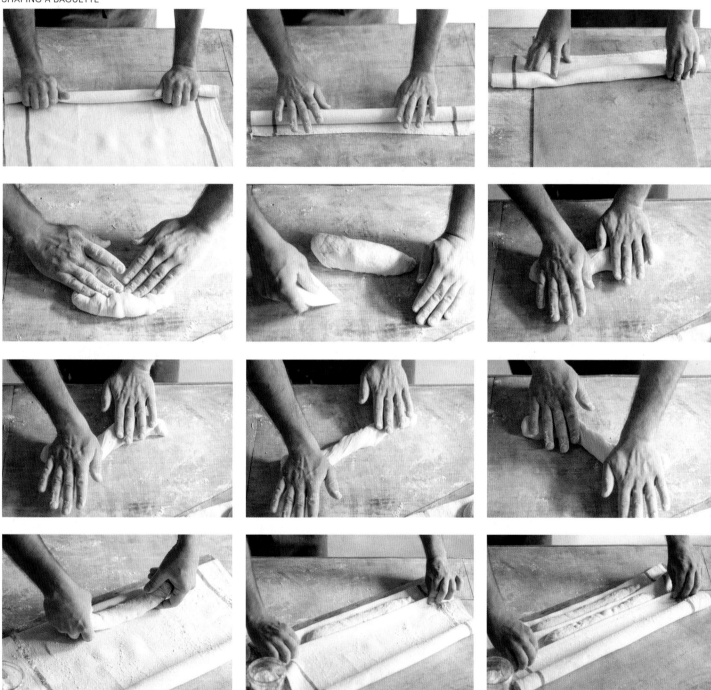

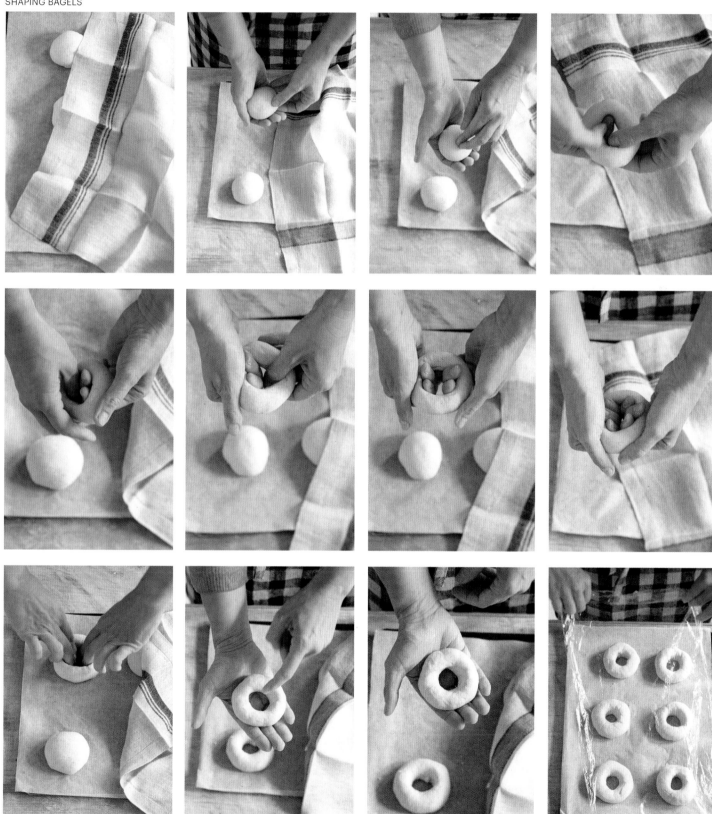

PROOFING

Proofing (also known as the second rise or proving) is another resting time. It generally takes between 30 minutes and 2 hours. For best results, you'll create ideal rising conditions, and also be able to determine the moment when the dough is ready for the oven.

Bannetons

Bannetons are baskets used to support the dough and help maintain its shape during proofing. They are available in different shapes and materials.

Lined cane bannetons: these are the most commonly used by professional French bakers. They are lined with a layer of linen that the baker dusts with flour before adding the dough. Whatever you do, don't wash the lining after use. You want to preserve the flora that will develop there (unless, of course, you see mold appear). Instead, simply scrape away any stuck dough, shake out any excess flour, and let it dry if necessary. (If you are using more than one banneton, let them dry individually; don't stack them.)

Rattan bannetons: rattan bannetons are unlined and leave a pretty pattern on the bread. They should be dusted with flour before use and cleaned with a slightly stiff brush.

Plastic bannetons: plastic bannetons might seem more hygienic, but they have one major drawback—flour won't stick to the sides, so they're not recommended for use with sticky doughs.

Salad bowls: if you don't have a banneton, a wide salad bowl lined with a flour-dusted dish towel will do nicely.

Proofing cloths (*couches*)

A proofing cloth, or *couche* in French, is a large piece of linen used to proof high-hydration doughs like ciabatta, or is arranged on a work surface in a series of accordion folds to proof long breads like baguettes. *Couches*, like banneton liners, should not be washed. Instead, let them air-dry thoroughly, then roll them up and store them somewhere cool and ventilated. Home bakers can also fashion a *couche* from a thick dish towel, preferably made of linen. Dust it with flour before putting the bread on it.

Loaf pans

When it comes to pans, bakers typically use rectangular loaf pans with straight or flared sides for breads with little or no gluten, as well as for *pain de mie*. For a perfectly square crumb, there's a special pan with a lid called a Pullman pan.

Baguette molds, which make transferring loaves to the oven easier, can be helpful for amateur bakers.

Loaf pans must be greased before receiving dough.

Baking sheets

A baking sheet is useful for individual breads like *fougasse* and focaccia, and is usually lined with parchment paper before baking, unless it's nonstick.

Method

1. Dust the banneton or *couche*, or grease the pan. Place the shaped dough seam-side up in the banneton or the pan (unless otherwise indicated), or seam-side down if using a *couche*.

2. Cover to prevent a crust from forming. Use a large upside-down container or a plastic bag (leave some air inside) to avoid the plastic coming into contact with the dough as it rises. If this is not possible, use a dish towel.

3. Proof dough for 30 minutes to 2 hours at room temperature. Use the poke test (see p. 169) to determine when the dough is ready to transfer to the oven.

THE POKE TEST

If the proofing time is too short, the dough won't build up enough CO_2 to rise correctly during baking. Conversely, if the proofing time is too long, the gluten network weakens and the bread may fall during baking.

Even professional bakers use the poke test to evaluate the dough's resistance and determine when it is ready for the oven.

Gently press your finger about ½ in. (1 cm) into the dough. If the dough is ready to bake, it will spring back slowly but retain a small indentation where you poked it. If no indentation forms, the dough is not ready; leave it to proof a little longer. If the indentation doesn't spring back at all, it's too late—the dough is over-proofed.

THE POKE TEST

SCORED BREAD

BAKED SCORED BREAD

Scoring

Scoring (or *grigne*) serves two purposes. It creates one or more openings through which steam and carbon dioxide, produced during fermentation, escape during baking, which helps bread to rise. It also gives the bread a pleasing appearance. Bakers use signature scoring marks to personalize or differentiate their bread.

These incisions require a steady and precise hand, acquired with experience.

Choosing the right tool

The blade used for scoring must be thin and very sharp.

Professional bakers use razor blades, called lames, attached to a blade holder, which gives the baker a steady grip for making decisive cuts. It usually gives the blade a slight curve as well, which makes it easier to slice into dough. Lames are available in specialty and kitchen supply stores at modest prices.

You can also use a scalpel blade, a box cutter, or a well-sharpened knife. Avoid serrated knives, which may tear the dough.

Scoring with a lame

The incision is made with the tip of the blade, which must penetrate the dough at an angle (between 25° and 45°) and to a depth of about ¼ in. (5 mm).

If the incision is too shallow, the *grigne* may close up during baking. If it is too deep, the bread may fall.

Method

1. Turn the dough out of the banneton onto a bread peel, a baking sheet, or into a Dutch oven, depending on the baking method (see p. 181).

2. Lightly dust the dough with flour. (This step is not necessary if the banneton was dusted beforehand.)

3. Immediately grasp your lame between two fingers, as though you were going to make a stroke with a pen.

4. Cut the dough with a single quick, decisive gesture, without sawing back and forth.

5. Immediately transfer the dough to the oven.

6. Carefully clean and dry your lame after use, and replace it regularly if you make bread often.

Scoring with scissors

Scoring with scissors creates a lovely "hedgehog" design that is typically used on *pain viennois*.

GOOD TO KNOW

Some doughs don't need to be scored. These include:
- high-hydration doughs (ciabatta, focaccia);
- doughs rich in fat (*pain de mie*);
- low-gluten and gluten-free doughs (einkorn, 100-percent rye);
- doughs baked seam-side up.

SCORING A BOX TOP

SCORING A CROSS

SCORING BAGUETTES

Decorative Finishes

——

Not all bakers choose to decorate their bread; some prefer to let bread express itself naturally. These decorative finishes are purely visual ways to personalize your bread.

EGG WASH

Egg wash adds shine to crust and prevents the surface of some breads, like pain viennois or burger buns, from drying out. It also produces a pleasing crispness.

Ingredients
- 1 whole egg

Method
1. Crack the egg into a high-sided bowl.
2. Whisk or, even better, use an immersion blender to obtain a smooth mixture.
3. Using a brush, apply the wash to the surface of the dough or doughs in a uniform fashion, wiping away excess.
4. Immediately transfer to the oven.

TIGER BREAD

Despite its slightly misleading name, "tiger bread" more closely resembles a leopard hide. The bread is brushed with a flour mixture during shaping. Then as it rises, the mixture cracks, producing a mottled effect when it bakes.

Ingredients

1 ¼ cups (6.25 oz./180 g) rice flour

¾ tsp (0.15 oz./4 g) salt

1 tsp (0.15 oz./4 g) sugar

0.15 oz./4 g fresh yeast

½ cup (4.5 oz./130 g) water

2¾ tsp (0.5 oz./12 g) neutral oil (grape-seed, vegetable, or canola)

Method

1. Place the rice flour, salt, and sugar in a bowl. Crumble in the yeast. Make a well in the mixture and mix in the water.

2. Shape the bread on a baking sheet lined with parchment paper.

3. Brush the dough with the wet mixture.

4. Leave to rise (proof).

5. Transfer to the oven without scoring.

SEEDS

To obtain an attractive result, seeds must be applied to the surface of dough in a single, uniform layer. Also consider the size of the seeds (see p. 69). Oleaginous (oil-containing) seeds like poppy, pumpkin, sunflower, flax, and sesame can be added directly to dough whereas grains (wheat, rye, millet, quinoa, etc.) must be soaked before using.

Method

1. Line two baking sheets with parchment paper.

2. Place a generous amount of seeds (a single variety or a combination) on one of the sheets.

3. Using a brush or mister, moisten the shaped dough, seam-side up.

4. Roll delicately in the seeds and place on the other baking sheet, seam-side up.

5. Immediately transfer to the oven.

Stencils

Specialty stores carry stencils in all kinds of patterns. Choose plastic stencils that won't stick to the dough. You can also make your own using a food-safe stencil sheet. Draw or trace your design onto the sheet and use a small utility or craft knife (like an X-Acto) to cut it out.

Method

1. Shape the dough and place in the banneton. Proof.
2. Turn the dough out of the banneton onto a bread peel, a baking sheet, or into a Dutch oven, depending on baking method (see p. 181).
3. Brush away any excess flour left on the dough from the banneton.
4. Gently press the stencil onto the undusted dough.
5. Sprinkle with flour using a fine-mesh sieve.
6. Carefully remove the stencil.
7. Score the bread around the design.
8. Transfer to the oven and bake without convection.

You can also reverse the process and apply a solid shape (a heart or leaf, for example) to the dough and sprinkle flour over the rest using a fine-mesh sieve. Carefully remove the shape when you have finished.

To create a dark pattern, use cocoa or charcoal powder.

DOUGH DESIGNS

To decorate bread with designs cut from dough (ears of wheat, leaves, flowers, etc.) use what is known as "dead dough," or dough made without yeast.

Ingredients

- 2 cups (9 oz./250 g) wheat flour (T65–T110)
- Scant ½ cup (3.5 oz./100 g) water
- 1 tsp (0.2 oz./5 g) salt
- 2 tbsp (1 oz./25 g) butter, softened
- To make the edible glue: 1 egg white + a generous ⅓ cup (1.5 oz./40 g) rye flour

Method

1. Place the first four ingredients in the bowl of a stand mixer fitted with the dough hook or paddle attachment.
2. Combine on low speed (speed 1) for 5 minutes.
3. Gather the dough into a ball, cover, and transfer to the refrigerator for at least 1 hour, or ideally overnight, before using.
4. Combine the egg white and rye flour in a small bowl.
5. Roll out the dough on a floured work surface to a thickness of ⅛–¼ in. (3–5 mm).
6. Cut out the desired shapes using a cookie cutter or knife.
7. Lightly brush the cutouts with the egg-flour mixture.
8. Carefully place the cutouts on the shaped bread dough. Bake dough as directed.

Baking

Baking is the last—but definitely not the least important—step in the bread-making process. It is the final reward for both the professional and amateur baker's efforts—it's also the moment when the dough's work during fermentation is expressed.

Amateur bakers are often frustrated by their first loaves. In their defense, it's nearly impossible to obtain the same result in a home oven as you would in a professional deck oven. The "deck" is the lower part of the oven, made of refractory stone, on which bread is directly baked. The stone has strong thermal inertia, which means the heat that is stored within it is easily transferred. This is what allows the bread to "split"—in other words, to rise and open along scoring marks—and cook through to the center.

Home ovens typically use heating elements that distribute heat from bottom to top, or have a convection element that circulates heat with a fan, and it is impossible to bake directly on the oven floor. Sharp temperature increases are also difficult to achieve, not to mention that much more heat is lost from a home oven than from a professional oven when the door is opened to put dough inside. However, a perfectly acceptable result can be achieved in a home oven using one of the following techniques.

USING A BAKING STONE

The best way to reproduce deck oven baking in a home oven is to use a baking stone, which simulates the stone "deck" of a deck oven.

Method
1. Position a rack at the lowest oven position.
2. Position a second rack above the first, and place the baking stone on that rack. Use caution; baking stones are often heavy.
3. Preheat the oven to 500°F (260°C/Gas Mark 10), or as high as your oven can go, at least 30 minutes before you want to put the bread in.

4. When the dough has finished proofing, turn it out of the banneton onto a floured bread peel and transfer directly to the stone.

5. Add steam (see below).

6. Quickly close the oven.

7. Midway through baking, lower the oven temperature to 450°F (230°C/Gas Mark 8).

8. When the bread is baked through, remove from the oven using a bread peel and let cool on a metal cooling rack.

Adding steam

When professional bakers transfer bread to a deck oven, they can also add steam, which is an essential part of crust formation. Steam slows down the drying process and prevents the dough from forming a crust too quickly. It also adds shine. It is difficult (and rather dangerous) to reproduce this injection of steam in a home oven. The most effective home-based method is to place a drip pan, heavy-duty baking sheet, or oven-safe skillet on a rack positioned under the rack holding the baking stone. (The pan will oxidize, so you won't want to use it for anything else.) After transferring the dough to the oven, pour hot water into the pan or skillet and immediately close the oven door. The steam created will be extremely hot; be very careful not to burn yourself. Wear oven mitts—and perhaps a pair of safety glasses as additional protection.

GOOD TO KNOW

- Home ovens sometimes offer convection heat, which guarantees uniform heat in the oven—and that's a good thing. But it also tends to dry out bread. If your oven has an adjustable convection fan, choose the lowest speed.

- Ovens usually offer several cooking methods. You'll have to experiment to determine which is best suited to baking your bread, but always choose the method that allows you to reach the highest temperature.

- Bread is baked in falling heat, which means that you begin with a hot oven and lower the temperature during baking: for example, the oven heat will start at 500°F (260°C/Gas Mark 10) and fall to 450°F (230°C/Gas Mark 8).

BAKING IN A DUTCH OVEN

This is our favorite method for home bread making, and it's practically foolproof. Although baking in a Dutch oven might seem less impressive than watching a loaf of bread expand beautifully in the oven (if all goes well!), it has the benefit of compensating for a home oven's shortcomings. When hot, a Dutch oven functions like a mini oven, evenly distributing heat, including from below. The lid also traps the steam escaping from the bread, which replaces the need to add steam to the oven.

Ideally, use a Dutch oven made from unglazed cast iron and with a metal knob. While it may be a sizeable investment, it will last forever. Use it only for bread, to keep it (and your bread) from absorbing unwanted odors. Transferring the dough into the Dutch oven and then to the oven for baking takes a little practice. To simplify the operation, choose a Dutch oven with a diameter that is at least ¾–2 in. (2–5 cm) greater than your banneton. Cast-iron combo cookers, which can be used as Dutch ovens, are another good option. Transferring bread into the shallow lid of a combo cooker is slightly easier than lowering your bread into a deeper Dutch oven.

Cast-iron combo cookers—made up of a shallow fry pan/lid and a deep skillet—are another good option. The dough can be loaded onto the shallow pan/lid, which makes transferring from the banneton easier. The deep skillet is then placed on top to form a cover. If you don't have a Dutch oven, you can transfer your bread to a baking stone, then cover it with a large stainless steel pot or oven-safe bowl. Be careful not to burn yourself when removing the pot or bowl.

Method

1. Cut out a circle of parchment paper big enough to line the bottom of the Dutch oven. Set the parchment paper aside.
2. Place the covered Dutch oven into the oven (remove the knob from the lid beforehand if it isn't made of metal). Preheat the oven to 500°F (260°C/Gas Mark 10) for at least 30 minutes.
3. When proofing is complete, carefully remove the Dutch oven from the oven using oven mitts or protective gloves and place on a heat-safe surface. Close the oven.
4. Still using oven mitts, remove the lid and place on a heat-safe surface, such as a stovetop.
5. Line the bottom of the pot with the parchment circle.
6. Turn the dough out of the banneton into the Dutch oven, being careful not to burn yourself on the rim of the vessel.
7. Score the bread.
8. Using oven mitts, put the lid on the Dutch oven, transfer it to the middle rack of the oven, and close the oven door.

9. After 20 minutes, remove the lid using oven mitts and place it on a heat-safe surface. Close the oven door, lower the temperature to 450°F (230°C/Gas Mark 8), and continue baking for 20 minutes.

10. When the bread is done, remove the Dutch oven from the oven and take the bread out, being careful not to burn yourself. Place the bread on a wire rack to cool.

WHEN IS BREAD DONE?

White, light golden, deeply golden—everyone has their preferences when it comes to evaluating doneness. Bread is usually considered done baking when it makes a hollow sound, similar to patting someone on the back, when tapped on its underside. Color is another good indicator of doneness: the bread should be golden brown, like a caramel. The ears (the ridges formed by scoring) can be lightly burnished. However, the bread should not be burned; otherwise the crust will have a bitter taste and develop acrylamide, a carcinogenic and neurotoxic substance. (You shouldn't let your toast burn for the same reason.)

BAKING OVER HOT COALS

Your home oven isn't the only thing that can bake bread. If you're barbecuing outside at home, or on a camping trip, barbecue coals or campfire embers can provide a heat source to cook your dough.

For best results, make a smaller loaf (using 2 cups (9 oz./250 g) of flour, for example) or rolls.

Method

1. Shape your dough into a ball and place it in a cast-iron Dutch oven or a well-oiled stainless steel baking dish. If you decide to make rolls, shape them into balls and place them in the Dutch oven, spacing them about ½ in. (1 cm) apart. Cover and let rise.

2. When the embers or coals are hot but no flames remain, place the Dutch oven or covered dish directly in the center of the embers, or on a rack just above them. Bake for at least 20 minutes without removing the lid (15 minutes for small breads/rolls). Remove the lid and continue baking until the bread is cooked through. If you have a barbecue with a lid, you can also use it to bake bread on a hot baking stone.

POACHING *BRETZELS* (OR BAGELS)

Poaching consists of plunging dough into a boiling water bath before baking, which gelatinizes the starch in the flour: upon contact with heat and water, the starch grains swell and dissolve, creating a firm, shiny surface, and leaving the interior soft.

Adding baking soda, honey, or malt extract to the water encourages the Maillard reaction (see p. 76) and a browning effect.

Method

1. Bring a large saucepan of water to a simmer.
2. Add baking soda, honey, or malt extract to the water, according to the recipe instructions.
3. One by one, immerse the pieces of raw dough into the water for several minutes each.
4. Remove from the water bath with a slotted spoon and drain well.
5. Arrange on a baking sheet lined with parchment paper.

BAKING WITH STEAM (*BAO* BUNS)

Baking with steam, like poaching, encourages the formation of a crust—thin, in this case—through the gelatinization of starch.

A steamer pot, steamer basket, or *couscoussier* work well. The shaped dough should be cooked on parchment paper to prevent it from sticking to the bottom of the cooking vessel.

Method

1. Heat water in the *couscoussier* or in a saucepan fitted with a steamer basket. The steamer basket should not touch the water.
2. Carefully arrange the *bao* buns on parchment paper in the pan, about ¾ in. (2 cm) apart.

Cutting and Serving Bread

—

There are many superstitions related to serving bread. In France, it's considered a bad omen to place a loaf upside down, and making the sign of the cross over bread (or scoring a cross into the bread) ensures that the family will never be without it. In reality, serving bread is mostly a matter of common sense.

CUTTING BREAD

People often say you should "break" bread. This Biblical reference was suited to matzo bread, which was thin as a pancake. These days, the term has expanded to symbolize the sharing of food, and we tend to slice our bread instead of breaking it.

Breadboards

Choose a wood breadboard or cutting board, which is visually pleasing and will last a lifetime.

If possible, use the board only for bread, to avoid transferring unwanted odors or germs to your bread.

Knives

The term "bread knife" usually refers to a large serrated knife, and is a relatively recent design. A century ago, people cut rustic country bread with a small sharp knife or a kind of billhook (a knife that curved at the tip), holding the bread against the chest with one hand and drawing the blade towards themselves with the other. Serrated knives appeared with the first modern loaves.

For all practical purposes, you need a well-sharpened, fairly long blade (around 8–12 in./20–30 cm) that will cut the bread in a single motion; avoid sawing back and forth, which damages the crumb. The knife should be rigid enough to keep from slipping. However, the word "bread knife" may refer to several different kinds of blades.

Pointed serrated edge blade: This blade has teeth of uneven height, delivering a clean incision that leaves no crumbs.

Scalloped or wavy-edged blade: Blades with scalloped edges cut most types of bread easily. However, they may tear bread that has many holes and produce crumbs during cutting.

Inverted scallop-edged blade: Inverted serrations protect bread with lots of holes and bread with delicate crumbs like *pain de mie*. This is the professional baker's preferred blade.

For rustic or country breads like *pain au levain*, a good smooth blade that has been well-sharpened will also do the job.

Alternatives

Bread slicers
Bread slicers consist of a cutting board and a pivoting blade. They are not adapted to all bread types and take up a lot of space.

Electric knives
Electric knives work very well on all kinds of bread and deliver a neat, clean cut.

Pizza wheel
As the name suggests, a pizza wheel slices pizza efficiently.

Scissors
Scissors are very practical for cutting thin crusts like *pissaladière* or *flammenküche*.

A nice slice

The best way to slice bread is not from above, which squashes it, but at an angle.

How to slice a levain-based bread, like a *boule*

Method
1. Place the loaf on a wood cutting board.
2. Hold the bread in one hand at a 45° angle.
3. Slice the bread with a decisive gesture, bringing the entire length of the blade towards you, avoiding any back-and-forth motion. Whatever you do, don't "saw" the bread.
4. Eat right away.
Another method:
1. Cut the loaf in two down the middle.
2. Place the bread crumb-side down on a cutting board.
3. Slice crosswise.

How thick should my slices be?

How thickly you slice your bread is a matter of taste—and depends on the bread. The recommended average thickness is one thumb's width—about half an inch, enough to chew on and hold a spread. *Pain de mie* can be sliced thinner, for example, but you can also cut a small *boule* into quarters. Long breads like baguette are typically cut into crosswise sections on the diagonal.

SHOULD BREAD BE EATEN HOT?

Who can resist the odor of warm bread and the impulse to immediately tear off a piece? It's all the more tempting when the bread is homemade and fresh out of the oven. Fight the urge! Bread needs time to rest after it comes out of the oven to let the steam escape (*ressuage*). For best air circulation and fastest cooling, place the bread on a wire rack and let cool between 30 minutes and 1 hour. (Rye and einkorn bread benefit from a little extra time to bring out their spiced notes.) During *ressuage*, the crust might seem particularly appetizing and crusty. But the crumb inside is still a little gummy and won't exude all of its aromas just yet; if you cut into the bread immediately, the crumb tends to clump together and is harder to digest. Plus, hot bread is very difficult to cut, and you may damage it if you take a knife to it at this stage.

 GOOD TO KNOW

Any guide to good manners will tell you that you shouldn't cut your bread at the table with your knife, or bite off a hunk with your teeth. Instead, break it into bite-sized pieces with your fingers. And don't lunge for the bread until after the soup or appetizer course—you don't want to ruin your appetite.

SERVING BREAD

A whole range of tableware has been created specifically for serving bread in restaurants and elegant table settings. Look for charming, old-fashioned varieties in antique shops and flea markets.

Bread plate

This small plate should be positioned above and to the left of the main plate.

Bread tongs

Tongs are used to remove bread from the basket (to avoid your fingers coming into contact with multiple slices).

Bread basket

Typically made of metal, wicker, or cane, a bread basket prevents the bread from coming into direct contact with the table or tablecloth, and collects crumbs. It is sometimes lined with a napkin or cloth, notably to keep toasted bread warm.

Crumb sweeper/crumb catcher

Crumb sweepers come in roller or blade form and are used mostly at restaurants to gather up crumbs after the main course or cheese course and before dessert.

Toast rack

A toast rack is used to hold slices of toast upright.

 GOOD TO KNOW

In the Middle Ages, bread itself was used as a dish. Meat was served on a large slice of bread called a *tranchoir* ("trencher"), which absorbed the juices. Often, the *tranchoir* was given to the poor or tossed to dogs after the meal. Sometimes, dining companions shared this slice of bread, giving rise to the French word *copain*, which means "friend."

Storing Bread

—

As soon bread is removed from the oven, it gradually begins to undergo changes. Only freezing can halt this race against time. Drying, crumbling, and mold are just some of the phenomena that bread undergoes as it turns stale. There is no miracle solution; nothing can replace fresh-baked bread.

The best place to store bread

All kinds of bread boxes, bins, and tools exist to "keep" bread. Originally their primary purpose was to protect bread from pests, rodents, and insects, and they didn't really contribute to longer shelf life. These days, you can use a bread box to store your bread, but avoid plastic ones, especially airtight designs that encourage mold growth. You can also store your bread cut side down on a wood cutting board or flat plate, covered with a clean dish towel.

Freezing bread

Bread should be frozen sliced rather than as whole loaves; slices will thaw more easily. However, thawed bread goes stale faster than fresh bread. Freeze it within a day of baking, after it has cooled completely, and eat it within the month. Past that time, the bread will deteriorate and lose its crust. You can also freeze pieces of raw dough just after shaping. Let them thaw 8 hours in the refrigerator, then proceed with proofing and baking.

Method
1. Slice the bread.
2. Divide into portions according to your needs (three slices together, for example).
3. Wrap each portion tightly in plastic wrap, or better yet, use a reusable zip-top plastic freezer bag, being sure to remove all the air.

4. Label with the type of bread and date of freezing.
5. Store in the freezer.

Refreshing bread

There are two techniques for softening stale bread:
- Preheat the oven to 350°F (180°C/Gas Mark 4). Place the bread on a baking sheet and cover with an similarly-sized upside-down pan (a cake pan for a baguette, a deep springform pan for a loaf). Heat for about 10 minutes.
- Place the bread on a microwave turntable along with a glass of water. Heat for 30 seconds on high power. Repeat for an additional 30 seconds if necessary.

TOAST

Stale bread has one clear advantage: it's ideal for making toast. Opinions differ as to which bread is best stale, but toasted baguette is a classic breakfast item in any Parisian bistro. "Toast" in French refers to toasted *pain de mie*. Slice the bread to a thickness equal to the toaster opening. The best toast is crisp on both sides but still soft in the center. Bread can also be toasted on just one side.

Stale bread is also ideal for French toast, known as *pain perdu* in France.

If you don't have a toaster, you can use your oven's grill/broiler or toast the bread on the stovetop in an ungreased pan. Watch carefully so your toast doesn't burn.

GOOD TO KNOW

Pain au levain has a longer shelf life than yeast-leavened bread. Levain retards the process of starch retrogradation, which slows drying as a result. And levain's acidity prevents mold growth.

Using Leftover Bread

It seems a shame to throw away bread. And yet the average French person discards about 9 lb. (4 kg) per year. The next time you find yourself with stale bread, try one of these ideas instead.

Bread crumbs
Place slices of stale bread in the toaster, or in a hot oven for about 10 minutes, until completely dry. Be careful not to let the bread burn. Let cool, and grind in a food processor to achieve the desired texture. Store the bread crumbs in an airtight container, preferably in the refrigerator or freezer.

Croutons
Cut leftover bread into small cubes with a well-sharpened knife. Place in a bowl. Drizzle in olive oil, add a pinch of salt, and toss to mix well. Bake 5 to 10 minutes in a 400°F oven (200°C/Gas Mark 6). (To make garlic croutons, rub slices of bread with a clove of garlic before cutting into cubes.)

Stuffing
Break bread into pieces and place them in a large bowl. Moisten with milk. Beat in an egg and add the mixture to a fish, meat, or vegetable stuffing.

Bread flour
Process hard bread finely to obtain a powder. Use as a flour replacement in cookies or crackers.

Crispbread
Slice leftover *pain de mie* into ¼-in. (7-mm) thick slices. Leave to air-dry 2 hours, then toast 10 minutes on each side in the oven at 350°F (180°C/Gas Mark 4). Turn the oven off, open the oven door to lower the temperature, and then close it again and leave the crispbread inside to cool completely. Store in a metal tin or other airtight container.

RECIPES
—

DIFFICULTY LEVEL

  Beginner

  Intermediate

★★★ Advanced

KEY TO THE SYMBOLS

  I've got time on my hands
(24-hour cycle)

  I'm in a rush
(same day)

  Levain

  Yeast

  Baking powder

  Gluten-free

ABOUT THE RECIPES

All of the following recipes (with the exception of those from professional bakers) have been developed in conditions typically found in a home kitchen, with an ambient temperature of around 68°F (20°C), and baked in a home oven.

INGREDIENTS

Butter: When an ingredient list calls for "butter," use unsalted butter unless otherwise specified.

Flour: The recipes in this book have been made with French-milled flours, which are classified by type (T numbers) according to their ash content—the higher the number, the more bran the flour contains. French-type flours are increasingly available outside of France, but they can be difficult to find, so flour equivalents have been provided. However, the specific type of French flour used to make the original recipes has been included in parentheses (T65, for example) if you'd like to source authentic flours.

Unless otherwise noted, the word "flour" in the ingredients lists refers to wheat flour. When a recipe calls for "bread flour" and a range is indicated in parentheses (T65–T80), you can either use bread flour or a white whole wheat flour. We strongly recommend using organic flour if possible.

Water: Unless otherwise indicated, use unchlorinated water at room temperature.

Levain: Before using levain in the bread-making process, it must be refreshed and should be at peak fermentation (*levain tout point*) before you mix it into the dough. In most of the recipes in this book, we have used liquid levain, i.e., levain that has been refreshed with equal parts flour and water. Unless we specify to use stiff levain, use liquid levain when you see "refreshed levain" in an ingredient list. (See Techniques pp. 130–31.)

Unless indicated otherwise, "levain" refers to wheat levain.

Yeast: Recipes that call for yeast (also known as commercial yeast/baker's yeast) will specify fresh yeast, active dry yeast, or instant yeast. If finding fresh yeast near you is a challenge, you can use active dry or instant yeast instead (and vice versa), but you'll need to adjust the amount.

As a general rule, if you are using active dry yeast, multiply the fresh yeast weight in grams by 0.4. If you are using instant yeast, multiply the fresh yeast weight in grams by 0.33. Incorporate the different types of yeast into the recipes as explained in Techniques (see p. 141).

Salt: The recipes in this book have been developed with unrefined, fine-grain sea salt.

Sugar: Unless otherwise indicated, the word "sugar" in this book refers to superfine sugar (baker's sugar).

Eggs: The recipes in this book have been made with hen's eggs equivalent in size to "large" eggs in the US and Canada and "medium" eggs in the UK, with an average weight of about 2 oz. (55–60 g) per egg.

EQUIPMENT

Any special equipment necessary for the recipes (loaf pan, thermometer, food processor, etc.) has been listed under the "Equipment" heading in the recipe. Stand mixers, baking stones, and baking sheets are considered basic equipment so are not listed.

TECHNIQUES

Kneading

All recipes that ask you to knead the dough with a stand mixer can also be kneaded by hand (see Techniques, pp. 143–44). Unless otherwise indicated, use a stand mixer fitted with the dough hook.

Kneading and fermentation times:

The times indicated are general guidelines and depend on many factors, especially the ambient temperature. To confirm that the dough has been kneaded sufficiently, do the windowpane test (p. 50), and to ensure it is perfectly proofed before baking, do the poke test (p. 169).

Transferring dough to the oven: Some recipes call for a bread peel or a *paline* (baguette transfer peel) to move loaves or baguettes into the oven. If you don't have a peel, you can remove the preheated baking stone or sheet from the oven (wear oven mitts!), carefully place or turn out the dough onto it, score as desired, and quickly return the stone or sheet to the oven. If you don't have a *paline*, you can carefully transfer your dough onto an inverted baking sheet lined with parchment paper, and slide the dough and parchment paper onto the baking stone in the oven.

Baking

The baking time and temperature may vary depending on your oven. Select the baking mode that you feel is most appropriate for bread making.

Many of the recipes calling for a baking stone can be prepared in a Dutch oven (see p. 184) and vice-versa.

Specific techniques used (kneading, folding, scoring, etc.) are listed at the bottom of each recipe. In addition, the following key words appear with asterisks in the recipes:

Autolyse p. 138
Bassinage (adding water during kneading) p. 150
Bulk fermentation p. 154
Frasage (mixing) p. 144
Poaching p. 186
Poke test p. 169
Poolish p. 137
Proofing pp. 166–68
Resting p. 158

Roland Feuillas

——

"The word 'Justice' should always be spelled with a capital 'J,' because it stands for a concept that deserves respect and reverence, and is therefore sacred in the literal sense of word. We should write 'Liberté,' 'Égalité,' 'Fraternité' with capitals for the same reasons [the French national motto is *Liberty, Equality, Fraternity*]. By the same token, shouldn't we write 'Bread' with a capital 'B'? The fundamental symbol of our cultural, historical, and spiritual sustenance has been poorly treated in the last several decades. Can it regain the reverence and respect it has always deserved and received, up until recently? What criteria must be met, from seed to loaf, to restore Bread's reputation to one worthy of being written with a capital letter? In 2004, I launched the project *Les maîtres de mon moulin* [The Masters of My Mill] as an attempt to solve this complex problem step by step and point by point. Our company's social objective is to bring together every participant in the farm-to-loaf chain in pursuit of a shared vision of overall values and principles. A guide, a leitmotif, an absolute referent quickly emerged: Nature. Clearly Nature also deserves reverence and respect, and to be spelled with a capital 'N'. Most important to us is to respect Nature, from seed to finished loaf; to assist, help, support, and respect Nature, not control and constrain; working with Nature, in other words, not against it. We consider the genetic heritage that has been passed down to us through the symbiotic convergences between the living world, soils, climate, and humankind as sacred, an inheritance to be maintained at any cost. We advocate abandoning the harmful assumption that yield and profit are the only reliable guides. Other paths are possible; a new paradigm is essential, most of all for Bread, the staple of all staples. Reinventing our relationship with Bread will result in a complete transformation of our diet and therefore of our society. We seek to revive Bread that is 100 percent made from Nature, guided by and created with the single, axiomatic goal of listening to and serving Nature. We seek to restore coherency to the fact that 'culture' is used to refer to cultivating both 'soil' and 'humanity.' This work is urgent and absolutely necessary."

In the early 2000s, Roland Feuillas left his corporate role and found a new vocation making bread at the foot of the windmill once owned by the lords of Cucugnan, in the village of the same name in the French region of Hautes Corbières in south-eastern France. Using freshly stone-ground heritage grains and natural levain, he makes bread with high nutritional value. Feuillas draws on his scientific background to master every step in the earth-to-hearth cycle, always with great respect for the living world.

www.farinesdemeule.com

Tourte de meule Stone-Ground Bread

Recipe by Roland Feuillas

———

Makes 1 loaf

Active time: 15 minutes
Bulk fermentation: 14–18 hours
Proofing: 1–2 hours
Cooking: 40 minutes

Ingredients

1¾ tsp (0.3 oz./9 g) salt

Scant 1½ cups (12.5 oz./350 g) water + 2 tbsp (1 oz./30 g) for *bassinage*

4 cups + 2 tbsp (1 lb. 2 oz./500 g) stoneground white whole wheat flour (T80)

5¼ oz. (150 g) refreshed levain

Equipment

Bread peel

A day before baking, place the salt, 1½ cups (12¼ oz./350 g) water, flour, and levain, in this order, in the bowl of the stand mixer fitted with the dough hook. Knead for 3 minutes on speed 1, followed by 3 minutes on speed 2. Drizzle the 2 tbsp (1 oz./30 g) water into the bowl during the 3 minutes on speed 2 (*bassinage**).

When the dough is smooth and elastic, turn it out onto a floured work surface. Fold the dough twice, then place it in a large tub. Cover tightly and let rest in the refrigerator for 14–18 hours (bulk fermentation*).

The next day, dust the rim of the tub with flour and ease the dough onto a floured work surface with the help of a bowl scraper.

Shape the dough into a loose ball or *bâtard* and place in a floured banneton or a large bowl lined with a well-floured towel. Cover and let rise at room temperature for 1–2 hours (proofing*).

Toward the end of the rising time, place a rack at the lowest oven position and place another rack directly above it. Place an empty heavy-duty baking sheet, oven-safe skillet, or drip pan on the lower rack, and a baking stone or heavy-duty baking sheet on the upper rack, and preheat the oven to 500°F (260°C/Gas Mark 10). Bring 1 cup (250 ml) of water to a simmer.

When the dough passes the poke test*, quickly invert the banneton over the floured peel and score the dough before sliding it onto the baking stone or sheet in the oven.

Carefully pour the simmering water into the baking sheet, skillet, or drip pan to create steam and quickly close the oven door.

Bake for 20 minutes at 500°F (260°C/Gas Mark 10), then lower the oven temperature to 430°F (220°C/Gas Mark 7). Continue to bake for an additional 20 minutes, until the bread is deeply golden and makes a hollow sound when tapped on the bottom.

Remove the bread from the oven and place it on a rack to cool.

LA BONNE IDÉE
You can also bake this bread in a Dutch oven (see Techniques p. 184).

Techniques
Refreshing levain
Kneading by hand or with a mixer
Stages of fermentation
Folding
Shaping
Scoring
Using a baking stone

Pain aux graines
Seeded Bread

———

Makes 1 loaf

Active time: 15 minutes
Soaking: Overnight
Bulk fermentation: 1–2 hours
Resting: 15 minutes
Proofing: 2 hours
Cooking: 40 minutes

Ingredients

3.5 oz. (100 g) assorted seeds (sesame, flax, millet, poppy, buckwheat, etc.) + 3.5 oz. (100 g) assorted seeds for topping (sesame, flax, millet, poppy, buckwheat, etc.)

Scant ½ cup water (3.5 oz./100 g) for soaking seeds + 1 cup (9 oz./250 g)

1¾ tsp (0.3 oz./9 g) salt

4 cups + 2 tbsp (1 lb. 2 oz./500 g) bread, white whole wheat, or light whole wheat flour (T65–T110)

3.5 oz. (100 g) refreshed levain

0.1 oz. (3 g) fresh yeast

Equipment

Bread peel

Techniques

Refreshing levain
Kneading by hand or with a mixer
Stages of fermentation
Folding
Decorative finishes
Scoring
Using a baking stone

A day before baking, preheat the oven to 400°F (200°C/Gas Mark 6). Spread 3.5 oz (100 g) of the seeds across a baking sheet and toast them in the oven until fragrant (about 10 minutes). Meanwhile, bring the scant ½ cup (3.5 oz./100 g) water to a boil in a saucepan. Transfer the seeds to a heat-resistant bowl and pour the water over them. Let cool, then cover bowl and let soak in the refrigerator overnight. The next day, drain the seeds if they have not absorbed all of the water.

Place the 1 cup water, salt, flour, and levain in the bowl of the stand mixer fitted with the dough hook. Crumble in the fresh yeast. Knead for 3 minutes on speed 1, followed by 4–6 minutes on speed 2. Add the soaked seeds and knead briefly until evenly distributed.

Shape the dough into a ball, place in a lightly oiled or flour-dusted bowl, and cover. Let rise in a warm place for 1–2 hours. Fold the dough twice during the rise time: once after 30 minutes, and again after 1 hour (bulk fermentation*). When the dough has nearly doubled in size, turn it out onto a floured work surface and quickly shape it into a ball. Cover loosely with a towel and let rest for 15 minutes (resting*).

Shape the dough into a ball and place it seam-side up in a flour-dusted banneton or a large bowl lined with a well-floured towel. Cover with a towel, or an inverted large bowl or tub, and let rise at room temperature for 2 hours (proofing*).

Toward the end of the rising time, place a rack at the lowest oven position and place another rack directly above it. Place an empty heavy-duty baking sheet, oven-safe skillet, or drip pan on the lower rack, and a baking stone or heavy-duty baking sheet on the upper rack, and preheat the oven to 500°F (260°C/Gas Mark 10). Bring 1 cup (250 ml) of water to a simmer.

When the dough passes the poke test*, quickly invert the banneton over the floured peel. Brush the dough with a little water and sprinkle with the remaining 3.5 oz (100 g) seeds, then score the dough and immediately place in the oven. Carefully pour the simmering water into the baking sheet, skillet, or drip pan to create steam and quickly close the oven door.

Bake for 20 minutes at 500°F (260°C/Gas Mark 10), then lower the oven temperature to 430°F (220°C/Gas Mark 7). Continue to bake for an additional 20 minutes, until the bread is deeply golden and makes a hollow sound when tapped on the bottom. Remove the bread from the oven and place it on a rack to cool.

LA BONNE IDÉE
You can also bake this bread in a Dutch oven (see Techniques p. 184).

Tourte de seigle

Auvergne Rye Loaf

—————

Makes 1 large or 2 small loaves

Active time: 15 minutes
Bulk fermentation: 14–18 hours
Proofing: 1–2 hours
Cooking: 40 minutes

Ingredients

1¾ tsp (0.3 oz./9 g) salt
Scant 1½ cups (12.5 oz./350 g) lukewarm water
4¾ cups (1 lb. 2 oz./500 g) rye flour
5.25 oz. (150 g) refreshed levain

Equipment

Bread peel

A day before baking, place the salt, water, flour, and levain, in this order, in the bowl of a stand mixer fitted with the paddle attachment. Mix for 3 minutes on speed 1. Alternatively, combine the ingredients with your hands. The dough will be very sticky.

Cover the bowl tightly or transfer dough to an airtight container. Let rest in the refrigerator for 14–18 hours (bulk fermentation*).

The next day, dust the rim of the bowl with flour and gently ease the dough onto a well-floured work surface with the help of a bowl scraper.

For two small loaves, divide the dough into two equal pieces. Shape dough into a loose ball without folding it. Place in a flour-dusted banneton or a large bowl lined with a well-floured towel.

Cover and let rise at room temperature for 1–2 hours (proofing*).

Toward the end of the rising time, place a rack at the lowest oven position and place another rack directly above it. Place an empty heavy-duty baking sheet, oven-safe skillet, or drip pan on the lower rack, and a baking stone or heavy-duty baking sheet on the upper rack, and preheat the oven to 500°F (260°C/Gas Mark 10). Bring 1 cup (250 ml) of water to a simmer.

When the dough passes the poke test*, quickly invert the banneton over the floured peel and slide the dough onto the baking stone or sheet in the oven.

Carefully pour the simmering water into the baking sheet, skillet, or drip pan to create steam and quickly close the oven door.

Bake for 20 minutes at 500°F (260°C/Gas Mark 10), then lower the oven temperature to 430°F (220°C/Gas Mark 7). Continue to bake for an additional 20 minutes, until the bread is deeply golden and makes a hollow sound when tapped on the bottom.

Remove the bread from the oven and place it on a rack to cool.

LA BONNE IDÉE
You can also bake this bread in a Dutch oven (see Techniques p. 184).

Techniques
Refreshing levain
Kneading by hand or with a mixer
Stages of fermentation
Using a baking stone

Pain au grand épeautre

Spelt Bread

———

Makes 1 loaf

Active time: 15 minutes

Bulk fermentation:
1½ hours + 14–18 hours

Proofing: 1–2 hours

Cooking: 40 minutes

Ingredients

1¾ tsp (0.3 oz./9 g) salt

Scant 1½ cups (12.5 oz./350 g) water

5 cups (1 lb. 2 oz./500 g) white whole wheat or light whole wheat spelt flour (T80–T110)

5.25 oz. (150 g) refreshed levain

Equipment

Bread peel

A day before baking, place the salt, water, flour, and levain, in this order, in the bowl of a stand mixer fitted with the dough hook. Knead for 3 minutes on speed 1, followed by 5 minutes on speed 2, or until you obtain a smooth dough.

Cover the bowl and let the dough rise for 1½ hours. Fold the dough twice during the rise time: once after 30 minutes, and once after 1 hour. Place in the refrigerator for 14–18 hours (bulk fermentation*).

The next day, dust the rim of the bowl with flour and gently ease the dough onto a floured work surface with the help of a bowl scraper.

Shape the dough into a loose round and place in a flour-dusted banneton or a large bowl lined with a well-floured towel. Let rise at room temperature for 1–2 hours (proofing*).

Toward the end of the rising time, place a rack at the lowest oven position and place another rack directly above it. Place an empty heavy-duty baking sheet, oven-safe skillet, or drip pan on the lower rack, and a baking stone or heavy-duty baking sheet on the upper rack, and preheat the oven to 500°F (260°C/Gas Mark 10). Bring 1 cup (250 ml) of water to a simmer.

When the dough passes the poke test*, quickly invert the banneton over the floured peel and score the dough before sliding it onto the baking stone or sheet in the oven.

Carefully pour the simmering water into the baking sheet, skillet, or drip pan to create steam and quickly close the oven door.

Bake for 20 minutes at 500°F (260°C/Gas Mark 10), then lower the oven temperature to 430°F (220°C/Gas Mark 7). Continue to bake for an additional 20 minutes, until the bread is deeply golden and makes a hollow sound when tapped on the bottom.

Remove the bread from the oven and place it on a rack to cool.

LA BONNE IDÉE

You can also bake this bread in a Dutch oven (see Techniques p. 184).

Techniques

Refreshing levain

Kneading by hand or with a mixer

Stages of fermentation

Folding

Scoring

Using a baking stone

Pain de ménage en cocotte et sans pétrie

No-Knead Dutch Oven Bread

___

Makes 1 loaf

Active time: 15 minutes

Bulk fermentation:
1 ½ hours + 8 hours–overnight

Proofing: 1 hour

Cooking: 35–40 minutes

Ingredients

0.35 oz. (10 g) fresh yeast

1⅔ cups (14 oz./400 g) lukewarm water

2½ cups (10.5 oz./300 g) white whole wheat or light whole wheat flour (T80–T110)

Scant 2 cups (7 oz./200 g) rye flour

1¾ tsp (0.3 oz./9 g) salt

Equipment

8–10-in. (2–4-qt./20–25-cm) round cast-iron or enamel Dutch oven

In a bowl, dissolve the yeast in the lukewarm water.

Combine the flours and salt in a large mixing bowl and make a well in the center. Gradually add the water-yeast mixture and stir (or mix with your hands) until well blended. The dough will be very sticky, so do not try to knead it.

Cover the bowl and let the dough rise for 1½ hours. Fold the dough three times during the rise time: once after 30 minutes, once after 1 hour, and once after 1½ hours. Cover the bowl and place in the refrigerator for at least 8 hours and up to overnight (bulk fermentation*).

Toward the end of bulk fermentation, cut out a circle of parchment paper big enough to line the bottom of the Dutch oven. Set the parchment paper aside.

Place the Dutch oven with lid on in the oven, and preheat to 500°F (260°C/Gas Mark 10) for at least 30 minutes.

Ease the dough onto a floured work surface without deflating it and gently shape it into a loose ball. Place the dough seam-side down in a floured banneton or a bowl lined with a well-floured towel. Cover and let rise for about 1 hour (proofing*).

When the dough passes the poke test*, carefully remove the Dutch oven using oven mitts (both the base and lid will be extremely hot) and place on a heat-resistant surface. Close the oven.

Working quickly, remove the oven top and place on a heat-safe surface. Line the pot with the parchment circle and turn the dough over into the pot (the seam will now be on the top). Dust the surface of the dough with flour and score it, then—using oven mitts—put the lid on the Dutch oven and place it in the oven.

Bake for 25 minutes without lifting the lid, then remove the lid, lower the oven temperature to 475°F (245°C/Gas Mark 9), and bake for an additional 10–15 minutes, until the loaf is deeply golden.

Remove the bread from the Dutch oven and place it on a rack to cool.

Techniques
Stages of fermentation
Folding
Scoring
Baking in a Dutch oven

Pain moulé à l'engrain

Einkorn Sandwich Loaf

————

Makes 1 loaf

Active time: 15 minutes
Bulk fermentation:
1–2 hours + 14–18 hours
Proofing: 1 hour
Cooking: 40 minutes

Ingredients

1¾ tsp (0.3 oz./9 g) salt
Scant 1½ cups (11.75 oz./330 g) water
4 cups (1 lb. 2 oz./500 g) einkorn flour + more for the pan
5.25 oz. (150 g) refreshed levain
Neutral oil, for the pan

Equipment

10–11 × 5-in. (26–28 × 12.7-cm) loaf pan

A day before baking, place the salt, water, flour, and levain, in this order, in the bowl of a stand mixer fitted with the dough hook. Knead for 3 minutes on speed 1, followed by 5 minutes on speed 2, or until you obtain a smooth dough.

Transfer to a dough tub or a separate large mixing bowl, cover, and let rise at room temperature for 1–2 hours (bulk fermentation*).

Lightly grease the loaf pan with oil and dust it with flour. After the first rise, dust the sides of the tub or bowl with flour and gently ease the dough onto a floured work surface with the help of a bowl scraper. Shape into a *bâtard* and place in the prepared loaf pan. Cover and place in the refrigerator for 14–18 hours.

The next day, remove the dough from the refrigerator and let sit at room temperature for 1 hour (proofing*).

Meanwhile, place a rack at the lowest oven position and place another rack directly above it. Place an empty heavy-duty baking sheet, oven-safe skillet, or drip pan on the lower rack and preheat the oven to 500°F (260°C/Gas Mark 10). Bring 1 cup (250 ml) of water to a simmer.

When the dough passes the poke test*, place the bread, without scoring, in the oven, then carefully pour the simmering water into the baking sheet, skillet, or drip pan to create steam and quickly close the oven door.

Bake for 20 minutes at 500°F (260°C/Gas Mark 10), then lower the oven temperature to 430°F (220°C/Gas Mark 7). Continue to bake for an additional 20 minutes, until golden.

Let the bread cool for 5 minutes in the pan, then turn it out onto a rack and let cool completely.

Techniques
Refreshing levain
Kneading by hand or with a mixer
Stages of fermentation
Shaping

Baguettes

Makes 4 small baguettes

Active time: 15 minutes

Autolyse: 3 hours

Bulk fermentation: 1½ hours + 15 hours

Resting: 30 minutes

Proofing: 30 minutes

Cooking: 18 minutes

Ingredients

4 cups + 2 tbsp (1 lb. 2 oz./500 g) bread flour (T65)

Scant 1½ cups (12.5 oz./350 g) water + 2 tsp (0.35 oz./10 g) for dissolving salt

1.75 oz. (50 g) refreshed levain

0.05 oz. (1 g) fresh yeast

Scant 1½ tsp (0.25 oz./7 g) salt

Equipment

Paline (baguette transfer peel)

Techniques

Refreshing levain

Kneading by hand or with a mixer

Stages of fermentation

Folding

Shaping

Scoring baguettes

Using a baking stone

A day before baking, place the flour and scant 1½ cups (12.5 oz./350 g) of water in the bowl of a stand mixer fitted with the dough hook. Mix for 1 minute on speed 1 (*frasage**). Cover the bowl and let the mixture rest for 3 hours (autolyse*).

Add the levain and crumble in the fresh yeast. Combine the salt and 2 tsp (0.35 oz./10 g) water in a bowl and stir or swish to dissolve, then add to the dough. Knead for 8 minutes on speed 1.

Cover the bowl and let the dough rise for 1½ hours. Fold the dough three times during the rise time: once after 30 minutes, once after 1 hour, and once after 1½ hours. Cover and place in the refrigerator for 15 hours (bulk fermentation*).

The next day, dust a work surface and the dough with flour. Turn the dough out onto the work surface, floured side down. With a bench scraper, divide dough into four equal pieces. Shape each piece into a rough oval and let rest at room temperature for 30 minutes (resting*).

Shape each piece of dough into an approximately 10-in. (25-cm) baguette, ensuring it will fit in your oven lengthwise (the baguettes will be easier to transfer to the oven if they're shorter). Place the shaped baguettes between the folds of a floured *couche*, or flour a towel and pleat it like an accordion around the baguettes. Let rest for 30 minutes (proofing*).

Meanwhile, place a rack at the lowest oven position and place another rack directly above it. Place an empty heavy-duty baking sheet, oven-safe skillet, or drip pan on the lower rack, and a baking stone or heavy-duty baking sheet on the upper rack, and preheat the oven to 500°F (260°C/Gas Mark 10). Bring 1 cup (250 ml) of water to a simmer.

When the dough passes the poke test*, using a lame, slash each baguette diagonally in two places. Roll the baguettes one at a time onto the *paline* and carefully transfer to the baking stone or sheet in the oven.

Carefully pour the simmering water into the baking sheet, skillet, or drip pan to create steam and quickly close the oven door.

Bake for 18 minutes, lowering the oven temperature to 450°F (240°C/Gas Mark 8) halfway through the baking time.

Remove the baguettes from the oven and place on a rack to cool.

Ciabattas

___

Makes 2 small ciabattas

Active time: 30 minutes
Poolish: Overnight
Autolyse: 20–30 minutes
Bulk fermentation: 2½ hours
Proofing: 1–2 hours
Cooking: 20–30 minutes

Ingredients

Poolish:
Scant ½ cup (3.5 oz./100 g) lukewarm water
0.05 oz. (1 g) fresh yeast
¾ cup + 2 tbsp (3.5 oz./100 g) bread or white whole wheat flour (T65–T80)

Ciabattas
2 oz. (60 g) refreshed levain
0.05 oz. (1 g) fresh yeast
¾ cup + 1 tbsp (7 oz./200 g) water + 1 tsp (0.16 oz./5 g) for dissolving salt
2½ cups (10.5 oz./300 g) bread or white whole wheat flour (T65–T80)
1¾ tsp (0.3 oz./9 g) salt
1 tbsp (0.5 oz./15 g) extra-virgin olive oil
Superfine semolina flour, for dusting

Equipment
Paline (baguette transfer peel)

Techniques
Refreshing levain
Kneading by hand or with a mixer
Stages of fermentation
Folding
Using a baking stone

A day before baking, prepare the poolish*: Pour the water into a bowl or container with enough space for rising and stir in the yeast to dissolve. Add the flour and stir to combine. Cover and let rest at room temperature overnight (10 hours).

Prepare the ciabattas: The next day, transfer the poolish to the bowl of a stand mixer fitted with the dough hook. Add the levain, yeast, ¾ cup + 1 tbsp (7 oz./200 g) water, and flour. Mix quickly until smooth, then cover and let rest at room temperature for 20–30 minutes (autolyse*).

Knead for 3 minutes on speed 1, then dissolve the salt in the 1 tsp water and add to the bowl. Knead for 3–5 minutes on speed 2, gradually drizzling in the olive oil with the mixer running. Knead until the dough is smooth, elastic, and shiny. Cover the bowl tightly and let the dough rise at room temperature for 2½ hours. Fold the dough three times during the rise time: once after 30 minutes, once after 1 hour, and once after 1½ hours. For the final hour, let the dough rest without folding it (bulk fermentation*).

Gently ease the dough out of the bowl onto a floured work surface. Quickly shape the dough into a rectangle and divide it in half lengthwise using a bench scraper. Generously dust a towel, preferably linen, with a combination of bread or all-purpose flour and superfine semolina flour. Gently place the two pieces of dough on the floured towel and make pleats on either side of each piece to maintain the shape. Dust the dough with flour, cover, and let rise at room temperature for 1–2 hours (proofing*).

Toward the end of the rising time, place a rack at the lowest oven position and place another rack directly above it. Place an empty heavy-duty baking sheet, oven-safe skillet, or drip pan on the lower rack, and a baking stone or heavy-duty baking sheet on the upper rack, and preheat the oven to 500°F (260°C/Gas Mark 10). Bring 1 cup (250 ml) of water to a simmer.

When the dough passes the poke test*, roll the ciabattas one at a time onto the *paline* and carefully transfer to the baking stone or sheet in the oven.

Carefully pour the simmering water into the skillet to create steam, quickly close the oven door, and reduce the heat to 450°F (240°C/Gas Mark 8).

Bake for 20–30 minutes, until lightly golden.

Remove the ciabattas from the oven and place on a rack to cool.

Pain de mie

Pullman Loaf

Makes 1 loaf

Active time: 30 minutes
Bulk fermentation: 1½ hours
Proofing: 1–1½ hours
Cooking: 25–30 minutes

Ingredients

0.2 oz. (5 g) fresh yeast
3½ tbsp (1.75 oz./50 g) water
¾ cup + 1 tbsp (7 oz./200 g) whole milk
2¾ cups (12.5 oz./350 g) bread flour (T65)
1.5 oz. (40 g) refreshed levain
2½ tsp (0.35 oz./10 g) sugar
Scant 1½ tsp (0.25 oz./7 g) salt
5 tbsp (2.5 oz./70 g) butter, diced, at room temperature + 1 tbsp (15 g) for the pan

Equipment

9 × 4-in. (23 × 10-cm) Pullman loaf pan

Dissolve the yeast in the water in a bowl, then place all the ingredients, except for the butter, in the bowl of a stand mixer fitted with the dough hook.

Knead for 5 minutes on speed 1, followed by 3–4 minutes on speed 2, until the dough pulls away from the sides of the bowl and is smooth and supple. Add the butter and knead on speed 1 until the butter is fully incorporated.

Cover the bowl and let the dough rise in a warm place for 1½ hours. Fold the dough twice during the rise time, once after 30 minutes and once after 1 hour (bulk fermentation*).

Grease the base and lid of the loaf pan with the remaining 1 tbsp butter. Turn the dough out onto a floured work surface and gently deflate it by shaping it into a ball.

Form the dough into a 9-in. (23-cm) log and place in the greased pan, seam-side down. Let rise in a warm place for 1–1 ½ hours, keeping a close eye on it (proofing*). The dough should rise to within ¼–½ in. (5 mm–1 cm) of the top edge of the pan, but must not stick to the lid.

Toward the end of the rising time, preheat the oven to 400°F (200°C/ Gas Mark 6).

When the dough passes the poke test*, put in the oven and bake for 25–30 minutes, then remove the lid and bake for an additional 5 minutes, or until the bread is uniformly golden.

Turn the bread out of the pan and place it on a rack to cool.

LA BONNE IDÉE
If you don't have a Pullman loaf pan, use a regular loaf pan and cover it with a weighted-down baking sheet.

Techniques
Refreshing levain
Kneading by hand or with a mixer
Stages of fermentation

★★

Pain au maïs

Cornmeal Bread

―――――

Makes 1 loaf

Active time: 15 minutes
Poolish: Overnight
Bulk fermentation: 1 hour + 15 hours
Proofing: 1–2 hours
Cooking: 35–40 minutes

Ingredients

Poolish:

⅓ cup (1.5 oz./45 g) finely ground cornmeal

Scant ¼ cup (1.75 oz./55 g) water

0.07 oz. (2 g) fresh yeast

Dough

0.1 oz (3 g) fresh yeast

2 cups (8.75 oz./245 g) white whole wheat flour (T80)

½ cup + 2 tsp (4.75 oz./135 g) water at 61°F (16°C) + 2 tsp (0.35 oz./10 g) for *bassinage*

1 tsp (0.25 oz./6 g) salt

Finely ground cornmeal for dusting

Equipment

8–10-in. (2–4-qt./20–25-cm) round cast-iron or enamel Dutch oven

Two days before baking, prepare the poolish*: Combine all of the ingredients in a bowl or container with enough space for rising. Cover and let sit at room temperature overnight.

The next day, transfer the poolish to the bowl of a stand mixer fitted with the dough hook. Add the fresh yeast, flour, ½ cup + 2 tsp (4.75 oz./135 g) water, and salt. Knead for 8 minutes on speed 1, then drizzle in the 2 tsp (0.35 oz./10 g) water with the mixer running (*bassinage**) and knead for an additional 2 minutes, still on speed 1.

Cover the bowl and let the dough rise in a warm place for 1 hour. Fold the dough once, after 30 minutes. Cover and place in the refrigerator for 15 hours (bulk fermentation*).

The next day, dust the dough and sides of the bowl with flour. Using a bowl scraper, ease the dough out of the bowl onto a floured work surface.

Shape the dough into a loose ball and place seam-side up in a floured banneton or a large bowl lined with a well-floured towel. Cover and let rise at room temperature for 1–2 hours (proofing*).

Toward the end of the rising time, cut out a circle of parchment paper big enough to line the bottom of your Dutch oven; set the parchment circle aside.

Place the Dutch oven with the lid on in the oven as you preheat it to 500°F (260°C/Gas Mark 10).

When the dough passes the poke test*, carefully remove the Dutch oven using oven mitts (both the base and lid will be extremely hot) and place on a heat-safe surface.

Working quickly, line the pot with the parchment paper circle and turn the dough over into the pot (the seam side will now be on the bottom). Dust the surface of the dough with cornmeal and quickly score it. Put the lid back on and place in the oven.

Bake for 25 minutes at 500°F (260°C/Gas Mark 10) without lifting the lid, then remove the lid, lower the oven temperature to 475°F (245°C/Gas Mark 9), and bake for an additional 10–15 minutes, until the loaf is deeply golden.

Remove the bread from the Dutch oven and place it on a rack to cool.

Many thanks to Matthieu Dalmais (B.O.U.L.O.M) for this recipe.

Techniques

Kneading with a mixer
Stages of fermentation
Folding
Scoring
Baking in a Dutch oven

Pain aux noix

Nut Bread

————

Makes 1 loaf

Active time: 20 minutes
Bulk fermentation: 1½ hours
Proofing: 1 hour
Cooking: 35–40 minutes

Ingredients

1¾ tsp (0.3 oz./9 g) salt

Scant 1½ cups (12.5 oz./350 g) water

2¾ cups (12.5 oz./350 g) bread or white whole wheat flour (T65–T80)

1½ cups (5.25 oz./150 g) chestnut flour

3.5 oz. (100 g) refreshed levain

0.2 oz. (5 g) fresh yeast

5 tbsp (2.5 oz./75 g) butter, diced, at room temperature

¾ cup (3.5 oz./100 g) walnut halves, roughly chopped

Equipment

Bread peel

Place the salt, water, bread flour, chestnut flour, and levain, in this order, in the bowl of a stand mixer fitted with the dough hook. Crumble in the fresh yeast, then knead for 3 minutes on speed 1, followed by 5–7 minutes on speed 2. At the end of the kneading time, knead in the butter until well incorporated, then mix in the walnuts.

Cover the bowl and let the dough rise in a warm place for 1½ hours. Fold the dough three times during the rise time: once after 30 minutes, once after 1 hour, and once after 1½ hours (bulk fermentation*).

Turn the dough out onto a floured work surface. Shape it into a *bâtard* or ball and place seam-side up in a floured banneton or a large bowl lined with a well-floured towel.

Cover and let rise at room temperature for 1 hour (proofing*).

Toward the end of the rising time, place a rack at the lowest oven position and place another rack directly above it. Place an empty heavy-duty baking sheet, oven-safe skillet, or drip pan on the lower rack, and a baking stone or heavy-duty baking sheet on the upper rack, and preheat the oven to 480°F (250°C/Gas Mark 9). Bring 1 cup (250 ml) of water to a simmer.

When the dough passes the poke test*, quickly invert the banneton over the floured peel and score the dough before sliding it onto the baking stone or sheet in the oven.

Carefully pour the simmering water into the baking sheet, skillet, or drip pan to create steam and quickly close the oven door.

Bake for 20 minutes at 480°F (250°C/Gas Mark 9), then reduce the heat to 430°F (220°C/Gas Mark 7) and continue to bake for an additional 20 minutes, until deeply golden.

Remove the bread from the oven and place it on a rack to cool.

LA BONNE IDÉE

You can also bake this bread in a Dutch oven (see Techniques p. 184).

Techniques

Refreshing levain
Kneading by hand or with a mixer
Stages of fermentation
Folding
Shaping
Scoring
Using a baking stone

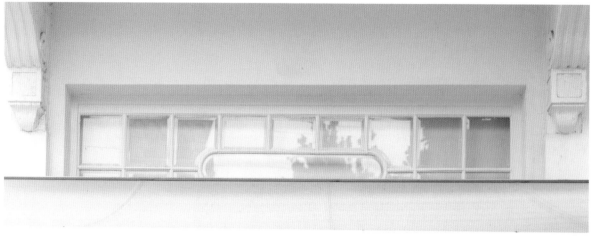

Julien Burlat
—

"Bread reminds me of my childhood. We spent weekends in a small village where we ate rustic bread baked in a wood-fired oven. When I started making bread for my restaurant, Dôme, in Antwerp, the goal wasn't to make bread per se, but rather to offer our clients something good. I didn't like any of the commercially available options; Belgian Flanders doesn't have the same culture of bread that we have in France. When I opened my second restaurant, Dôme-sur-Mer, I had to hire an assistant to make enough bread to supply both establishments. I thought to myself: why not go further and sell a little of our bread as well? That's when bread took on a larger role in my business. We opened a bakery, Domestic, then a second one. We kept the bakeries when my wife, Sophie, and I decided to sell our restaurants. There's a line out the door on Saturday mornings—people have taken to us. Our bread has a certain exotic quality for the Flemish; it reminds them of France, where they travel for vacation. We also supply restaurants in Antwerp. Our bread is enjoyable to eat; it has good texture. In the ten years I've been learning about bread, I've also realized, through the people I've met and the things I've read, that the entire industry needs an overhaul. I work increasingly with Belgian heritage wheats, like the one produced by Graines de Curieux in the Belgian region of Ardennes. Perhaps, like meat, we should eat less bread, but ensure it is only good bread."

Originally from Saint-Étienne, France, Julien Burlat trained under French chefs Pierre Gagnaire, Alain Ducasse at Hôtel de Crillon, and Bernard Pacaud at L'Ambroisie, before opening his own restaurant, Dôme, in Antwerp, Belgium, in 2001 (which earned a Michelin star), then Dôme-sur-Mer. Two boulangeries-patisseries, Domestic and Cuisinette Domestic, followed, also located in Antwerp. Since then, Burlat has closed his two restaurants to focus on other projects, including a collaboration with the Zannier family, which runs a luxury hospitality group. He oversees the group's kitchens, notably at Chalet Zannier in Megève, France, as well as first-class establishments in Cambodia and Vietnam.

www.domestic-bakkerij.be

Pain intégral 100 Percent Whole Wheat Bread
Recipe by Julien Burlat

Makes 2 loaves

Active time: 15 minutes
Bulk fermentation: 3 hours
Proofing: 1 hour + 12–24 hours
Cooking: 40 minutes

Ingredients

4 tsp (0.75 oz./20 g) salt
2½ cups (1 lb. 5 oz./600 g) water
8¾ cups (2¼ lb./1 kg) organic dark/100 percent whole wheat flour
3.5 oz. (100 g) refreshed levain

A day before baking, place the salt, water, flour, and levain in the bowl of a stand mixer fitted with the dough hook. Knead for 5 minutes on speed 1, followed by 8 minutes on speed 2.

Cover the bowl and let the dough rise at room temperature for 3 hours. Fold the dough twice during the rise time: once after 1 hour and once after 2 hours (bulk fermentation*).

Turn the dough out onto a floured work surface and divide it into two equal pieces using a bench scraper. Shape into *bâtards* or balls and place in generously floured bannetons, or in two separate large bowls, each lined with a well-floured towel. Let rest at room temperature for 1 hour, then cover and place in the refrigerator for 12–24 hours (proofing*).

The next day, place a rack at the lowest oven position and place another rack directly above it. Place an empty heavy-duty baking sheet, oven-safe skillet, or drip pan on the lower rack, and a baking stone or heavy-duty baking sheet on the upper rack, and preheat the oven to 500°F (260°C/Gas Mark 10). Bring 1 cup (250 ml) of water to a simmer.

When the dough passes the poke test*, put on oven mitts, remove the baking stone or sheet from the oven and carefully invert the bannetons over it, then return to the oven.

Carefully pour the simmering water into the baking sheet, skillet, or drip pan to create steam and quickly close the oven door.

Bake for 20 minutes at 500°F (260°C/Gas Mark 10), then reduce the heat to 450°F (230°C/Gas Mark 8) and continue to bake for an additional 20 minutes.

Remove the bread from the oven and place it on a rack to cool.

LA BONNE IDÉE
You can also bake this bread in a Dutch oven (see Techniques p. 184).

Techniques
Refreshing levain
Kneading with a mixer
Stages of fermentation
Folding
Shaping
Using a baking stone

Alex Croquet

———

"To make bread is to bring forth a world that you can literally feel when kneading the dough. It has character: it is resistant, smooth, elastic, and extensible. Fermentation is life. In the oven, the bread offers up its whole life, opening like a rosebud. Water and heat combine to form steam, taking fermentation to its culmination in a landscape of crevasses, summits, and peaks.

"My passion for levain developed as I worked with dough and occasionally found myself in sticky situations, so to speak. I'm so fascinated by levain, which I no longer see as an ingredient, but as a living thing. It's a member of the family, and it's always on my mind. I only forgot to feed it once, and it was as if I had forgotten to pick up my son from school! Now, *faluche* is a yeast-leavened bread; it took me ten years to develop a liking for it. I never included *faluche* in my tastings because it is very easy to make and has nowhere near the aromatic complexity of *pain au levain*. Only the flavor of the wheat flour comes through. But it reveals the mildness of bread. *Faluche* is typical of the Nord [the northernmost department of France], which is often associated with the bitterness of beer and endives. But we also have sweet tooths. *Faluche* resembles us: it's white and mild-flavored because it has no crust—which is the height of irony for someone like me who loves crust so much, especially when it fades from deep brown to ochre, until it disappears into the crumb.

"*Faluche* is eaten alone as a snack or at breakfast. It would never occur to us to eat it alongside another dish or as part of a meal. It looks like a little cloud or a pillow—everything about it is round, including how it tastes, looks, and feels."

Alex Croquet uses his extensive, empirical knowledge to select organic flour, care for his levains like treasures, and dynamize water using a waterfall installed in his laboratory. In his bakery in Wattignies in northern France, he has befriended many chefs, including Emmanuel Renaut and Alexandre Gauthier, whom he has taught the art of bread making. He also has a bakery in Lille, France.

www.alexcroquet.fr

Faluche

Recipe by Alex Croquet

___

Makes 6 *faluches*

Active time: 15 minutes
Autolyse: 1 hour
Bulk fermentation: 1½ hours
Resting: 15 minutes
Proofing: 1½ hours
Cooking: 8 minutes

Ingredients

4 cups + 2 tbsp (1 lb. 2 oz./500 g) bread flour (T65)
1⅓ cups (11.5 oz./325 g) water, divided
0.25 oz. (7 g) fresh yeast
1¾ tsp (0.3 oz./9 g) salt

Place the flour and 1¼ cups (10.5 oz./300 g) of the water in the bowl of a stand mixer fitted with the dough hook. Mix for 1 minute on speed 1 (*frasage**), then let rest for 1 hour (autolyse*).

Dissolve the fresh yeast in 1 tbsp (0.5 oz./15 g) of the water. Dissolve the salt in the remaining 2 tsp (0.35 oz./10 g) water.

Pour the dissolved yeast and salt into the bowl of the stand mixer with the other ingredients and mix for 2 minutes on speed 1. Cover the bowl and let the dough rise for 1½ hours. Fold the dough three times during the rise time: once after 30 minutes, once after 1 hour, and once after 1½ hours (bulk fermentation*).

Dust the work surface and the top of the dough with flour. Turn the bowl over onto the work surface, then turn the dough over so it's floured-side up. Divide the dough into six equal pieces using a bench scraper and shape each into a ball. Let rest at room temperature for 15 minutes (resting*).

Using the heel of your hand or a rolling pin, gently flatten the dough, without crushing it, into ½-in. (1-cm) thick circles. To obtain perfect circles, frequently rotate the dough a quarter-turn as you work.

Transfer the rounds of dough to a baking sheet lined with parchment paper. Run a dough docker over each round, or pierce them all over with a fork dipped in water.

Cover and let rise for 1½ hours (proofing*).

Toward the end of the rising time, preheat the oven to 480°F (250°C/Gas Mark 9).

When the dough passes the poke test*, bake the *faluches* for 8 minutes. They should remain pale, so do not let them brown.

Techniques
Kneading with a mixer
Stages of fermentation
Shaping

Pain Brié

Normandy Bread

───────

Makes 1 loaf

Active time: 20 minutes
Poolish: 2 hours
Bulk fermentation: 30 minutes
Proofing: 1 hour
Chilling: 10–15 minutes
Cooking: 20–25 minutes

Ingredients

Poolish
⅔ cup (5.25 oz./150 g) water
0.07 oz. (2 g) fresh yeast
1 cup + 2 tbsp (5.25 oz./150 g) all-purpose flour (T55)

Bread
5 tsp (1 oz./25 g) water
0.1 oz. (3 g) fresh yeast
¾ cup + 2 tbsp (3.5 oz./100 g) all-purpose flour (T55)
1 tbsp (0.75 oz./20 g) butter, at room temperature
1 tsp (0.2 oz./5 g) salt

Equipment

Bread peel

Prepare the poolish*: Heat the water to about 77°F (25°C). Place in a medium bowl, add the yeast, and stir or swish to dissolve. Stir in the flour until just combined. Cover and let sit at room temperature for about 2 hours, until bubbly on top.

Prepare the bread: Place the 5 tsp (1 oz./25 g) water in the bowl of a stand mixer fitted with the dough hook and crumble in the fresh yeast. Mix to dissolve the yeast, then add the poolish, flour, butter, and salt.

Knead for 3 minutes on speed 1, followed by 3–5 minutes on speed 2. Cover and let rest at room temperature for about 30 minutes (bulk fermentation*).

Turn the dough out onto a floured work surface and shape it into a ball or a very short *bâtard*. Cover and let rise for 1 hour (proofing*).

Meanwhile, place a rack at the lowest oven position and place another rack directly above it. Place an empty heavy-duty baking sheet, oven-safe skillet, or drip pan on the lower rack, and a baking stone or heavy-duty baking sheet on the upper rack, and preheat the oven to 450°F (230°C/ Gas Mark 8). Bring 1 cup (250 ml) of water to a simmer.

At the end of proofing, refrigerate the dough for 10–15 minutes to firm it up before baking.

When the dough passes the poke test*, remove it from the refrigerator and place it on the floured peel. Holding a lame at a slight angle, make three to five quick parallel slits, about ¼ in. (5 mm) deep, from one end of the dough to the other.

Slide the dough onto the baking stone or sheet. Carefully pour the hot water into the skillet to create steam and quickly close the oven door.

Bake for 20–25 minutes, until deeply golden. Toward the end of the baking time, crack the oven door open for 5–10 minutes to lower the temperature and encourage the bread to develop a thick crust.

Remove the bread from the oven and place it on a rack to cool.

Techniques
Kneading by hand or with a mixer
Stages of fermentation
Shaping
Scoring
Using a baking stone

Fougasse

—

Makes 1 large or 2 small *fougasses*

Active time: 20 minutes
Bulk fermentation: 2 hours
Resting: 30 minutes
Proofing: 1 hour
Cooking: 15–18 minutes

Ingredients

⅔ cup (9 oz./160 g) water

1 tsp (0.2 oz./5 g) salt

2 cups (9 oz./250 g) bread or white whole wheat flour (T65–T80)

0.2 oz. (5 g) fresh yeast

2 tsp (5 g) dried herbs and/or spices (thyme, oregano, herbes de Provence, etc.)

2 tbsp (1 oz./30 g) extra-virgin olive oil + 1 tbsp (0.5 oz./15 g) for brushing

1.75 oz. (50 g) pitted and coarsely chopped olives and/or thinly sliced sundried tomatoes (optional)

Toppings (optional)

1.75 oz. (50 g) bacon, cut into thin strips (lardons)

Grated Emmental cheese

Place the water, salt, and flour in the bowl of a stand mixer fitted with the dough hook. Crumble in the yeast in very small pieces and add the herbs/spices. Knead for 5 minutes on speed 1, followed by 5–7 minutes on speed 2. About halfway through the 5–7 minutes, drizzle in the 2 tbsp (1 oz./30 g) olive oil with the mixer running. At the end of the kneading time, add the olives and/or sundried tomatoes, if using, and mix for 1 minute on speed 1, until well incorporated.

Cover the bowl and let the dough rise in a warm place for 2 hours. Fold the dough twice during the rise time (bulk fermentation*).

Meanwhile, if you'd like to top your *fougasse* with bacon, fry the bacon in a skillet until browned and crisp. Drain on paper towels and let cool completely before using.

Turn the dough out onto a floured work surface. For two *fougasses*, divide the dough into two equal pieces using a bench scraper. Shape each piece into a *bâtard*, cover with a damp towel, and let rest for 30 minutes (resting*).

Using the palm of your hand or a rolling pin, flatten the dough into one or two ovals with a thickness of about ¾ in. (2 cm). Place on a baking sheet lined with parchment paper. Using a bench scraper or a spatula, make several diagonal slits in the dough, cutting all the way through and making a pattern that resembles a palm leaf. Stretch the slits open with your fingers, making them wide so that they won't close up during baking.

Cover with a damp towel and let rise at room temperature for 1 hour (proofing*).

If you're adding toppings, brush the dough with water to moisten it and sprinkle with the bacon and/or cheese.

Toward the end of the rising time, preheat the oven to 450°F (230°C/ Gas Mark 8).

When the dough passes the poke test*, bake the *fougasse(s)* for 15–18 minutes, until golden. Slide onto a rack with the parchment paper underneath and brush with a little olive oil.

Serve warm or at room temperature.

Techniques

Kneading by hand or with a mixer
Stages of fermentation
Folding
Shaping
Scoring

Préfou

Vendée Garlic Bread

_____

Makes 2 *préfous*

Active time: 30 minutes
Bulk fermentation: 1–2 hours
Proofing: 30 minutes
Cooking: 15 minutes + 5–7 minutes

Ingredients

Bread
⅔ cup (5.25 oz./150 g) water
1 tsp salt
2 tbsp sugar
2 cups (9 oz./250 g) all-purpose flour
0.35 oz. (10 g) fresh yeast
1 tbsp + 1 tsp (0.70 oz./20 g) butter,
at room temperature

Garlic-Parsley Butter
7 tbsp (3.5 oz./100 g) salted butter,
at room temperature
4 cloves garlic, finely chopped
1 bunch parsley, finely chopped
Salt

Equipment

Food processor

Prepare the bread: Place the water, salt, sugar, and flour in the bowl of a stand mixer fitted with the dough hook. Crumble in the fresh yeast. Knead for 3 minutes on speed 1, followed by 4–6 minutes on speed 2. Add the butter halfway through the 4–6 minutes with the mixer running.

Shape the dough into a ball, place in a lightly oiled or flour-dusted bowl, and cover. Let rise for 1–2 hours, until doubled in volume. Fold the dough twice during the rise time: once after 30 minutes, and once after 1 hour (bulk fermentation*).

Turn the dough out onto a floured work surface and divide it into two equal pieces using a bench scraper.

Shape each piece of dough into a baguette and flatten gently with a rolling pin. Place on a baking sheet lined with parchment paper, cover, and let rest for 30 minutes (proofing*).

Meanwhile, preheat the oven to 400°F (200°C/Gas Mark 6).

When the dough is visibly puffy and passes the poke test*, place it in the oven and bake it for about 15 minutes. Watch closely—the bread should remain pale, so do not let it brown.

Remove the bread from the oven and let it cool completely on a rack.

Prepare the garlic-parsley butter: Place the butter, garlic, and parsley in the food processor and pulse until well combined. Add salt to taste if necessary.

Assemble the *préfous*: Cut each piece of bread in two lengthwise and spread the bottom halves generously with the garlic-parsley butter. Cover with the top halves.

Cut the *préfous* crosswise into thick slices (a generous ¾ in./1 cm), without cutting all the way through. Cover tightly and refrigerate until serving.

Just before serving, preheat the oven to 350°F (180°C/Gas Mark 4).

Remove the plastic wrap and place the *préfous* in the oven on a baking sheet lined with parchment for 5–7 minutes to warm them and allow the butter to soften. Serve hot.

 GOOD TO KNOW
Préfou comes from the Vendée region of France. It's a take on garlic bread, and can be served cold or hot.

Techniques
Kneading by hand or with a mixer
Stages of fermentation
Folding
Shaping

Bretzels

Alsatian Pretzels

_____

Makes 8 _bretzels_

Active time: 35 minutes

Bulk fermentation: 1½ hours

Cooking: 3 minutes per _bretzel_ (poaching) + 15–20 minutes (baking)

Ingredients

Bretzels

⅔ cup (5.25 oz./150 g) water

⅔ cup (5.25 oz./150 g) whole milk

2¼ tsp (7 g) active dry yeast

4 cups + 2 tbsp (1 lb. 2 oz./500 g) all-purpose flour

2 tsp (0.35 oz./10 g) salt

3 tbsp (1.5 oz./40 g) salted butter, diced

1 egg yolk

1 tsp water

Fleur de sel

Poaching liquid

4 cups (1 liter) water

2 tsp (0.35 oz./10 g) salt

¼ cup (2 oz./55 g) baking soda

Prepare the _bretzel_ dough: Combine the water and milk in a saucepan and heat to lukewarm. Add the yeast and stir or swish to dissolve. Let sit for 10 minutes, until foamy.

Place the flour, salt, yeast mixture, and butter in the bowl of a stand mixer fitted with the dough hook. Knead for 5–7 minutes on speed 1, until the dough is smooth and elastic. Cover the bowl and let the dough rise for about 1½ hours, until doubled in volume (bulk fermentation*).

Toward the end of the rising time, preheat the oven to 400°F (200°C/ Gas Mark 6).

When the dough passes the poke test*, divide it into eight equal pieces and shape each into a ball. Using your hands, roll each piece of dough into a rope and shape into a _bretzel_.

Prepare the poaching liquid: Combine the water, salt, and baking soda in a medium stockpot or Dutch oven and bring to a boil.

Poach and bake the _bretzels_: Carefully lower one _bretzel_ at a time into the poaching liquid and let cook for about 3 minutes. Remove with a slotted spoon and place on a baking sheet lined with parchment paper.

Whisk together the egg yolk and water in a bowl to make an egg wash. Brush over the _bretzels_ and sprinkle with _fleur de sel_.

Bake for 15–20 minutes, until deeply golden. Place on a rack to cool.

Enjoy warm or at room temperature.

Techniques

Kneading by hand or with a mixer

Stages of fermentation

Shaping

Poaching

Taloas
Basque-Style Tortillas
———

Makes 8 *taloas*

Active time: 50 minutes
Bulk fermentation: 1 hour
Proofing: 20 minutes
Cooking: 25 minutes

Ingredients

3.25 oz. (90 g) drained canned corn
Scant 1½ cups (12.5 oz./350 g) lukewarm water
1 tsp fresh yeast
3¼ cups (14 oz./400 g) bread or white whole wheat flour (T65–T80)
⅔ cup (2.5 oz./75 g) corn flour (not cornmeal)
½ cup (2.5 oz./75 g) stone-ground polenta
2 tsp fine salt
2 tbsp sugar
2 pinches *piment d'Espelette*
2 tbsp extra-virgin olive oil
1 tsp baking powder

Equipment

Immersion blender

Place the canned corn in a bowl and process it to a very fine puree using the immersion blender.

Place the water in a bowl, crumble in the yeast, and stir or swish to dissolve.

Place the bread flour, corn flour, polenta, corn puree, salt, sugar, *piment d'Espelette*, olive oil, and baking powder in the bowl of a stand mixer fitted with the dough hook. Add the yeast-water mixture and knead for 5 minutes on speed 1. Cover the bowl tightly and let the dough rise at room temperature for 1 hour (bulk fermentation*).

Toward the end of the rising time, preheat the oven to 480°F (250°C/Gas Mark 9) with a baking sheet inside. Alternatively, you can cook the *taloas* in a skillet or on a griddle (see instructions below).

Divide the dough into eight pieces, weighing 5.25–6 oz. (150–170 g) each. On a corn-flour-dusted surface, roll each piece to a thickness of about 1⁄16 in. (1–2 mm). Cover with a towel and let rise at room temperature for 20 minutes (proofing*).

When the dough passes the poke test*, remove the hot baking sheet from the oven and line it with a sheet of parchment paper. Place the *taloas* on it (bake them in batches if they don't all fit on the baking sheet). Bake for 6 minutes, then place on a rack to cool.

Alternatively, heat an ungreased skillet or griddle to medium-low heat and cook the *taloas* one at a time for 3 minutes on each side. Adjust the heat as necessary if the *taloas* are cooking too quickly or slowly.

Many thanks to Julien Duboué (at Corn'R) for this recipe.

Techniques
Kneading by hand or with a mixer
Stages of fermentation
Shaping

Socca

Chickpea-Flour Flatbread

___

Makes 2 soccas

Active time: 5 minutes
Resting: 30 minutes
Cooking: 30 minutes

Ingredients

3 cups (9 oz./250 g) chickpea flour
1 heaping tsp finely chopped dried rosemary
1½ tbsp (0.75 oz./20 g) extra-virgin olive oil + 2 tbsp for the pan
2 cups (1 lb. 2 oz./500 g) water
1 tsp (0.2 oz./5 g) salt

Equipment

10-in. (25-cm) nonstick tart pan

Place the chickpea flour, rosemary, 4½ tsp (0.75 oz./20 g) olive oil, water, and salt in a large mixing bowl. Stir until well combined and smooth. Cover and let rest for 30 minutes (resting*).

The oven and the broiler is used in cooking. Preheat the oven to 480°F (250°C/Gas Mark 9) and pour 1 tbsp of the olive oil into the tart pan. When the oven has nearly reached the desired temperature, place the tart pan inside.

Pour half of the *socca* batter into the hot pan, to a thickness of about ⅛ in. (3 mm). Place the *socca* under the broiler for 8–15 minutes, until it's completely cooked—it should pull away from the sides of the pan and be charred in places. Keep a close eye on it and remove it as soon as it's ready.

Turn the *socca* out onto a rack and cover it with a large mixing bowl to retain the heat. Repeat the process for the second socca.

Many thanks to Isabelle Guerre for this recipe.

Sarah Bertin

——

"I work with the living world, which is complex. I don't have a proofing cabinet; I work with the surrounding environment as it is. I just adjust course, and constantly adapt my process to account for external factors so my bread will turn out well. This requires finding a balance between scientific knowledge of bread and a more intuitive understanding.

"I want to remain independent and work with other independent artisans in order to continue making my bread—I don't want to make someone else's bread.

"I want to decide what bread I make, to choose my ingredients without having someone else tell me what recipe to follow, and to sell a healthy product intended to be eaten every day. I try to bring a spirit of goodwill to the way I make bread, and I think people sense that.

"*Pain de campagne*, country bread, is everyday bread that goes well with everything; it's a rustic bread that has personality, and it's the kind I make most often. It's a rather mild bread with a supple, pleasant crumb. I start with white whole wheat (*semi-complète*) flour and add rye, and a variable quantity of levain, depending on the season. It has a beautiful crust. I like to eat beautiful things. We also eat with our eyes. Using a really great flour is only one part of the equation and cannot compensate for poor baking or a dense crumb without holes. Plus the crust has a large impact on taste. For me, bread must be both good and beautiful."

After studying to be a graphic designer, Sarah Bertin traveled and took some time for self-discovery. She finally found her path as a baker. After studying at Thomas Teffri-Chambelland's École Internationale de Boulangerie (International Baker School) in Noyers-sur-Jabron, in the Alpes-de-Haute-Provence region of France, she earned a vocational degree in 2012 and established her bakery the following year. Based in the village of Céré-la-Ronde, near the Château de Chenonceau, she makes organic bread that she sells at the farmers' market in Blois, among other places.

mademoiselle2013@gmail.com

★★

Pain de campagne French Country Bread
Recipe by Sarah Bertin
———

Makes 1 large loaf

Active time: 15 minutes
Bulk fermentation: 2–3 hours
Proofing: 2 hours
Cooking: 40 minutes

Ingredients

3 cups (1½ lb./750 g) water

6 cups + 2 tbsp (1½ lb./740 g) white whole wheat or light whole wheat flour (T80–T110)

1½ cups (5.75 oz./160 g) dark rye flour (T130)

9.25 oz. (260 g) refreshed levain

1 tbsp (0.75 oz./18 g) salt

Equipment

Bread peel

Place the water, flours, and levain in the bowl of a stand mixer fitted with the dough hook. Mix to combine, then add the salt and knead for 3–4 minutes on speed 1. Cover the bowl and let the dough rise for 2–3 hours. Fold the dough twice during the rise time (bulk fermentation*).

Turn the dough out onto a floured work surface. Shape it into a ball and place in a floured banneton or a large bowl lined with a well-floured towel. Cover and let rise in a warm place for 2 hours (proofing*).

Toward the end of the rising time, place a rack at the lowest oven position and place another rack directly above it. Place an empty heavy-duty baking sheet, oven-safe skillet, or drip pan on the lower rack, and a baking stone or heavy-duty baking sheet on the upper rack, and preheat the oven to 500°F (260°C/Gas Mark 10). Bring 1 cup (250 ml) of water to a simmer.

When the dough passes the poke test*, quickly invert the banneton over the floured peel and score the dough before sliding it onto the baking stone or sheet in the oven.

Carefully pour the simmering water into the skillet to create steam and quickly close the oven door.

Bake for 20 minutes at 500°F (260°C/Gas Mark 10), then reduce the heat to 430°F (220°C/Gas Mark 7) and bake for an additional 20 minutes, until the bread is deeply golden and makes a hollow sound when tapped on the bottom.

Remove the bread from the oven and place it on a rack to cool.

LA BONNE IDÉE
You can also bake this bread in a Dutch oven (see Techniques p. 184).

Techniques
Refreshing levain
Kneading by hand or with a mixer
Stages of fermentation
Folding
Scoring
Using a baking stone

Juan Arbelaez
—

"I'm originally from Colombia, where we eat breads made from manioc or corn, like arepas and tortillas, low-gluten breads that are staples of every meal. When I arrived in France, I was fascinated by the importance of sitting down to eat, and especially of gathering together around the famous baguette. I discovered a wonderful ritual in bread, and the tradition captured my imagination. I began exploring bread and eventually fell in love. I am fascinated by the variety. It's an incredible thing to be able to make so many different breads with so few ingredients. Today my dream would be to open a bakery. Four years ago, I realized that bread and wine have always been seen as the Sancho Panzas of meals—in other words, as constant companions. I wanted to celebrate both wine and bread, like *Don Quixote*, so I founded the restaurant Levain in Boulogne-Billancourt, where we revisited recipes that had been 'bastardized' by brasseries, like the *tartine*. When we opened Yaya, in Saint-Ouen, I started making my Kalios olive oil bread, based on the idea of using, instead of throwing out, the oil from jars of Kalamata olives. When we opened Yaya Secrétan, I started my own levain, showing up every day to feed it. It's our baby, and we wanted to make exceptional bread with it. So we decided to start by using organic flour and cold overnight fermentation. We shape the bread by eye without a scale and flavor it with oregano from the mountains. We serve it with meze, and I know a few people who would be happy just eating that for lunch!"

Juan Arbelaez, who runs seven restaurants in Paris, quickly gained a wealth of impressive professional experience. Born in Bogotá, the young Colombian chef began his career in Paris working alongside Pierre Gagnaire at his restaurant, and with Éric Briffard at the Hotel George V, and Éric Frechon at Le Bristol. Since a run on the French version of the reality competition series *Top Chef*, he has opened Plantxa, Levain, Maya, Vida, Froufrou, Yaya Saint-Ouen, and Yaya Halle Secrétan.

www.juan-arbelaez.com

Pain à l'huile d'olive et à l'origan Olive Oil Bread with Oregano

Recipe by Juan Arbelaez

Makes 1 large loaf

Active time: 20 minutes
Bulk fermentation:
3 hours + 12–24 hours
Proofing: 30 minutes
Cooking: 40 minutes

Ingredients

2 tsp (0.35 oz./10 g) salt
2 cups (1 lb. 2 oz./500 g) water
6 cups + 3 tbsp (1½ lb./750 g) bread flour (T65)
2 tsp (0.35 oz./10 g) honey
3.25 oz. (90 g) refreshed levain
0.5 oz. (15 g) fresh yeast
Scant ½ cup (100 ml) fruity extra-virgin olive oil, preferably Koroneiki (use the Kalios brand if you can find it)
3 tbsp (0.35 oz./10 g) dried oregano

Equipment

Bread peel

A day before baking, place the salt, water, flour, honey, and levain in the bowl of a stand mixer fitted with the dough hook. Crumble in the fresh yeast, then knead for 5 minutes on speed 1, followed by 8 minutes on speed 2. Drizzle in the olive oil halfway through the 8 minutes. At the end of the kneading time, add the oregano and knead briefly until evenly distributed.

Cover the bowl and let the dough rise at room temperature for 3 hours. Fold the dough twice during the rise time: once after 1 hour, and once after 2 hours. Cover the bowl well and place the dough in the refrigerator for 12–24 hours (bulk fermentation*).

Toward the end of the rising time, place a rack at the lowest oven position and place another rack directly above it. Place an empty heavy-duty baking sheet, oven-safe skillet, or drip pan on the lower rack, and a baking stone or heavy-duty baking sheet on the upper rack, and preheat the oven to 500°F (260°C/Gas Mark 10). Bring 1 cup (250 ml) of water to a simmer.

Turn the dough out onto a floured work surface and shape it into a ball. Cover with a towel and let rest for 30 minutes (proofing*).

When the dough passes the poke test*, gently transfer it to the floured peel and score it before sliding it onto the baking stone or sheet in the oven. Carefully pour the simmering water into the baking sheet, skillet, or drip pan to create steam and quickly close the oven door.

Bake for 20 minutes at 500°F (260°C/Gas Mark 10), then reduce the heat to 450°F (230°C/Gas Mark 8) and continue to bake for an additional 20 minutes, until deeply golden.

Remove the bread from the oven and place it on a rack to cool.

Juan Arbelaez makes this bread for his restaurant Yaya Halle Secrétan. The recipe has been adapted for home bakers.

LA BONNE IDÉE
You can also bake this bread in a Dutch oven (see Techniques p. 184).

Techniques
Refreshing levain
Kneading with a mixer
Stages of fermentation
Folding
Scoring
Using a baking stone

★★

Petites baguettes noires au sésame

Charcoal-Sesame Baguettes

———

Makes 2 small baguettes

Active time: 15 minutes

Autolyse: 1 hour

Bulk fermentation: 1½ hours

Resting: 30 minutes

Proofing: 1½ hours

Cooking: 20 minutes

Ingredients

2¾ cups (12.5 oz./350 g) bread flour (T65)

Scant 1 cup (8 oz./225 g) water

2.5 oz. (70 g) refreshed levain

0.07 oz. (2 g) fresh yeast

0.5 oz. (15 g) activated charcoal powder (*charbon végétal*)

Scant 1½ tsp (0.25 oz./7 g) salt

⅓ cup (1.75 oz./50 g) white sesame seeds

Equipment

Paline (baguette transfer peel)

Techniques

Refreshing levain

Kneading by hand or with a mixer

Stages of fermentation

Folding

Shaping

Scoring

Decorative finishes

Place the flour and water in the bowl of a stand mixer fitted with the dough hook. Mix for 3 minutes on speed 1, then cover the bowl and let rest for 1 hour (autolyse*).

Add the levain and crumble in the fresh yeast, then add the charcoal powder and salt. Knead for 3 minutes on speed 1, followed by 3–5 minutes on speed 2.

Shape the dough into a ball and place it in a lightly oiled or flour-dusted bowl. Cover the bowl and let the dough rise for 1½ hours. Fold the dough twice during the rise time: once after 30 minutes, and once after 1 hour (bulk fermentation*).

When the dough has doubled in volume, turn it out on to a floured work surface. Divide into two equal pieces using a bench scraper, then quickly shape each piece into a rough oval. Cover with a towel and let rest at room temperature for 30 minutes (resting*).

Scatter the sesame seeds across a small tray. Shape each piece of dough into a baguette. With the seam facing up, brush or mist the sides and ends of each baguette with a little water and gently roll the dough in the sesame seeds to coat.

Place the two baguettes between the folds of a floured *couche*, or use a floured towel, pleated like an accordion around the baguettes. Cover with a towel and let rise for 1½ hours (proofing*).

Toward the end of the rising time, place a rack at the lowest oven position and place another rack directly above it. Place an empty heavy-duty baking sheet, oven-safe skillet, or drip pan on the lower rack, and a baking stone or heavy-duty baking sheet on the upper rack, and preheat the oven to 500°F (260°C/Gas Mark 10). Bring 1 cup (250 ml) of water to a simmer.

When the dough passes the poke test*, using a lame, slash each baguette diagonally in two places. Roll the baguettes one at a time onto the *paline* and carefully transfer to the baking stone or sheet in the oven.

Carefully pour the simmering water into the baking sheet, skillet, or drip pan to create steam and quickly close the oven door.

Bake for 20 minutes, then remove from the oven and place on a rack to cool.

Pain à la pomme de terre et au romarin

Potato-Rosemary Rolls

————

Makes 6 rolls

Active time: 30 minutes
Bulk fermentation: 2 hours
Proofing: 1–1½ hours
Cooking: 20 minutes + 25 minutes

Ingredients

14 oz. (400 g) waxy potatoes
1 egg
2 tbsp (1 oz./30 g) whole milk
0.35 oz. (10 g) fresh yeast
2¾ cups (12.5 oz./350 g) bread or white whole wheat flour (T65–T80)
1¾ tsp (0.3 oz./9 g) salt
6 tbsp (3 oz./90 g) butter, diced, at room temperature
1 egg yolk, lightly beaten
1 sprig rosemary

Peel and rinse the potatoes and steam or boil them until just tender (about 15–20 minutes). Drain well and mash. Let cool slightly, then add the egg and stir until well combined. Let cool completely before using.

In a saucepan, heat the milk to lukewarm and stir in the yeast to dissolve.

Place the flour, salt, mashed potatoes, and yeast mixture in the bowl of a stand mixer fitted with the dough hook. Knead for 3 minutes on speed 1, followed by 3 minutes on speed 2. Add the butter and knead for an additional 2 minutes, until the dough is smooth and elastic.

Shape the dough into a ball and place in a lightly oiled or flour-dusted bowl. Cover the bowl and let the dough rise at room temperature for 2 hours. Fold the dough once every 30 minutes (bulk fermentation*).

Turn the dough out on to a floured work surface and divide it into six equal pieces using a bench scraper. Shape each piece into a ball and place on a baking sheet lined with parchment paper, forming a ring (leave a little space between each ball to allow for expansion). Let rise at room temperature for 1–1½ hours (proofing*).

Toward the end of the rising time, place a rack in the center of the oven and place another rack directly below it. Place an empty heavy-duty baking sheet, oven-safe skillet, or drip pan on the lower rack and preheat the oven to 450°F (230°C/Gas Mark 8). Bring 1 cup (250 ml) of water to a simmer.

When the dough passes the poke test*, brush the surface of the rolls with the egg yolk, then chop the rosemary leaves and sprinkle over the tops. Place the baking sheet in the oven, then carefully pour the simmering water into the baking sheet, skillet, or drip pan to create steam and quickly close the oven door.

Bake for 25 minutes, until deeply golden. If the tops are browning too quickly, lower the oven temperature.

Let the rolls cool on a rack.

Techniques
Kneading by hand or with a mixer
Stages of fermentation
Folding
Shaping
Decorative finishes

Petits pains au potimarron et graines de courge

Red Kuri Squash Rolls

───────

Makes 6 rolls

Active time: 30 minutes
Bulk fermentation: 2 hours
Proofing: 1–1½ hours
Cooking: 25–30 minutes + 25 minutes

Ingredients

Red kuri squash puree

14 oz. (400 g) red kuri squash (or use kabocha or butternut)
¼ cup (1.75 oz./50 g) extra-virgin olive oil
2 tsp (0.5 oz./15 g) honey

Rolls

⅓ cup (2.5 oz./75 g) lukewarm water
0.35 oz. (10 g) fresh yeast
2¾ cups (12.5 oz./350 g) white whole wheat or light whole wheat flour (T80–T110)
1 tsp (0.2 oz./5 g) salt
1 tbsp (0.5 oz./15 g) extra-virgin olive oil
¾ cup (3.5 oz./100 g) hulled pumpkin seeds

Equipment

Food processor

Prepare the squash puree: Preheat the oven to 350°F (180°C/Gas Mark 4). Peel the squash and cut it into big pieces. Place on a baking sheet and drizzle with the olive oil and honey. Bake for 25–30 minutes, until completely tender.

Using a food processor, pulse the squash to a smooth puree. Let cool completely before using.

Prepare the rolls: Combine the water and fresh yeast in a bowl and stir or swish to dissolve.

Place the flour, salt, squash puree, and yeast mixture in the bowl of a stand mixer fitted with the dough hook. Knead for 3 minutes on speed 1, followed by 3 minutes on speed 2.

Add the olive oil and knead for an additional 2 minutes on speed 2, until the dough is smooth and elastic.

Shape the dough into a ball and place in a lightly oiled or flour-dusted bowl. Cover the bowl and let the dough rise at room temperature for 2 hours. Fold the dough once every 30 minutes (bulk fermentation*).

Turn the dough out onto a floured work surface and divide it into six equal pieces using a bench scraper. Shape each piece into a ball and place on a baking sheet lined with parchment paper.

Score the top of each roll with a cross and sprinkle with the pumpkin seeds. Let rise at room temperature for 1–1½ hours (proofing*).

Toward the end of the rising time, place a rack in the center of the oven and place another rack directly below it. Place an empty heavy-duty baking sheet, oven-safe skillet, or drip pan on the lower rack and preheat the oven to 450°F (230°C/Gas Mark 8). Bring 1 cup (250 ml) of water to a simmer.

When the dough passes the poke test*, place the baking sheet in the oven, then carefully pour the simmering water into the baking sheet, skillet, or drip pan to create steam and quickly close the oven door.

Bake for 25 minutes, until golden.

Let the rolls cool on a rack.

Techniques
Kneading by hand or with a mixer
Stages of fermentation
Folding
Shaping
Scoring
Decorative finishes

Petits pains feuilletés

Puff Pastry Rolls

———

Makes 6–8 rolls

Active time: 30 minutes

Poolish: 20 minutes

Bulk fermentation:
30 minutes + 2 hours

Chilling: 30 minutes

Proofing: 30 minutes–1 hour

Cooking: 15–20 minutes

Ingredients

Poolish

2 tbsp (1 oz./30 g) lukewarm water

3 tbsp (1 oz./30 g) all-purpose flour (T55)

0.35 oz. (10 g) fresh yeast, crumbled

1¼ tsp (0.2 oz./5 g) sugar

Rolls

¾ cup (6.25 oz./180 g) water

1½ tsp (0.25 oz./8 g) fine salt

2¾ cups (12.5 oz./350 g) all-purpose flour (T55)

7 tbsp (3.5 oz./100 g) butter, diced, at room temperature, divided

1 stick + 1½ tbsp (4.5 oz./130 g) European-style butter (at least 84% butterfat), well chilled

Fleur de sel

Equipment

6–8 × 2½-in. (6-cm) baking rings, 1¼–1½ in. (3–4 cm) deep, or a 6-cup muffin pan

LA BONNE IDÉE

For a special event or holiday meal, grate truffle over the rolls.

| **Techniques**
| Kneading by hand or with a mixer
| Stages of fermentation
| Folding
| Shaping

Prepare the poolish: Combine the water, 3 tbsp (1 oz./30 g) flour, yeast, and sugar (poolish*). Let sit for 20 minutes to activate the yeast.

Prepare the rolls: Place the ¾ cup (6.25 oz./180 g) water, salt, 2¾ cups (12.5 oz./350 g) flour, and the poolish in the bowl of a stand mixer fitted with the dough hook. Knead for 3 minutes on speed 1, followed by 4–6 minutes on speed 2. Add 5 tbsp (2.5 oz./70 g) of the room-temperature butter halfway through the 4–6 minutes. Cover the bowl and let the dough rise at room temperature for 30 minutes. Fold the dough, then re-cover the bowl and place in the refrigerator for 2 hours (bulk fermentation*).

Remove the butter from the refrigerator and place it between two sheets of parchment paper. Using a rolling pin, flatten the butter into an approximately 4-in. (10-cm) square. Turn the dough out onto a floured work surface and roll it into a rectangle twice as long as the square of butter. Place the butter in the center of the dough and fold the sides of the dough over the butter to meet in the middle. Press to seal the ends of the dough, completely enclosing the butter. Rotate the dough 90° clockwise, and roll it into a rectangle three times as long as it is wide. Fold the dough in three—this is known as a single turn. Rotate the dough 90° clockwise, so that the seam is facing right. Roll the dough once again into a rectangle three times as long as it is wide, dusting the work surface and dough with flour as needed to prevent sticking. Fold in three as above, then cover and chill for 30 minutes in the refrigerator. Place the chilled dough on a floured surface with the seam facing left. Roll into a rectangle three times as long as it is wide, then make a double turn: fold the short ends in to meet in the center, then fold the dough in half.

If you are using baking rings, place them on a baking sheet lined with parchment paper.

Roll the dough into a large square with a thickness of about ⅛ in. (3–4 mm), then cut the square into strips, ¾–1¼ in. (2–3 cm) wide. Roll up each strip as tightly as possible, then place the rolls flat in the baking rings or in the cavities of a muffin pan. Cover with a towel and let rise for 30 minutes–1 hour (proofing*).

Preheat the oven to 400°F (200°C/Gas Mark 6). When the dough passes the poke test*, place the rolls in the oven and bake for 15–20 minutes, until puffed and golden.

Melt the remaining 2 tbsp (1 oz./30 g) butter in a saucepan over low heat. Simmer gently without stirring until a foam forms on the surface. Skim off the foam and let the milk solids sink to the bottom to obtain clarified butter. As soon as you take out of the oven, remove the baking rings, or turn the rolls out of the muffin pan. Place on a rack, brush with the clarified butter, sprinkle with *fleur de sel*, and enjoy warm.

Ficelles à la mimolette

Mimolette Ficelles

_____

Makes eight *ficelles*

Active time: 20 minutes
Bulk fermentation: 1½ hours
Resting: 15 minutes
Proofing: 1 hour
Cooking: 15 minutes

Ingredients

1¾ tsp (0.3 oz./9 g) salt

Scant 1½ cups (12.5 oz./350 g) water

4 cups + 2 tbsp (1 lb. 2 oz./500 g) bread or white whole wheat flour (T65–T80)

5 tbsp (2.5 oz./75 g) butter, at room temperature

3.5 oz. (100 g) refreshed levain

0.2 oz. (5 g) fresh yeast

7 oz. (200 g) Mimolette *jeune* (young) cheese, roughly grated and divided

Place the salt, water, flour, butter, and levain, in this order, in the bowl of a stand mixer fitted with the dough hook. Crumble in the fresh yeast and knead for 3 minutes on speed 1, followed by 5–7 minutes on speed 2. At the end of the kneading time, add 5.25 oz. (150 g) of the grated Mimolette and knead briefly until evenly distributed.

Cover the bowl and let the dough rise in a warm place for 1½ hours. Fold the dough three times during the rise time: once after 30 minutes, once after 1 hour, and once after 1½ hours (bulk fermentation*).

Line two inverted baking sheets with parchment paper. Turn the dough out onto a floured work surface and divide it into eight equal pieces using a bench scraper. Shape each piece into a ball, cover, and let rest for 15 minutes (resting*). Shape the pieces of dough into *ficelles* (thin baguettes) and place seam-side down on the prepared baking sheets, four per sheet. Cover and let rise for 1 hour (proofing*).

Toward the end of the rising time, place a rack at the lowest oven position and place another rack directly above it. Place an empty heavy-duty baking sheet, oven-safe skillet, or drip pan on the lower rack, and a baking stone or heavy-duty baking sheet on the upper rack, and preheat the oven to 480°F (250°C/Gas Mark 9). Bring 1 cup (250 ml) of water to a simmer.

When the dough passes the poke test*, brush the *ficelles* with a little water and sprinkle with the remaining Mimolette. Taking great care, slide one batch of *ficelles* with the parchment paper underneath onto the baking stone. Carefully pour the simmering water into the baking sheet, skillet, or drip pan to create steam and quickly close the oven door.

Bake for 10 minutes at 480°F (250°C/Gas Mark 9), then lower the oven temperature to 430°F (220°C/Gas Mark 7) and continue to bake for an additional 5 minutes. Remove the first batch of *ficelles* from the oven and place on a rack to cool, then repeat with the second batch.

Techniques
Refreshing levain
Kneading by hand or with a mixer
Stages of fermentation
Folding
Shaping
Using a baking stone

Pain du brasseur

Brewer's Bread

Makes 1 loaf

Active time: 20 minutes
Bulk fermentation: 1½ hours
Proofing: 1–1½ hours
Cooking: 35–40 minutes

Ingredients

Scant 1½ tsp (0.25 oz./7 g) salt

1 cup (9 oz./250 g) stout beer

2¼ cups (9.75 oz./275 g) white whole wheat or light whole wheat flour (T80–T110)

Scant 1¼ cups (3.5 oz./100 g) barley flour

3.5 oz. (100 g) refreshed levain

0.1 oz. (3 g) fresh yeast

1 tbsp barley malt syrup (optional)

Equipment

A large round cast-iron or enamel Dutch oven

Place the salt, beer, flours, and levain, in this order, in the bowl of a stand mixer fitted with the dough hook. Crumble in the fresh yeast and add the barley malt syrup, if using. Knead for 3 minutes on speed 1, followed by 5–7 minutes on speed 2.

Cover the bowl and let the dough rise in a warm place for 1½ hours. Fold the dough three times during the rise time: once after 30 minutes, once after 1 hour, and once after 1½ hours (bulk fermentation*).

Turn the dough out onto a floured work surface and gently shape it into a boule without deflating it. Place seam-side up in a floured banneton or a large bowl lined with a well-floured towel. Cover and let rise at room temperature for 1–1½ hours (proofing*).

Toward the end of the rising time, cut out a circle of parchment paper big enough to line the bottom of a cast-iron or enamel Dutch oven. Set the parchment paper circle aside.

Place the Dutch oven with the lid on in the oven as you preheat it to 500°F (260°C/Gas Mark 10).

When the dough passes the poke test*, carefully remove the Dutch oven using oven mitts (both the base and lid will be extremely hot) and place on a heat-safe surface.

Working quickly, line the pot with the parchment paper circle and turn the dough over into the pot (the seam will now be on the bottom). Dust the surface of the dough with flour and score it, then put the lid on the Dutch oven and place it in the oven.

Bake for 25 minutes without lifting the lid, then remove the lid, lower the oven temperature to 475°F (245°C/Gas Mark 9), and bake for an additional 10–15 minutes, until the loaf is deeply golden.

Remove the bread from the Dutch oven and place it on a rack to cool.

Techniques

Refreshing levain
Kneading by hand or with a mixer
Stages of fermentation
Folding
Scoring
Baking in a Dutch oven

Galets aux algues et au sarrasin

Buckwheat and Seaweed Rolls

———

Makes 8–10 rolls

Active time: 20 minutes

Hydrating seaweed: 10–15 minutes

Bulk fermentation: 1½ hours

Proofing: 1½ hours

Cooking: 15–20 minutes

Ingredients

1 oz. (25 g) dried seaweed, such as wakame or nori

1 tsp (0.2 oz./5 g) salt

1 generous cup (9.5 oz./270 g) water

1 tbsp sunflower oil

2¼ cups (9.75 oz./275 g) bread or white whole wheat flour (T65–T80)

¾ cup + 2 tbsp (3.5 oz./100 g) buckwheat flour

3.5 oz. (100 g) refreshed levain

0.1 oz. (3 g) fresh yeast

Place the seaweed in a bowl with water and let it sit for 10–15 minutes to rehydrate.

Meanwhile, place the salt and water, in this order, in the bowl of a stand mixer fitted with the dough hook. Let sit for 5 minutes, then stir or swish to dissolve. Add the oil, flours, and levain, then crumble in the fresh yeast. Knead for 3 minutes on speed 1, followed by 5–7 minutes on speed 2.

At the end of the kneading time, drain the seaweed well, squeezing it gently to remove excess water. If you've used big pieces of seaweed, chop it finely. Add to the dough and knead briefly until evenly distributed.

Cover the bowl and let the dough rise in a warm place for 1½ hours. Fold the dough three times during the rise time: once after 30 minutes, once after 1 hour, and once after 1½ hours (bulk fermentation*).

Turn the dough out onto a floured work surface. Using the palm of your hand, press down gently on the dough to flatten it to a thickness of ¾ in. (2 cm). Divide the dough into eight to ten square-shaped pieces, about 1.75 oz. (50 g) each, using a bench scraper. Place on a baking sheet lined with parchment paper, cover, and let rise for 1½ hours (proofing*).

Toward the end of the rising time, place a rack in the center of the oven, and place another rack below it. Place an empty heavy-duty baking sheet, oven-safe skillet, or drip pan on the lower rack, and a baking stone or heavy-duty baking sheet on the upper rack, and preheat the oven to 450°F (230°C/Gas Mark 8). Bring 1 cup (250 ml) of water to a simmer.

When the dough passes the poke test*, score each piece of dough, then place the baking sheet in the oven on the center rack. Carefully pour the simmering water into the baking sheet, skillet, or drip pan to create steam and quickly close the oven door. Bake for 15–20 minutes, until golden.

Let cool on a rack.

Techniques

Refreshing levain

Kneading by hand or with a mixer

Stages of fermentation

Folding

Scoring

Épis au sésame

Sesame Wheat Stalk Bread

────────

Makes 2 small baguettes

Active time: 15 minutes
Autolyse: 3 hours
Bulk fermentation: 1½ hours + 15 hours
Resting: 30 minutes
Proofing: 30 minutes
Cooking: 18 minutes

Ingredients

2 cups (9 oz./250 g) bread flour (T65)
Scant ¾ cup (6 oz./175 g) water
for autolyse + 2 tsp (0.35 oz./10 g)
for dissolving salt
1 oz. (25 g) refreshed levain
1 oz. (25 g) fresh yeast
¾ tsp (0.15 oz./4 g) salt
⅔ cup (3.5 oz./100 g) white and/or black
sesame seeds

Techniques

Refreshing levain
Kneading by hand or with a mixer
Stages of fermentation
Folding
Shaping
Decorative finishes
Oven baking

Place the flour and scant ¾ cup (6 oz./175 g) water in the bowl of a stand mixer fitted with the dough hook. Mix for 1 minute on speed 1 (*frasage**), then cover and let rest for 3 hours (autolyse*).

Add the levain and crumble in the fresh yeast. Place the salt and 2 tsp (0.35 oz./10 g) water in a small bowl and stir or swish to dissolve, then add to the dough. Knead for 8 minutes on speed 1.

Cover the bowl and let the dough rise for 1½ hours. Fold the dough twice during the rise time, once after 30 minutes and once after 1 hour. Cover the bowl well and place in the refrigerator for 15 hours (bulk fermentation*).

When you are ready to proceed, dust a work surface and the top of the dough with flour. Turn the dough out onto the work surface and divide it into two equal pieces using a bench scraper. Shape each piece into a rough oval and let rest at room temperature for 30 minutes (resting*).

Shape each piece of dough into an approximately 10-in (25-cm) baguette, ensuring it will fit in your oven lengthwise (the baguettes will be easier to transfer to the oven if they're shorter). Place the shaped baguettes between the folds of a floured *couche*, or use a floured towel, pleated like an accordion around the baguettes. Let rest for 30 minutes (proofing*).

Meanwhile, place a rack at the lowest oven position and place another rack directly above it. Place an empty heavy-duty baking sheet, oven-safe skillet, or drip pan on the lower rack, and a baking stone or heavy-duty baking sheet on the upper rack, and preheat the oven to 500°F (260°C/Gas Mark 10). Bring 1 cup (250 ml) of water to a simmer.

When the dough passes the poke test*, scatter the sesame seeds across a baking sheet. Lightly brush one or both of the baguettes with water to moisten and quickly roll in the sesame seeds to coat the top(s). Place on an inverted baking sheet lined with parchment paper.

Cut the dough to resemble a wheat stalk (*épi*) using kitchen shears. To do this, make a series of quick cuts into the dough at an angle, cutting about three-quarters of the way to the bottom of the dough and alternating sides. As you go, fold the cut dough out to the side like kernels of wheat (see p. 163).

Slide the *épis* with the parchment paper underneath onto the baking stone or sheet in the oven. Carefully pour the simmering water into the baking sheet, skillet, or drip pan to create steam and quickly close the oven door.

Bake for 18 minutes, lowering the oven temperature to 450°F (240°C/Gas Mark 8) halfway through the baking time.

Place on a rack to cool.

Pains burger

Hamburger Buns

————

Makes 6 buns

Active time: 20 minutes
Blooming yeast: 10 minutes
Bulk fermentation: 1½ hours
Proofing: 1 hour
Cooking: 15 minutes

Ingredients

1 cup (9 oz./250 g) lukewarm whole milk + more for glazing
0.5 oz. (12 g) fresh yeast
3¼ cups (14 oz./400 g) all-purpose flour
1 egg
5 tsp (0.75 oz./20 g) sugar
1½ tsp (0.25 oz./8 g) salt
3 tbsp (1.5 oz./40 g) butter, diced, at room temperature
⅓ cup (1.75 oz./50 g) white sesame seeds

Place the lukewarm milk in a bowl and crumble in the fresh yeast. Stir to dissolve and let sit for 10 minutes.

Place the flour, egg, sugar, and salt in the bowl of a stand mixer fitted with the dough hook. Mix for 3 minutes on speed 1. Add the milk-yeast mixture and mix for 3 minutes on speed 2, then add the butter. Knead for 5 minutes on speed 3. Cover and let the dough rise for 1½ hours. Fold the dough once, after 1 hour (bulk fermentation*).

Turn the dough out onto a floured work surface. Using a bench scraper, divide the dough into six pieces weighing about 4.25 oz. (120 g) each. Shape each piece into a ball and place on a baking sheet lined with parchment paper. Flatten each ball slightly, cover, and let rise for 1 hour (proofing*).

Toward the end of the rising time, place a rack at the lowest oven position and place another rack directly above it. Place an empty heavy-duty baking sheet, oven-safe skillet, or drip pan on the lower rack and preheat the oven to 350°F (180°C/Gas Mark 4). Bring 1 cup (250 ml) of water to a simmer.

When the dough passes the poke test*, brush the buns with a little milk and sprinkle with sesame seeds.

Place the baking sheet in the oven, then carefully pour the simmering water into the baking sheet, skillet, or drip pan to create steam and quickly close the oven door. Bake for 15 minutes, until golden.

Cool the buns on a rack.

Techniques
Kneading by hand or with a mixer
Stages of fermentation
Folding
Shaping
Decorative finishes

Pains vapeur à la ciboule et au sésame

Steamed Sesame-Scallion Buns

———

Makes 6 buns

Active time: 20 minutes
Blooming yeast: 20 minutes
Bulk fermentation: 1½ hours
Resting: 10 minutes
Cooking: 15 minutes

Ingredients

¼ cup + 3 tbsp (3.75 oz./110 g) lukewarm water, divided
2 tbsp (1 oz./25 g) sugar, divided
1 tsp (0.1 oz./3 g) active dry yeast
1⅔ cups (7 oz./200 g) bread flour (T65)
Scant ¼ tsp (0.05 oz./1 g) salt
2 scallions, thinly sliced
3 tbsp (1 oz./30 g) white sesame seeds

Equipment

Steamer pot, steamer basket, or *couscoussier*

Place 5 tsp (0.75 oz./20 g) of the water in a bowl and add 1 tbsp of the sugar and the yeast. Stir or swish to dissolve and let sit for about 20 minutes, until foamy.

Place the flour, remaining sugar, salt, and yeast mixture in the bowl of a stand mixer fitted with the dough hook. Knead for 3 minutes on speed 1, followed by 3–5 minutes on speed 2. At the end of the kneading time, add the scallions and knead briefly until evenly distributed. Cover the bowl and let the dough rise at room temperature for about 1½ hours (bulk fermentation*).

Meanwhile, cut out six 4-in. (10-cm) squares of parchment paper and place on a baking sheet.

Turn the dough out onto a floured work surface and divide it into six equal pieces using a bench scraper. Shape each piece into a ball and place one on each parchment paper square. Brush lightly with water to moisten and sprinkle with the sesame seeds. Cover and let rest while you prepare the steamer (resting*).

Pour several inches of water into a steamer pot or a saucepan with a steamer basket set over it (the basket should not touch the water). Bring the water to a rapid simmer.

When the dough passes the poke test*, place the buns in the steamer basket with the parchment paper underneath, leaving about ¾ in. (2 cm) between the buns. Steam for 15 minutes and test for doneness with the tip of a knife.

Remove the steamer or saucepan from the heat and let the buns rest in the steamer basket for a few minutes before serving them warm.

Techniques
Kneading by hand or with a mixer
Stages of fermentation
Shaping
Baking with steam

Nathaniel Doboin and Thomas Teffri-Chambelland

"Rice is the second most cultivated grain in the world, yet it isn't used to make bread like all the other grains are. So making bread with rice is above all a creative challenge. It's a wonderful experience to embark upon a path with no clear guideposts. More than anything, we want to break a taboo rather than take up a challenge, while maintaining a healthy and organic approach. The way we conceive of bread is different; it's as if a newcomer has been invited to take a seat at the family table, bringing their own personality, taste, demands, and limits.

"We also want to give bakers the desire to broaden the horizons of an industry where the path is well-trodden. It's a way of breaking with tradition; not of rejecting it, but of serving it. Our concept doesn't oppose tradition, but complements it.

"We didn't want to make gluten-free the basis of a communication strategy or a dogma. Nor did we want to open a pharmacy or pretend to be doctors. We made a definite choice, but we don't lead gluten-free lives. We don't suffer from celiac disease. We like rice and we like bread. Many people stop by the bakery without knowing that our bread is gluten-free, and we appreciate this mix of customers.

"We work directly with three Italian short-grain rice farmers. We own our own mill and grind our own flours. Chambelland is also a story about people, one that stretches from the Po plateau to Paris. We make bread that nourishes people, that puts a smile on the faces of those who buy from us, and who provide a living for our employees. In short, it's a meaningful business."

Thomas Teffri-Chambelland, a trained biologist turned baker, also founded the École Internationale de Boulangerie (International Baker School). In partnership with Nathaniel Doboin, a globe-trotting businessman with experience in advertising, he created a new bread-making sector based on rice flour. Today Chambelland runs two bakeries, one in Paris and one in Brussels, and produces flour available for purchase at local organic stores.

www.chambelland.com

Pain au riz et au sarrasin Brown Rice and Buckwheat Bread

Recipe from Chambelland

___

Makes 1 loaf

Active time: 15 minutes
Bulk fermentation: 1¼ hours
Cooking: 40–50 minutes

Ingredients

2½ cups (10.5 oz./300 g) Chambelland plain bread mix or gray flour blend (see La Bonne Idée)

Scant 1½ tsp (0.25 oz./7 g) salt

1¼ cups (10.5 oz./300 g) lukewarm water (100°F/38°C)

0.15 oz. (4 g) fresh yeast

Scant 1½ tsp (0.25 oz./6 g) extra-virgin olive oil

Oil for the pan, if needed

Buckwheat flour, for dusting

Equipment

8 × 4 × 2 ½-in. (20 × 10 × 6.3-cm) loaf pan, preferably nonstick

Instant-read thermometer

Place the bread mix or gray flour blend in the bowl of a stand mixer fitted with the paddle beater. Mix for 10 minutes on speed 1, then crumble in the fresh yeast and mix for an additional 2 minutes on speed 1. Drizzle in the olive oil and continue to blend for another 2 minutes, until the mixture is uniform and smooth. It will have the consistency of a thick béchamel.

If your loaf pan is not nonstick, lightly grease it with oil. Pour the dough into the pan and let ferment at room temperature for 1¼ hours in a draft-free place (bulk fermentation*).

Preheat the oven to 450°F (240°C/Gas Mark 8). Dust the surface of the dough with a little buckwheat flour, then score with a crisscross pattern.

When the dough passes the poke test*, bake for 20 minutes at 450°F (240°C/Gas Mark 8), then lower the oven temperature to 400°F (200°C/Gas Mark 6) and continue to bake for 20–30 minutes, until the crust is deeply golden and the internal temperature of the bread registers at least 204°F (96°C) on the thermometer.

Turn the bread out of the pan and place it on a rack to cool.

LA BONNE IDÉE

If you are based in France or Belgium, you can purchase Chambelland's plain bread mix (*préparation pour pain*) in Chambelland bakeries and select natural food stores, or online via the company's website (https://www.chambelland.com/en/grocery-items/).

You can make your own gluten-free gray flour blend for this recipe by combining 7 cups (2 lb./900 g) brown rice flour, ¾ cup + 2 tbsp (3.5 oz./100 g) buckwheat flour, and 3 tsp (0.5 oz./12 g) psyllium husk powder. Store any unused mix in an airtight container in a cool, dry place for future loaves.

Techniques
Kneading by hand or with a mixer
Stages of fermentation
Scoring

Olivier Vandromme

"I became a baker by eating bread, and by wondering about what goes on inside a loaf. I did things backwards, really. I originally trained as a pastry chef. When I began an apprenticeship with Alex Croquet, the way I viewed bread completely changed. I spent all my time off in the bakery. I discovered that baking is a very technical craft, and constantly evolving, contrary to what pastry chefs may think. I acquired my bakery in 2008. Back then, I had already begun using organic flours and natural levains, and now I work increasingly with local flours derived from heritage grains. Above all, I seek to celebrate these ingredients in the breads that I make. I don't claim to have created a recipe; I work with the complexity of a single ingredient, and I highlight the grain as much as possible. I also like richer breads, like this rye tourte with honey, figs, and hazelnuts.

"I use ingredients that I like in my bread, which I make sure is accessible to everyone, both in terms of price and taste. This is bread you can eat at any time of day, from breakfast to an afternoon snack. Personally, I like to take it when I go hiking."

Originally from the north of France, and a trained pastry chef-chocolatier, Olivier discovered bread at Alex Croquet's bakery in Wattignies (see p. 233), where he spent ten years before earning his baker's vocational certificate. He opened his bakery in 2008 in Wambrechies, near Lille, France. He makes bread according to a credo of working with high-quality raw ingredients, preferably organic and local. He is especially interested in heritage grain varieties.

16 rue du Pont-Levis, Wambrechies, France

Pain de seigle au miel, à la figue, et à la noisette

Fig, Hazelnut, and Honey Rye Bread

Recipe by Olivier Vandromme

Makes 1 loaf

Active time: 15 minutes
Bulk fermentation: 1½ hours
Proofing: 15 minutes
Cooking: 45–50 minutes

Ingredients

Generous ¾ cup (6.75 oz./195 g) water
heated to 113°F (45°C)
1¾ tsp (0.3 oz./9 g) salt
1 tbsp (0.75 oz./20 g) honey
2⅓ cups (8.75 oz./245 g) dark rye flour
6 oz. (170 g) refreshed levain
0.05 oz. (1 g) fresh yeast, crumbled
¼ cup (2 oz./50 g) whole hazelnuts
2 oz. (50 g) dried figs, chopped

Equipment

Bread peel

Pour the water into the bowl of a stand mixer fitted with the dough hook, then add the salt, honey, flour, levain, and yeast. Knead for 10 minutes on speed 1, adding the hazelnuts and figs 2 minutes before the end of the kneading time.

Cover the bowl and let the dough rise at room temperature for 1½ hours (bulk fermentation*).

Toward the end of the rising time, place a rack at the lowest oven position and place another rack directly above it. Place an empty heavy-duty baking sheet, oven-safe skillet, or drip pan on the lower rack, and a baking stone or heavy-duty baking sheet on the upper rack, and preheat the oven to 500°F (260°C/Gas Mark 10). Bring 1 cup (250 ml) of water to a simmer.

Turn the dough out onto a floured work surface and quickly shape it into a *bâtard* or ball, without overworking it. Let rest on the work surface for 15 minutes (proofing*).

When the dough passes the poke test*, transfer it to the floured peel and slide it onto the baking stone or sheet in the oven. Carefully pour the simmering water into the baking sheet, skillet, or drip pan to create steam and quickly close the oven door.

Bake for 45–50 minutes, until deeply browned, lowering the oven temperature to 450°F (230°C/Gas Mark 8) halfway through the baking time.

Remove the bread from the oven and place it on a rack to cool.

LA BONNE IDÉE
You can also bake this bread in a Dutch oven (see Techniques p. 184).

Techniques
Refreshing levain
Kneading by hand or with a mixer
Stages of fermentation
Shaping
Using a baking stone

Pain au cacao

Chocolate Bread

Makes 1 large or 2 small loaves

Active time: 15 minutes
Bulk fermentation: 2 hours
Proofing: 1 hour
Cooking: 20–30 minutes

Ingredients

Scant 2½ tsp (0.5 oz./12 g) salt

Scant 1½ cups (12.5 oz./365 g) water

4 cups + 2 tbsp (1 lb. 2 oz./500 g) bread or white whole wheat flour (T65–T80)

Generous ¼ cup (1 oz./30 g) unsweetened cocoa powder

2½ tbsp (1 oz./30 g) sugar

2 oz. (60 g) refreshed levain

0.25 oz. (6 g) fresh yeast, crumbled

7 oz. (200 g) dark or milk chocolate chips, pistoles, wafers, or discs

Equipment

Bread peel

Place the salt, water, flour, cocoa powder, sugar, levain, and fresh yeast, in this order, in the bowl of a stand mixer fitted with the dough hook. Knead for 3 minutes on speed 1, followed by 3 minutes on speed 2. Alternatively, knead for 10 minutes by hand.

Add the chocolate and knead for another minute until evenly distributed.

Cover the bowl and let the dough rise for 2 hours in a place that is warm (around 77°F/25°C), but not warm enough to melt the chocolate. Fold the dough three times during the rise time (bulk fermentation*).

Turn the dough out onto a floured surface and shape it into a ball. If you'd like to make two smaller loaves, divide the dough into two equal pieces using a bench scraper. Shape each piece of dough into a *bâtard* and place seam side down on a sheet of parchment paper. Cover with a towel and let rise in a warm place for 1 hour (proofing*).

Toward the end of the rising time, place a rack at the lowest oven position and place another rack directly above it. Place an empty heavy-duty baking sheet, oven-safe skillet, or drip pan on the lower rack, and a baking stone or heavy-duty baking sheet on the upper rack, and preheat the oven to 450°F (240°C/Gas Mark 8).

When the dough passes the poke test*, transfer it with the parchment paper underneath onto the peel and score down the center. Slide the dough and parchment paper onto the baking stone or sheet in the oven. Carefully pour the simmering water into the baking sheet, skillet, or drip pan to create steam and quickly close the oven door.

Bake for 20–30 minutes, depending on the size of the bread, until deeply browned.

Remove the bread from the oven and place it on a rack to cool.

LA BONNE IDÉE

Add raisins or candied or dried cherries along with the chocolate.

You can also bake this bread in a Dutch oven (see Techniques p. 184).

Techniques
Refreshing levain
Kneading by hand or with a stand mixer
Folding
Stages of fermentation
Shaping
Scoring
Using a baking stone

Pain de coco

Coconut Bread

————

Makes 1 loaf

Active time: 15 minutes

Bulk fermentation: 3–4 hours
(or 12 hours)

Proofing: 2–3 hours

Cooking: 30 minutes

Ingredients

Scant ½ cup (3.5 oz./100 g) water

¾ cup + 1 tbsp (7 oz./200 g) coconut milk

2 tsp (0.35 oz./10 g) salt

Generous 2 tbsp (1 oz./30 g) muscovado sugar

2 cups (9 oz./250 g) all-purpose flour (T55)

2 cups (9 oz./250 g) bread or white whole wheat flour (T65–T80)

7 oz. (200 g) refreshed levain

1 tbsp. (15 g) coconut oil or butter, for the pan + more coconut oil for the top of the bread

⅔ cup (1.75 oz./50 g) unsweetened shredded coconut, fresh or dried

Equipment

10–11 × 5-in. (26–28 × 12.7-cm) loaf pan

Combine the water and coconut milk in a saucepan or microwave-safe bowl and heat to lukewarm over low heat or in the microwave. Pour into the bowl of a stand mixer fitted with the dough hook and add the salt, sugar, flours, and levain. Knead for 5–8 minutes on speed 1, until the dough is soft and elastic.

Cover the bowl and let the dough rise in a warm place for 3–4 hours, until doubled in volume, if you wish to bake it on the same day (bulk fermentation*). Alternatively, let the dough cold ferment for 12 hours in the refrigerator.

Gently ease the dough out of the bowl onto a floured work surface. Divide it into three equal pieces using a bench scraper and shape each piece into a loose ball.

Grease the loaf pan with coconut oil or butter and place the balls of dough in it. Let rise in a warm place for 2–3 hours (proofing*).

Toward the end of the rising time, place a rack at the lowest oven position and place another rack directly above it. Place an empty heavy-duty baking sheet, oven-safe skillet, or drip pan on the lower rack and preheat the oven to 450°F (240°C/Gas Mark 8). Bring 1 cup (250 ml) of water to a simmer.

Brush the top of the loaf with a thin layer of coconut oil and sprinkle with the shredded coconut.

Place the loaf pan in the oven, then carefully pour the simmering water into the baking sheet, skillet, or drip pan to create steam and quickly close the oven door. Immediately lower the oven temperature to 400°F (200°C/Gas Mark 6).

Bake for about 30 minutes, until deeply golden.

Let the bread cool for 5 minutes in the pan, then turn it out onto a rack and let cool completely.

LA BONNE IDÉE

Add candied tropical fruit to the dough, such as pineapple, mango, or papaya. Cut the fruit into pieces and incorporate it into the dough at the end of the kneading time.

Techniques

Refreshing levain

Stages of fermentation

Kneading by hand or with a mixer

Shaping

Decorative finishes

Pain roulé au thé matcha

Matcha Swirl Bread

―――――

Makes 1 loaf

Active time: 40 minutes
Blooming yeast: 30 minutes
Bulk fermentation: 1 hour
Proofing: 1 hour
Cooking: 20–25 minutes

Ingredients

1¼ cups (10.5 oz./300 g) lukewarm water

2¼ tsp (0.25 oz./7 g) active dry yeast

Generous ¼ cup (3 oz./90 g) honey, divided

4 cups + 2 tbsp (1 lb. 2 oz./500 g) bread flour (T65)

1¾ tsp (0.3 oz./9 g) salt

¼ cup (1 oz./30 g) powdered whole milk

3 tbsp (1.5 oz./45 g) butter, diced, at room temperature + more for the pan

Neutral oil, for greasing dough balls

3 tsp (0.35 oz./10 g) matcha powder

1½ tbsp (0.5 oz./15 g) white sesame seeds

Equipment

9 × 4-in. (23 × 10-cm) loaf pan

Combine the water, yeast, and a scant ¼ cup (3 oz./80 g) of the honey in the bowl of a stand mixer fitted with the dough hook. Stir or swish to dissolve the yeast and honey and let sit for about 30 minutes to activate the yeast. When the mixture is foamy, add the flour, salt, powdered milk, and butter. Knead for 3 minutes on speed 1, followed by 5 minutes on speed 2.

Divide the dough into two equal pieces. Shape one of the pieces into a ball, grease it lightly with oil, place in a separate bowl, and cover. Return the second piece of dough to the mixer bowl, add the matcha powder, and knead on speed 1 until well incorporated—the dough should have a uniform green hue. Shape into a ball, grease lightly with oil, return to the mixer bowl, and cover. Let both pieces of dough rise at room temperature for 1 hour (bulk fermentation*).

Turn the dough out onto a floured work surface. Taking care not to deflate the dough too much, gently roll each piece into a rectangle of the same size and ¼ in. (5 mm) thick. Stack one rectangle on top of the other. If necessary, brush lightly with water to make the two layers stick together. Divide the rectangle in half lengthwise, and stack the resulting two pieces on top of one another. Roll out again into a rectangle nearly as long as the loaf pan (about 8 in./20 cm). If necessary, trim the dough into an even rectangle using a bench scraper.

Starting with a long edge, roll the dough up into a tight log. Grease the loaf pan with butter and place the dough in it, seam-side down. Let rise for 1 hour (proofing*).

Toward the end of the rising time, preheat the oven to 400°F (200°C/Gas Mark 6).

When the dough passes the poke test*, heat the remaining honey until liquefied and brush it over the top of the loaf, then sprinkle with the sesame seeds. Bake for 20–25 minutes, until golden.

Let the bread cool for 5 minutes in the pan, then turn it out onto a rack and let cool completely.

Techniques
Kneading by hand or with a mixer
Stages of fermentation
Shaping
Decorative finishes

Pains roulés au pavot

Poppy Seed Swirl Rolls

─────────

Makes 5–6 rolls

Active time: 30 minutes
Blooming yeast: 30 minutes
Bulk fermentation: 1 hour
Proofing: 1 hour
Cooking: 20–25 minutes

Ingredients

1¼ cups (10.5 oz./300 g) lukewarm water
2¼ tsp (0.25 oz./7 g) active dry yeast
Generous ¼ cup (3 oz./90 g) honey, divided
4 cups + 2 tbsp (1 lb. 2 oz./500 g) bread flour (T65)
1¾ tsp (0.3 oz./9 g) salt
¼ cup (1 oz./30 g) powdered whole milk
3 tbsp (1.5 oz./45 g) butter, diced, at room temperature
Neutral oil, for greasing dough balls and the pan
2 tsp (0.5 oz./15 g) blackstrap molasses
¼ cup (1 oz./30 g) poppy seeds, divided

Equipment

6-cup muffin pan

Combine the water, yeast, and a scant ¼ cup (3 oz./80 g) of the honey in the bowl of a stand mixer fitted with the dough hook. Stir or swish to dissolve the yeast and honey and let sit for about 30 minutes to activate the yeast. When the mixture is foamy, add the flour, salt, powdered milk, and butter. Knead for 3 minutes on speed 1, followed by 5 minutes on speed 2.

Divide the dough into two equal pieces. Shape one of the pieces into a ball, grease it lightly with oil, place in a separate bowl, and cover. Return the second piece of dough to the mixer bowl and add the molasses and half of the poppy seeds. Knead on speed 1 until the seeds and molasses are well incorporated—the dough should have a uniform brown color. Shape into a ball, grease lightly with oil, return to the mixer bowl, and cover. Let both pieces of dough rise at room temperature for 1 hour (bulk fermentation*).

Turn the dough out onto a floured work surface. Taking care not to deflate the dough too much, gently roll each piece into a rectangle of the same size and ¼ in. (5 mm) thick. Stack one rectangle on top of the other. If necessary, brush lightly with water to make the two layers stick together. Sprinkle with half of the remaining poppy seeds, then divide the rectangle in half lengthwise, and stack the resulting two pieces on top of one another. Sprinkle with the remaining poppy seeds, then roll into an 8-in. (20-cm) rectangle. If necessary, cut the dough into an even rectangle using a bench scraper.

Starting with a long edge, roll the dough up into a tight log. Cut the log into equal slices, 1¼–1½ in. (3–4 cm) thick.

Lightly grease the muffin pan with oil and lay the slices of dough flat in the cavities. Let rise for 1 hour (proofing*).

Toward the end of the rising time, preheat the oven to 400°F (200°C/Gas Mark 6).

When the dough passes the poke test*, heat the remaining honey until liquefied and brush it over the rolls. Bake for 20–25 minutes, until golden.

Turn the rolls out of the pan and let them cool on a rack.

Techniques

Kneading by hand or with a stand mixer
Stages of fermentation
Shaping
Decorative finishes

Pain à la pistache et aux fruits secs

Pistachio Bread with Dried Fruit and Nuts

———

Makes 1 loaf

Active time: 15 minutes

Bulk fermentation: 1–2 hours

Resting: 15 minutes

Proofing: 2 hours

Cooking: 40 minutes

Ingredients

Scant 1½ cups (12.5 oz./350 g) water

1¾ tsp (0.3 oz./9 g) salt

4 cups + 2 tbsp (1 lb. 2 oz./500 g) bread or white whole wheat flour (T65–T80)

1.75 oz. (50 g) refreshed levain

0.1 oz. (3 g) fresh yeast

¼ cup (1.75 oz./75 g) pistachio butter

Generous ¾ cup (3.5 oz./100 g) shelled pistachios, roughly chopped

¼ cup (1.75 oz./50 g) hazelnuts, roughly chopped

¼ cup (1.75 oz./50 g) almonds, roughly chopped

Scant ½ cup (1.75 oz./50 g) dried cranberries

Generous ⅓ cup (1.75 oz./50 g) plump dried apricots, quartered

Equipment

Bread peel

Place the water, salt, flour, and levain in the bowl of a stand mixer fitted with the dough hook. Crumble in the fresh yeast. Knead for 3 minutes on speed 1, followed by 4–6 minutes on speed 2.

Add the pistachio butter, nuts, and dried fruits and knead briefly until evenly distributed.

Shape the dough into a ball, place it on a floured work surface, and cover loosely. Let rise in a warm place for 1–2 hours (bulk fermentation*).

When the dough has risen significantly, quickly shape it into a ball. Cover with a towel and let rest for 15 minutes (resting*).

Shape the dough into a ball again and place it seam-side down in a floured banneton or a large bowl lined with a well-floured towel. Cover with a towel or a large container placed upside down and let rise for 2 hours (proofing*).

Toward the end of the rising time, place a rack at the lowest oven position and place another rack directly above it. Place an empty heavy-duty baking sheet, oven-safe skillet, or drip pan on the lower rack, and a baking stone or heavy-duty baking sheet on the upper rack, and preheat the oven to 500°F (260°C/Gas Mark 10). Bring 1 cup (250 ml) of water to a simmer.

When the dough passes the poke test*, quickly invert the banneton over the floured peel and score the dough before sliding it onto the baking stone or sheet in the oven.

Carefully pour the simmering water into the baking sheet, skillet, or drip pan to create steam and quickly close the oven door.

Bake for 20 minutes, then reduce the heat to 430°F (220°C/Gas Mark 7) and continue to bake for an additional 20 minutes, until deeply golden.

Remove the bread from the oven and place it on a rack to cool.

LA BONNE IDÉE

You can also bake this bread in a Dutch oven (see Techniques p. 184).

Techniques

Refreshing levain

Stages of fermentation

Kneading by hand or with a mixer

Shaping

Scoring

Using a baking stone

Baguettes viennoises aux pépites de chocolat

Vienna Bread with Chocolate Chips

———

Makes 2 small baguettes

Active time: 20 minutes
Bulk fermentation: 1 hour
Resting: 15 minutes
Proofing: 1–1½ hours
Cooking: 20–30 minutes

Ingredients

⅔ cup (5.25 oz./150 g) whole milk
0.25 oz. (7 g) fresh yeast
1.75 oz. (50 g) refreshed levain
1 generous tbsp (15 g) sugar
2 cups (9 oz./250 g) bread flour (T65)
1 tsp (0.2 oz./5 g) salt
3 tbsp (1.5 oz./40 g) butter, diced, at room temperature
Generous ½ cup (3.5 oz./100 g) chocolate chips, or 1 (3.5-oz./100-g) chocolate bar, roughly chopped
1 egg yolk, lightly beaten

Pour the milk into the bowl of a stand mixer fitted with the dough hook. Crumble in the fresh yeast and stir or swish to dissolve, then stir in the levain. Add the sugar, flour, and salt. Knead for 10 minutes on speed 1, followed by 5–10 minutes on speed 2, until the dough pulls away from the sides of the bowl. About halfway through the 5–10 minutes, add the butter with the mixer running. Add the chocolate chips and knead briefly until evenly distributed.

Shape the dough into a ball, place it in a lightly oiled or flour-dusted bowl, and cover. Let rise for 1 hour in a place that is warm, but not warm enough to melt the chocolate (bulk fermentation*).

Turn the dough out onto a floured work surface and divide it into two equal pieces. Cover with a towel and let rest for 15 minutes (resting*).

Shape each piece of dough into a short baguette and place seam-side down on a baking sheet lined with parchment paper.

Brush the dough with a thin layer of egg yolk, then chill in the refrigerator for 10 minutes to firm it up a bit. Brush with another layer of egg yolk and score with kitchen shears, making several parallel diagonal cuts across the top of the dough.

Let rise in a warm place for 1–1½ hours (proofing*).

Toward the end of the rising time, place a rack in the center of the oven and place another rack directly below it. Place an empty heavy-duty baking sheet, oven-safe skillet, or drip pan on the lower rack and preheat the oven to 400°F (200°C/Gas Mark 6). Bring 1 cup (250 ml) of water to a simmer.

When the dough passes the poke test*, place the baking sheet in the oven, then carefully pour the simmering water into the baking sheet, skillet, or drip pan to create steam and quickly close the oven door.

Bake for 20–30 minutes, until deeply golden.

Slide the bread onto a rack with the parchment paper underneath and let cool.

LA BONNE IDÉE

You can swap out the chocolate chips for dried fruit of your choice, such as raisins or a blend of tropical fruits.

Techniques

Refreshing levain
Kneading by hand or with a mixer
Stages of fermentation
Shaping
Scoring

Benoîtons raisins secs-cannelle

Cinnamon-Currant Benoîtons

————

Makes about 10 *benoîtons*

Active time: 20 minutes
Bulk fermentation: 1–2 hours
Proofing: 1 hour
Cooking: 15 minutes

Ingredients

Scant 1½ cups (12.5 oz./350 g) water
1¾ tsp (0.3 oz./9 g) salt
2⅔ cups (10.5 oz./300 g) dark/100 percent whole wheat flour (T150)
Scant 2 cups (7 oz./200 g) rye flour
2¾ tsp (0.25 oz./7 g) ground cinnamon
3.5 oz. (100 g) refreshed levain
0.35 oz. (10 g) fresh yeast
2 tbsp (1 oz./30 g) butter, diced, at room temperature
2 cups (10.5 oz./300 g) Zante currants

Place the water, salt, flours, cinnamon, and levain in the bowl of a stand mixer fitted with the dough hook. Crumble in the fresh yeast. Knead for 3 minutes on speed 1, followed by 4–6 minutes on speed 2. Halfway through the 4–6 minutes, add the butter with the mixer running. At the end of the kneading time, add the currants and knead briefly until evenly distributed.

Shape the dough into a ball, place in a lightly oiled or flour-dusted bowl, and cover. Let the dough rise for 1–2 hours, until doubled in volume. Fold the dough twice during the rise time: once after 30 minutes, and once after 1 hour (bulk fermentation*).

Turn the dough out onto a floured work surface and gently roll it or press it with your hand into a roughly 16-in. (40-cm) square, ¾ in. (2 cm) thick.

Cut the square in half, then cut each half lengthwise into 1¼-in. (3-cm) wide strips. As you cut the strips, place them on a baking sheet lined with parchment paper and keep them covered. Let rise for 1 hour (proofing*).

Toward the end of the rising time, place a rack in the center of the oven and place another rack directly below it. Place an empty heavy-duty baking sheet, oven-safe skillet, or drip pan on the lower rack and preheat the oven to 400°F (200°C/Gas Mark 6). Bring 1 cup (250 ml) of water to a simmer.

When the dough passes the poke test*, place the baking sheet in the oven, then carefully pour the simmering water into the baking sheet, skillet, or drip pan to create steam and quickly close the oven door.

Bake for 15 minutes, until golden.

Let the *benoîtons* cool on a rack.

LA BONNE IDÉE
You can replace the currants and cinnamon with chocolate chips or chopped walnuts or hazelnuts. For a savory version, add chopped olives and a teaspoon of oregano.

Techniques
Refreshing levain
Kneading by hand or with a mixer
Stages of fermentation

Pain noisettes et chocolat

Chocolate and Hazelnut Bread

—————

Makes 1 large loaf

Active time: 20 minutes
Bulk fermentation: 1½ hours
Proofing: 1 hour
Cooking: 40 minutes

Ingredients

½ cup (3.5 oz./100 g) hazelnuts
1¼ cups (10.5 oz./300 g) whole milk
0.35 oz. (10 g) fresh yeast
3.5 oz. (100 g) refreshed levain
Generous 2 tbsp (1 oz./30 g) muscovado
or turbinado sugar
4 cups + 2 tbsp (1 lb. 2 oz./500 g) bread
or white whole wheat flour (T65–T80)
1¾ tsp (0.3 oz./9 g) salt
Scant ½ cup (2.5 oz./75 g) hazelnut
butter, preferably organic
½ bar (1.75 oz./50 g) dark chocolate,
roughly chopped

Equipment

Bread peel

Techniques

Refreshing levain
Kneading by hand or with a mixer
Stages of fermentation
Shaping
Scoring
Using a baking stone

Toast the hazelnuts in an ungreased skillet for 4–5 minutes over medium heat, swirling the skillet often to prevent burning. Let cool, then chop roughly.

Pour the milk into the bowl of a stand mixer fitted with the dough hook. Crumble in the fresh yeast and stir or swish to dissolve, then add the levain, sugar, flour, and salt. Knead for 5 minutes on speed 1.

Add the hazelnut butter and knead for 5–8 minutes on speed 2. At the end of the kneading time, add the hazelnuts and chocolate and knead briefly until evenly distributed.

Shape the dough into a ball, place in a lightly oiled or flour-dusted bowl, and cover. Let rise for 1½ hours in a place that is warm, but not warm enough to melt the chocolate (bulk fermentation*).

When the dough has risen significantly, turn it out onto a floured work surface. Gently shape the dough into a ball without deflating it and place it seam-side down in a floured banneton or a large bowl lined with a well-floured towel. Cover and let rise at room temperature for 1 hour (proofing*).

Toward the end of the rising time, place a rack at the lowest oven position and place another rack directly above it. Place an empty heavy-duty baking sheet, oven-safe skillet, or drip pan on the lower rack, and a baking stone or heavy-duty baking sheet on the upper rack, and preheat the oven to 480°F (250°C/Gas Mark 9). Bring 1 cup (250 ml) of water to a simmer.

When the dough passes the poke test*, quickly invert the banneton over the floured peel and score the dough before sliding it onto the baking stone or sheet in the oven.

Carefully pour the simmering water into the baking sheet, skillet, or drip pan to create steam and quickly close the oven door.

Bake for 20 minutes at 480°F (250°C/Gas Mark 9), then reduce the heat to 430°F (220°C/Gas Mark 7) and continue to bake for another 20 minutes, until deeply golden.

Remove the bread from the oven and place it on a rack to cool.

LA BONNE IDÉE
You can also bake this bread in a Dutch oven (see Techniques p. 184).

Pain muesli

Muesli Bread

___

Makes 1 loaf

Active time: 20 minutes
Bulk fermentation: 1½ hours
Proofing: 1 hour
Cooking: 30–40 minutes

Ingredients

1¾ tsp (0.3 oz./9 g) salt
1¼ cups (10.5 oz./300 g) whole milk
1½ tbsp (1 oz./30 g) honey
5 cups (1 lb. 2 oz./500 g) white spelt flour (T80)
3.5 oz. (100 g) refreshed levain
0.25 oz. (7 g) fresh yeast
1⅓ cups (5.25 oz./150 g) muesli
⅔ cup (3.5 oz./100 g) raisins
Butter, for the pan
Generous ½ cup (1.75 oz./50 g) rolled oats

Equipment

10–11 × 5-in. (26–28 × 12.7-cm) loaf pan

Place the salt, milk, honey, flour, and levain, in this order, in the bowl of a stand mixer fitted with the dough hook. Crumble in the fresh yeast. Knead for 3 minutes on speed 1, followed by 5–7 minutes on speed 2. At the end of the kneading time, add the muesli and raisins and knead briefly until evenly distributed.

Cover the bowl and let rise in a warm place for 1½ hours. Fold the dough three times during the rise time: once after 30 minutes, once after 1 hour, and once after 1½ hours (bulk fermentation*).

Lightly grease the loaf pan with butter, then turn the dough out onto a floured work surface. Without deflating the dough, shape it into a *bâtard* that is roughly the same size as the pan. Transfer to the pan, cover, and let rise for 1 hour (proofing*).

Toward the end of the rising time, place a rack at the lowest oven position and place another rack directly above it. Place an empty heavy-duty baking sheet, oven-safe skillet, or drip pan on the lower rack and preheat the oven to 480°F (250°C/Gas Mark 9). Bring 1 cup (250 ml) of water to a simmer.

When the dough passes the poke test*, brush the surface of the dough with water and sprinkle with the rolled oats. Place in the oven, then carefully pour the simmering water into the baking sheet, skillet, or drip pan to create steam and quickly close the oven door.

Bake for 15 minutes at 480°F (250°C/Gas Mark 9), then reduce the heat to 450°F (230°C/Gas Mark 8) and continue to bake for an additional 15–25 minutes, until the bread is deeply browned.

Let the bread cool for 5 minutes in the pan, then turn it out onto a rack and let cool completely.

Techniques
Refreshing levain
Kneading by hand or with a mixer
Stages of fermentation
Shaping
Decorative finishes

Pain d'épices

French Spiced Loaf

Makes 1 spiced loaf

Active time: 15 minutes
To infuse honey: 24 hours
Cooking: 50 minutes
Maturing: 3–4 days

Ingredients

Spice-infused honey
Scant ¾ cup (6 oz./175 g) water
Generous ½ cup (7 oz./200 g) chestnut honey
1 oz. (30 g) star anise pods
2 cinnamon sticks
1 tsp ground cinnamon
1 tsp ground ginger
1 tsp ground nutmeg
½ tsp ground cloves
2 oz. (60 g) candied orange peel

Spiced loaf
2⅓ cups (9 oz./250 g) rye flour
2¾ tsp (0.35 oz./10 g) baking powder
1 tsp (0.2 oz./5 g) baking soda
4 tbsp (1.75 oz./50 g) brown sugar (light or dark)
Scant ¼ tsp (1 g) salt
Butter, for the pan

Equipment
8 × 4-in. (20 × 10-cm) loaf pan

The day before baking, prepare the spice-infused honey: Combine the water and honey in a saucepan and bring to a boil. Remove from the heat and stir in the spices and the candied orange peel. Cover and let infuse for 24 hours.

The next day, prepare the spiced loaf: Preheat the oven to 350°F (180°C/Gas Mark 4) and grease the loaf pan with butter.

Strain the spice-infused honey through a fine-mesh sieve into a bowl.

Stir together the flour, baking powder, baking soda, brown sugar, and salt in a large mixing bowl. Make a well in the center and pour in the spice-infused honey. Stir just until well combined and smooth.

Pour in the batter into the prepared pan, place in the oven, and immediately reduce the heat to 325°F (160°C/Gas Mark 3). Bake for 50 minutes, until the cake is golden and a knife inserted into the center comes out clean.

Let the bread cool for 10 minutes in the pan, then turn it out onto a rack and wrap while still warm with plastic wrap or reusable food wrap.

Before enjoying the spiced loaf, let it sit for 3–4 days at room temperature, well wrapped, to allow the flavors to develop.

Cécile Khayat and Victoria Effantin

———

"We love to eat; we're fascinated by gastronomy. We noticed that things were progressing when it came to food, but not with bread, even though it's the ultimate French product. We wanted to create the bakery of our dreams, the one we would want to have just around the corner. We got off to a rocky start. At the time, there were very few modern artisan bakeries. We didn't have much experience, we wanted to do everything ourselves, and we were women, which meant expectations were even higher. Since then, we've created a unique team of people who stand out from the crowd. Our business vision encompasses the well-being of our team and creating a strong brand identity. You could say we've taken a sensitive approach, perhaps a feminine one.

"*Mamiche* is a welcoming name that combines the words '*mamie*' (grandma) and '*miche*' (loaf). Our bread is rustic. We didn't want anything fussy. The crust is crunchy and the crumb has good chew and a mild flavor, since our levain is not too sour. We're not really into making 'fancy weekend treats.' We make large loaves that we sell by weight, an approach that surprised a lot of people at first, but one that allows us to buy what we need. We take a responsible and pragmatic approach. We're a neighborhood bakery making everyday bread at everyday prices."

After earning a vocational certificate in pastry making and a business degree from the École Supérieure de Commerce de Paris, Cécile Khayat dreamed of opening her own bakery. Victoria Effantin was working in food marketing and considering a similar project. She left her job to earn a vocational certificate in bread making, and the two women developed their idea together before opening Mamiche, a neighborhood bakery in Paris, in 2017. They create a range of high-quality, homemade breads and pastries with a laid-back, playful spirit. They have since opened a second location in Paris.

www.mamiche.fr

Petites baguettes chocolat beurre salé

Mini Chocolate and Salted Butter Baguettes

Recipe from Mamiche

———

Makes 5–6 baguettes

Active time: 15 minutes
Resting: 30 minutes
Proofing: 30 minutes
Cooking: 15 minutes

Ingredients

1 lb. 2 oz. (500 g) baguette dough, after bulk fermentation (see recipe p. 219)

1 stick + 2 tbsp (5.25 oz./150 g) salted butter, at room temperature

Scant 1 cup (5.25 oz./150 g) chocolate chips

3⅓ cups (1 lb. 7 oz./650 g) sugar

2 cups (1 lb. 2 oz./500 g) water

Place the baguette dough on a floured work surface. Using a bench scraper, divide the dough into five or six pieces weighing about 2.5 oz. (70–75 g) each.

Quickly shape each piece into a rough oval, cover with a towel, and let rest at room temperature for 30 minutes (resting*).

Cut the butter into small pieces. Shape each piece of dough into a small baguette—as you shape the dough, incorporate 1–2 tbsp (20–25 g) of butter and a small handful of chocolate chips into each piece. Sprinkle with *fleur de sel*.

Place on a baking sheet lined with parchment paper, cover, and let rise at room temperature for ½ hour (proofing*).

For the glaze, combine the sugar and water in a saucepan and bring to a boil over high heat, stirring often to dissolve the sugar. Let boil for 30 seconds and remove from the heat. Let cool completely.

Place a rack in the center of the oven and place another rack directly below it. Place an empty heavy-duty baking sheet, oven-safe skillet, or drip pan on the lower rack and preheat the oven to 480°F (250°C/Gas Mark 9). Bring 1 cup (250 ml) of water to a simmer.

When the dough passes the poke test*, place the baguettes in the oven, then carefully pour the simmering water into the baking sheet, skillet, or drip pan to create steam and quickly close the oven door. Bake for 10–15 minutes, until golden.

Transfer the baguettes to a rack and brush them with the sugar-water glaze.

Enjoy warm or at room temperature.

Techniques
Stages of fermentation
Shaping
Decorative finishes

Magda Gegenava

—

"We love cheese in Georgia; we eat it with everything. And we also like bread. We have all kinds of bread. There's one in particular that we cook in a traditional Georgian oven called a *tone*. No bakery in the world smells so good. The scent that wafts out makes you think: Give me one!

"All Georgian women cook and everything is homemade. When we really want to eat well, we eat at home. We go out to a restaurant to have fun; it's not like here in France where the meal is the most important part of going out. That's why I invented the term 'homemade gastronomy' to describe the food I make.

"I came to France with my family as a refugee in 2014. In my country I was a dentist. In my former profession, no one ever said thank you; no one likes their dentist. But people are happy when I cook! I don't weigh anything; instead I taste things to see if I like them, and they turn out different every time. For example, I make *khinkali*, Georgian ravioli, and *khachapuri*, a very important dish in Georgia that is served in every house when guests are invited. Each region has its own version. On the Black Sea coast, it resembles a boat and people say that a fisherman's wife created it. The egg yolk symbolizes the sun. The traditional form is round and the crust covers the cheese. It's always served as a sharing plate, but for the French, I make single portions, and I garnish the edges with cheese because personally, I don't like eating the crust alone. And I always accompany it with a very sweet Georgian lemonade."

Magda Gegenava, the former director of a dental clinic in Tbilisi, fled her country for political reasons. She settled first in Ukraine, where she opened a small fruit and vegetable shop before arriving in France in 2014. She was invited to be the guest chef for La Résidence, the restaurant at the Refugee Food Festival, held from June to December 2018. Then she ran a pop-up restaurant at the Grand Marché Stalingrad at La Rotonde, in Paris, from April to October 2019. She opened her own Georgian restaurant in Paris in the same year.

The mission of the Refugee Food Festival is to change popular conceptions about refugees through food, to assist them in their search for employment, and to introduce the public to flavors from around the world. Organized by the association Food Sweet Food, this culinary festival takes place in a dozen European cities each year in June. The Refugee Food Festival has been helping Magda move towards her professional goal since 2018.

www.chez-magda.com

Khachapuri GEORGIA

Georgian Cheese Bread
Recipe by Magda Gegeneva

────────

Makes 5 khachapuri

Active time: 30 minutes

Bulk fermentation: 3–4 hours, or overnight

Cooking: 15 minutes per batch

Ingredients

Dough

1 lb. 2 oz. (500 g) all-purpose or pastry flour (T45–T55), sifted

1½ tsp (0.2 oz./5 g) instant yeast

1¼ cups (10.5 oz./300 g) lukewarm water

¼ cup (1.75 oz./50 g) sunflower oil

1 tsp (0.2 oz./5 g) salt

Assembly

1 lb. 2 oz. (500 g) low-moisture mozzarella (or *sulguni*, a brined Georgian cheese)

6 oz. (170 g) feta

1–2 eggs, lightly beaten

For serving

5 eggs

Prepare the dough: Place the flour, yeast, water, oil, and salt in the bowl of a stand mixer fitted with the dough hook. Knead for 5–7 minutes, until a slightly sticky ball forms. Alternatively, knead the dough by hand in a large mixing bowl. Cover the bowl and let the dough rise in a warm place for 3–4 hours, until doubled in volume, or let it rest overnight in the refrigerator (bulk fermentation*).

Preheat the oven to 480°F (250°C/Gas Mark 9).

Line two baking sheets with parchment paper. Roughly chop the mozzarella. Transfer to a large mixing bowl, crumble in the feta, and add one of the eggs. Stir until well combined. If the mixture seems stiff or dry, add the second egg.

Turn the dough out onto a floured work surface and divide it into five pieces weighing about 7 oz. (200 g) each. Cover with plastic wrap or a towel. Take out one piece of dough at a time and roll it into a rectangle measuring about 6 × 8 in. (15 × 20 cm). Carefully transfer to one of the prepared baking sheets.

Line both of the long edges of the rectangle with a little of the cheese mixture and roll up the dough around the cheese to enclose it fully. Pinch the corners of the short ends together so that they join, making a boat-like shape. Fill the center with about 2 heaping tbsp of the cheese mixture.

Repeat with the remaining pieces of dough until you've filled both baking sheets, without packing the *khachapuri* too closely together.

Bake for 15 minutes, rotating the baking sheets from front to back and top to bottom if necessary to ensure even browning.

As soon as you remove the *khachapuri* from the oven, crack an egg into the center. If you like, you can break the yolk and return the *khachapuri* to the oven for 2–3 minutes, until the egg is set, or quickly stir the egg into the hot cheese mixture with a fork to cook it.

Serve warm.

Techniques

Kneading by hand or with a mixer

Stages of fermentation

Gua baos CHINA

Taiwanese Pork Belly Buns

___

Makes 6 *gua baos* (*bao* buns)

Active time: 30 minutes
Bulk fermentation: 1½–2 hours
Resting: 20 minutes
Proofing: 1 hour
Cooking: 50 minutes

Ingredients

Bao bun dough
⅔ cup (5.25 oz./150 g) low-fat milk
2½ cups (10.5 oz./300 g) bread flour (T65)
1 tsp (0.1 oz./3 g) instant yeast
1 tsp baking powder
Scant ¼ tsp (1 g) salt
5 tsp (0.75 oz./20 g) sugar

Caramelized pork belly
10.5 oz. (300 g) pork belly
1 tbsp neutral oil
2 cloves garlic, finely chopped
1 tbsp grated fresh ginger
1 tsp five-spice powder
½ tsp cinnamon
1 star anise pod
1 tbsp sugar
Scant ½ cup (100 ml) water
Scant ½ cup (100 ml) rice vinegar
Scant ½ cup (100 ml) soy sauce

Assembly
Kimchi and/or assorted vegetables
(grated carrot, thinly sliced scallions, etc.)
Fresh cilantro leaves
2 tbsp (0.75 oz./20 g) roasted, salted
peanuts, roughly chopped

Equipment

Steamer pot, steamer basket,
or *couscoussier*
Dutch oven or large saucepan

Techniques
Kneading by hand or with a mixer
Stages of fermentation
Shaping
Baking with steam

Prepare the bun dough: Place the milk, bread flour, yeast, baking powder, salt, and sugar in the bowl of a stand mixer fitted with the dough hook. Knead for 5–6 minutes on speed 2, until the dough is smooth and elastic.

Cover the bowl and let the dough rise for 1½–2 hours, until doubled in volume (bulk fermentation*).

Turn the dough out onto a floured work surface and divide it into six equal pieces using a bench scraper. Shape each piece into a loose ball, cover, and let rest for 20 minutes (resting*).

Meanwhile, cut out twelve 4-in. (10-cm) squares of parchment paper.

Roll each piece of dough into a 3 × 6-in. (8 × 16-cm) oval. Place a parchment paper square on each piece of dough, covering the dough halfway lengthwise. Fold the other half of the dough over the paper. Place each folded bun on a separate parchment paper square.

Transfer the buns to the steamer basket with the parchment paper underneath, leaving about ¾ in. (2 cm) between them. Let rise for 1 hour (proofing*).

Prepare the caramelized pork belly: Remove the skin from the pork belly and cut the meat into ½-in. (1-cm) slices.

Heat the oil in a Dutch oven or saucepan over medium-high heat and add the pork belly. Cook until browned on all sides, then stir in the remaining ingredients. Reduce the heat to low and let simmer, covered, for 40 minutes, until the meat is meltingly tender and caramelized. Add water as needed during the cooking process if the mixture appears dry.

Steam and assemble the buns: Steam the buns for 10 minutes over low-medium heat, to prevent them from cracking, until puffed and cooked all the way through. Divide the caramelized pork belly between the *bao* buns and garnish with kimchi and/or your vegetables of choice. Sprinkle with the cilantro and peanuts and serve right away.

Matzos ISRAEL

Makes 3 matzos

Active time: 20 minutes

Cooking: 15 minutes

Ingredients

¾ cup + 2 tbsp (3.5 oz./100 g) bread
or white whole wheat flour (T65–T80)

Scant ½ tsp (2 g) salt

3½ tbsp (1.75 oz./50 g) water

Preheat the oven to 400°F (200°C/Gas Mark 6).

Stir together the flour and salt in a large mixing bowl and make a well in the center. Gradually add the water, kneading it in with your hands as you pour. Continue kneading until the dough forms a smooth ball that is not at all sticky. Add a little more water if necessary if the dough is too firm.

Divide the dough into three pieces and shape each into a ball. On a floured surface, roll each piece of dough into a very thin round. Transfer to a baking sheet, either nonstick or lined with parchment paper.

Pierce the rounds all over with a fork or dough docker and bake for 10–15 minutes, until pale golden.

Let cool.

Techniques

Kneading by hand

Shaping

Arepas VENEZUELA

Venezuelan-Style Corn Cakes

———

Makes 4 arepas

Active time: 10 minutes
Cooking: 15 minutes

Ingredients

1 cup (5.25 oz./150 g) precooked cornmeal, preferably *masarepa*

Scant ¼ tsp (1 g) salt

⅔ cup (5.25 oz./150 g)– ¾ cup + 1 tbsp (7 oz./200 g) water

2 tbsp vegetable oil

Preheat the oven to 350°F (180°C/Gas Mark 4) and line a baking sheet with parchment paper.

Stir together the cornmeal and salt in a bowl and make a well in the center. Gradually add the water, stirring or kneading with your hands until a supple, slightly tacky dough forms (neither crumbly nor sticky).

Divide the dough into four equal pieces and shape into balls. Working on parchment paper, flatten each ball into a 3–4-in. (8–10-cm) disk, ¾ in. (1.5 cm) thick, using the palm of your hand.

Heat the oil in a skillet over medium to medium-high heat. Add the arepas and cook on both sides until the crust is dry and lightly charred in places.

Transfer the arepas to the prepared baking sheet and bake for 10 minutes, until cooked through. Fill the arepas as soon as they are cooked, or wrap them in a towel to keep them warm. To serve, slice the arepas open and add your choice of filling, like a sandwich.

Techniques
Kneading by hand or with a mixer
Shaping

Soda Bread IRELAND

Makes 1 loaf

Active time: 10 minutes

Cooking: 30–40 minutes

Ingredients

2 cups (9 oz./250 g) 100 percent whole wheat flour (T180)

¾ cup + 2 tbsp (3.5 oz./100 g) bread flour (T65)

¾ cup (2 oz./60 g) rolled oats

1 tsp (0.2 oz./5 g) baking soda

1 tsp (0.2 oz./5 g) salt

1¼ cups (10.5 oz./300 g) buttermilk

Preheat the oven to 400°F (200°C/Gas Mark 6). In a large mixing bowl, combine the flours, oats, baking soda, and salt. Make a well in the center and gradually pour in the buttermilk. Knead with your hands until a moist, but not sticky, dough comes together. Alternatively, knead in a stand mixer fitted with the dough hook for 5 minutes on speed 2.

Shape the dough into a ball and place on a baking sheet lined with parchment paper. Lightly dust the top of the dough with flour and score a cross into the surface. Bake for 30–40 minutes, until golden.

Remove the bread from the oven and place it on a rack to cool.

LA BONNE IDÉE

You can also bake this soda bread in a Dutch oven (see Techniques p. 184).

Techniques

Kneading by hand or with a mixer

Shaping

Scoring

Shokupan JAPAN

Japanese Milk Bread

—

Makes 1 loaf

Active time: 20 minutes
Tangzhong: Overnight
Bulk fermentation: 1–2 hours
Proofing: 1–2 hours
Cooking: 30 minutes

Ingredients

Tangzhong
Scant ½ cup (3.5 oz./100 g) water
2 tbsp (0.75 oz./20 g) all-purpose
or pastry flour (T45–T55)

Shokupan
⅔ cup (5 oz./140 g) whole milk
¼ cup (1.75 oz./50 g) sugar
1 egg
2¾ cups (12.5 oz./350 g) all-purpose
or pastry flour (T45–T55)
2 tbsp (1 oz./30 g) powdered whole milk
Scant 1½ tsp (0.25 oz./7 g) salt
0.5 oz. (15 g) fresh yeast
2 tbsp (1 oz./30 g) butter, at room
temperature + more for the pan
1 tbsp (0.5 oz./15 g) butter, melted
or clarified (optional)

Equipment

Instant-read thermometer
9 × 4-in. (23 × 10-cm) loaf pan

The day before baking, prepare the *tangzhong*: Combine the water and flour in a saucepan. Cook over low heat, whisking constantly, until the mixture is thick and registers 149°F (65°C) on the thermometer. Transfer to a bowl, cover, and let cool. Let rest in the refrigerator overnight.

The next day, remove the *tangzhong* from the refrigerator 1 hour before starting the *shokupan* dough to allow it to come to room temperature.

Prepare the *shokupan*: Place the milk, sugar, egg, flour, powdered milk, and salt in the bowl of a stand mixer fitted with the dough hook. Add the *tangzhong* and crumble in the fresh yeast.

Knead for 3 minutes on speed 1, followed by 6–8 minutes on speed 2. Halfway through the 6–8 minutes, add the butter with the mixer running. Knead until the dough is smooth and elastic.

Shape the dough into a ball and place it in a lightly oiled bowl. Cover the bowl and let the dough rise in a warm place for 1–2 hours, until doubled in volume. Fold the dough twice during the rise time: once after 30 minutes, and once after 1 hour (bulk fermentation*).

Grease the loaf pan with butter. Turn the dough out onto a floured work surface and divide it into four equal pieces using a bench scraper. Roll each piece into a circle with a thickness of ¼ in. (5 mm). Fold two sides of each circle in toward the center to form rough rectangles. Starting with a short end, roll each piece up tightly like a cinnamon roll. Place in the prepared loaf pan with the seam facing down and the swirls facing the pan sides. Cover and let rise in a warm place for 1–2 hours (proofing*).

Toward the end of the rising time, preheat the oven to 350°F (180°C/Gas Mark 4).

When the dough passes the poke test*, bake it for 30 minutes, until deeply golden.

Let the loaf cool for a few minutes in the pan, then turn it out onto a rack to cool. If you'd like to glaze the bread, brush it with the melted butter while it is still hot.

Techniques
Kneading with a stand mixer or by hand
Stages of fermentation
Folding
Shaping
Decorative finishes

Pita Bread MIDDLE EAST AND MEDITERRANEAN

____

Makes 10 pitas

Active time: 15 minutes

Bulk fermentation: 2 hours

Resting: 30 minutes–1 hour + 10 minutes

Cooking: 30 minutes

Ingredients

Scant 1½ cups (12.5 oz./350 g) water

2½ tsp (0.25 oz./8 g) instant yeast

4 cups + 2 tbsp (1 lb. 2 oz./500 g) all-purpose flour, divided

5 tsp (0.75 oz./20 g) sugar

1¾ tsp (0.3 oz./9 g) salt

4½ tsp (0.75 oz./20 g) extra-virgin olive oil

Place the water and yeast in the bowl of a stand mixer fitted with the dough hook and stir or swish to dissolve. Add half of the flour and the sugar and knead for 2 minutes on speed 1, just to combine the ingredients. Let rest for 20 minutes, then add the remaining flour and the salt. Knead for 3 minutes on speed 1, followed by 5–7 minutes on speed 2. Toward the end of the 5–7 minutes, drizzle in the olive oil with the mixer running.

Cover the bowl and let the dough rise in a warm place for 2 hours until nearly doubled in volume. Fold the dough twice during the rise time (bulk fermentation*).

Turn the dough out onto a floured work surface and divide it into ten pieces weighing 3.5 oz. (100 g) each. Cover with a damp towel and let rest for 30 minutes–1 hour (resting*).

Using a rolling pin or the palm of your hand, roll or flatten each piece of dough into a circle with a thickness of ¹⁄₁₆–¼ in. (2–5 cm). Let rest uncovered on a floured cutting board or baking sheet for 10 minutes (resting*).

Heat a heavy-bottomed nonstick or well-seasoned cast-iron skillet over high heat. Place one pita at a time in the skillet and cook until slightly puffed, then turn it over and cook until completely puffed and charred in places.

Stack the finished pitas under a towel or in a plastic bag to keep them soft until filling and serving.

Techniques
Kneading by hand or with a mixer
Stages of fermentation
Folding
Shaping

Chapatis INDIA

Indian Flatbread

Makes 6 *chapatis*

Active time: 10 minutes
Cooking: 5 minutes

Ingredients

¾ cup + 2 tbsp (3.5 oz./100 g) bread flour (T65)

¾ cup + 2 tbsp (3.5 oz./100 g) white whole wheat or light whole wheat flour (T80–T110)

½ tsp (0.1 oz./3 g) salt

⅔ cup (5.25 oz./150 g) lukewarm water

Sunflower oil

Combine the flours and salt in a large mixing bowl. Add the water and work with your hands to form a soft, pliable, and slightly sticky dough. Divide the dough into six pieces weighing about 1.75 oz. (50 g) each and shape each piece into a ball.

Flatten each ball slightly between your hands, then press down to make an indentation in the center. Add a few drops of sunflower oil and a pinch of flour to the indentation, then gather into a ball again. Flatten each ball into a thick 2½-in. (7-cm) disk.

Place a little all-purpose or bread flour on a plate and dip in one dough disk at a time, coat the dough lightly all over. Shake off any excess flour, then roll the dough into a very thin circle. Repeat with the remaining disks.

Set a heavy-bottomed skillet over medium-high heat and cook the *chapatis* for several seconds on each side, until browned in places.

Stack the finished *chapatis* under a towel right away to keep them soft.

Techniques
Kneading by hand or with a mixer
Shaping

Knäckebröd SWEDEN

Swedish Crispbread

———

**Makes 1 large
or 10 small *knäckebröd***

Active time: 15 minutes
Resting: 30 minutes
Cooking: 7–8 minutes

Ingredients
Scant ⅓ cup (2.5 oz./70 g) water
Generous ½ cup (5 oz./140 g) heavy cream
1⅓ cups (6.25 oz./180 g) rye flour
1½ cups (6.25 oz./180 g) white whole wheat or light whole wheat flour (T80–T110)
½ tsp (0.1 oz./3 g) salt
1 tsp (0.1 oz./3 g) instant yeast

Equipment
Instant-read thermometer

Combine the water and cream in a saucepan and warm over low heat to 113°F (45°C).

Whisk together the flours and salt in a large mixing bowl, then whisk in the yeast.

Make a well in the center and gradually add the water-cream mixture. Knead with your hands for 2–3 minutes, until the dough comes together. Shape the dough into a ball, then cover the bowl and let the dough rise in a warm place for 30 minutes (resting*).

Meanwhile, preheat the oven to 450°F (230°C/Gas Mark 8).

Turn the dough out onto a floured work surface and roll it to a thickness of ⅛ in. (3 mm). Place a large plate over the dough and cut around it to make a circle, or use a small plate or other circular object to cut out ten small circles. Gather the scraps and use them to make another crispbread or crackers.

Transfer the dough to a baking sheet, either nonstick or lined with parchment paper. Pierce the dough all over with a fork or dough docker and cut out a small round hole in the center of each circle using a small glass or a cookie cutter.

Bake for 5 minutes, then flip over using a spatula and bake for an additional 2–3 minutes, until lightly golden.

Let cool completely on a rack, then store in an airtight container in a dry place.

Techniques
Kneading by hand or with a mixer
Shaping

Vollkornbrot GERMANY

German Rye Bread

——————

Makes 1 loaf

Active time: 30 minutes
Soaker: 24 hours
Rye levain: 10–12 hours
Soaking inclusions: 15 minutes
Bulk fermentation: 1½ hours
Proofing: 12–16 hours
Cooking: 1 hour + 15 minutes
Maturing: 24 hours

Ingredients

Soaker
½ cup (4.25 oz./125 g) water
Scant 1 cup (4.25 oz./125 g) rye chops

Refreshed rye levain
Scant ½ cup (1.75 oz./50 g) rye chops
Scant ½ cup (1.75 oz./50 g) rye flakes
½ cup (4.25 oz./120 g) water
1.75 oz. (50 g) levain
Scant ⅓ cup (1 oz./30 g) dark rye
or pumpernickel flour

Dough
Generous ¾ cup (3.5 oz./100 g) rye
flakes
Generous ½ cup (3 oz./80 g) sunflower
seeds
Scant ½ cup (3 oz./80 g) pumpkin seeds
¾ cup + 1 tbsp (7 oz./200 g) lukewarm
water
Scant ½ cup (3.5 oz./100 g) room-
temperature water
Scant 1½ cups (5 oz./150 g) dark rye
or pumpernickel flour, plus more for the
pan
Scant 2½ tsp (0.5 oz./12 g) salt
Neutral oil, for the pan

Equipment
10 × 4-in. (26 × 10-cm) loaf pan
Food processor

Techniques
Kneading by hand or with a mixer
Stages of fermentation
Decorative finishes

Two days before baking, prepare the soaker: Bring the water to a boil. Place the rye chops in a heat-resistant bowl and pour the boiling water over them. Let cool to room temperature, then cover tightly and let soak for 24 hours.

Two days before baking, prepare the rye levain: Place the rye chops and rye flakes in the bowl of a food processor and pulse to chop roughly. Transfer to a bowl and add the water, levain, and rye flour. Stir to blend, cover loosely, and let ferment at room temperature for 10–12 hours.

The next day, prepare the dough: Place the rye flakes, sunflower seeds, and pumpkin seeds in a bowl, reserving some seeds for the top of the bread. Stir to blend. Add the ¾ cup + 1 tbsp (7 oz./200 g) lukewarm water and let soak for 15 minutes.

Place all of the rye levain in the bowl of a stand mixer fitted with the dough hook. Add the soaked flakes and seeds, along with the soaking liquid, then add the scant ½ cup (3.5 oz./100 g) room-temperature water, rye flour, and salt. Knead for 3–5 minutes on speed 1 until all the ingredients are well blended—the dough will be dense and sticky.

Cover the bowl and let the dough rise for 1½ hours, without folding (bulk fermentation*).

Grease the loaf pan with oil and dust it with flour. Transfer the dough to the pan and press it down into the corners using your fingertips or the back of a spatula. Cover the top of the dough with the reserved seeds and dust with flour. Cover and let rest in the refrigerator for 12–16 hours for the final rise (proofing*).

The next day, when you are ready to bake the bread, preheat the oven to 500°F (260°C/Gas Mark 10). Place the loaf pan in the oven and immediately reduce the heat to 450°F (230°C/Gas Mark 8). When the dough passes the poke test*, bake for 1 hour, then turn the oven off and leave the bread in the oven, without opening the door, for an additional 15 minutes.

Let the bread cool for 5 minutes in the pan, then turn it out onto a rack and let cool completely.

When the bread has cooled completely, wrap in plastic wrap or reusable food wrap and leave it to "mature" for 24 hours before enjoying.

Focaccia ITALY

Makes 1 focaccia

Active time: 20 minutes
Autolyse: 20–30 minutes
Bulk fermentation: 3 hours
Proofing: 2 hours
Cooking: 30 minutes

Ingredients

Dough

2¾ cups (12.5 oz./350 g) pastry, all-purpose, or bread flour (T45–T65)

1¼ cups (10.5 oz./300 g) water

3.5 oz. (100 g) refreshed levain

0.2 oz. (5 g) fresh yeast

1½ tsp (0.25 oz./8 g) salt dissolved in 1 tbsp water

1 tbsp (0.5 oz./15 g) extra-virgin olive oil

Olive oil, for the pan (see Good to Know)

Garnishes

Halved cherry tomatoes, chopped fresh rosemary, quartered olives, etc.

Extra-virgin olive oil

Fleur de sel

Prepare the dough: Place the flour, water, and levain in the bowl of a stand mixer fitted with the dough hook. Crumble in the fresh yeast. Mix for 2 minutes on speed 1 to combine the ingredients, then cover the bowl and let rest for 20–30 minutes (autolyse*).

Knead the dough for 4–6 minutes on speed 2, then reduce the speed to 1 and add the salt/water mixture and the 1 tbsp (0.5 oz./15 g) extra-virgin olive oil with the mixer running. Return to speed 2 and continue to knead for 5–7 minutes, until the dough is soft and elastic, but still quite wet.

Cover the bowl and let the dough rise in a warm place for 3 hours. Fold the dough once every 30 minutes (bulk fermentation*).

Line a baking sheet with parchment paper and generously grease the paper and sides of the baking sheet with olive oil. Turn the dough out onto the baking sheet. Grease your hands with oil and press the dough to flatten it and spread it across the baking sheet, taking care not to tear it. If the dough is too springy, let it rest for 20 minutes, then continue.

Dimple the surface of the dough all over using your fingertips. Drizzle with extra-virgin olive oil and let rise for 2 hours (proofing*). After 1 hour, dimple the dough again as above.

Toward the end of the rising time, place a rack in the center of the oven and place another rack directly below it. Place an empty heavy-duty baking sheet, oven-safe skillet, or drip pan on the lower rack and preheat the oven to 450°F (230°C/Gas Mark 8). Bring 1 cup (250 ml) of water to a simmer.

Arrange the cherry tomatoes over the dough and sprinkle with rosemary. Add olives, if you wish, or any other toppings of choice.

Place the focaccia in the oven, then carefully pour the simmering water into the baking sheet, skillet, or drip pan to create steam and quickly close the oven door. Bake for 30 minutes, until golden.

Slide the focaccia out onto a rack, drizzle with extra-virgin olive oil, and sprinkle with *fleur de sel*. Serve warm.

GOOD TO KNOW

There's no need to use extra-virgin olive oil for greasing the pan. Instead, use a refined olive oil, typically labeled simply as "olive oil," which has a higher smoke point than extra-virgin. Save your finest extra-virgin olive oil for drizzling over the focaccia when it's fresh out of the oven.

You can skip the levain and make focaccia with yeast only. In this case, you'll need to use 0.35 oz. (10 g) of fresh yeast.

Techniques

Refreshing levain
Kneading by hand or with a mixer
Stages of fermentation

Bagels UNITED STATES

Makes 6–8 bagels

Active time: 30 minutes
Poolish: 2 hours
Bulk fermentation: 30 minutes
Chilling: 20 minutes
Proofing: 20–40 minutes + overnight
Poaching: 6–8 minutes
Cooking: 15 minutes

Ingredients

Poolish
Scant ¾ cup (6 oz./170 g) water
0.07 oz. (2 g) fresh yeast
1 cup + scant ½ cup (6 oz./170 g) bread flour

Dough
1 cup + 2½ tbsp (5.5 oz./155 g) bread flour
1 tbsp (0.5 oz./12 g) sugar
1 tsp (0.2 oz./5 g) salt

Poaching liquid
1 tbsp barley malt syrup, or a scant 2 tsp (12 g) honey
1 tsp (5 g) baking soda

Toppings
White or black sesame seeds, dried onion flakes, poppy seeds, fleur de sel, etc.

Equipment
Dutch oven or large saucepan

Techniques
Kneading by hand or with a mixer
Stages of fermentation
Shaping
Poaching

The day before baking, prepare the poolish: Place the water and yeast in a large bowl and stir or swish to dissolve. Add the flour and stir until well blended. Cover the bowl and let rise for about 2 hours, until doubled in volume (poolish*).

When the poolish is ready, prepare the dough: Place the flour, sugar, salt, and poolish in the bowl of a stand mixer fitted with the dough hook. Knead on speed 1 for 10 minutes, scraping down the sides of the bowl often using a bowl scraper. If you like, finish kneading the dough by hand. It will be quite firm, but should be supple. Cover the bowl and let the dough rest for 30 minutes (bulk fermentation*).

Divide the dough into six to eight pieces weighing about 2.25 oz. (65 g) each using a bench scraper. As you cut, place the pieces on a baking sheet and keep covered with plastic wrap or a towel to prevent them from drying out. Shape each piece into a ball, re-cover, and chill in the refrigerator for 20 minutes to firm up the dough.

Line a separate baking sheet with parchment paper, then remove the dough from the refrigerator. Working with one piece of dough at a time, poke a hole in the center of each ball with two fingers and rotate it like a wheel to enlarge the opening—the final hole should have a diameter of about 2 in. (5 cm).

Place the shaped bagels on the prepared baking sheet, leaving plenty of space between them, and keeping them covered as you work to prevent a crust from forming.

Let rise for 20–40 minutes. To confirm that the bagels have risen adequately, do the float test: place one bagel in a bowl of cold water—if it floats, it's ready. Cover the baking sheet and place in the refrigerator overnight (12 hours) (proofing*).

The next day, preheat the oven to 430°F (220°C/Gas Mark 7).

Prepare the poaching liquid: Fill a Dutch oven or large saucepan with about 4 in. (10 cm) of water, add the barley malt syrup and baking soda, and bring to a boil. Lower the heat to maintain the liquid at a simmer.

Carefully lower as many bagels as will fit comfortably in the pot into the simmering liquid. Cook them for 1 minute on the first side, flip them over, and cook for 30 seconds on the other side (poaching*). Using a slotted spoon, transfer the bagels to a rack to let them drain.

Line the baking sheet with a clean piece of parchment paper and place the bagels on it. Combine your toppings of choice in a bowl and sprinkle generously over the bagels. Bake for 15 minutes, until golden.

Let the bagels cool completely on a rack before slicing and filling.

Polarbrød SCANDINAVIA

Scandinavian Soft Flatbread

_____

Makes 5–6 _polarbrød_

Active time: 10 minutes
Bulk fermentation: 2 hours
Proofing: 30–40 minutes
Cooking: 5 minutes

Ingredients

2 cups (9 oz./250 g) bread flour (T65)
3½ tsp (0.4 oz./11 g) instant yeast
¾ tsp (0.1 oz./3 g) sugar
½ tsp (0.1 oz./3 g) salt
¼ cup (1.5 oz./40 g) crème fraîche
½ cup (4.25 oz./120 g) water

Combine the flour and yeast in a large mixing bowl. Stir in the sugar and salt, then make a well in the center and add the crème fraîche. Stirring, gradually pour in the water.

Knead the dough with your hands until smooth, then shape it into a ball. Place in a lightly oiled bowl, cover, and let rise at room temperature for 2 hours, until doubled in volume (bulk fermentation*).

Turn the dough out onto a floured work surface and roll it to a thickness of ¼ in. (5 mm). Cut out five or six circles using a bowl (choose the size according to how you plan to use the bread). Place circles on a baking sheet lined with parchment paper and pierce all over with a fork or dough docker. Cover and let rise for 30–40 minutes (proofing*).

Set an ungreased, heavy-bottomed skillet over medium heat. Place one round of dough at a time in the skillet, pierced side down, and pierce the second side. As soon as the bread is cooked underneath and pale golden in places, flip it over and cook for a few more seconds until pale golden on the second side. The bread should remain pale, so reduce the heat if it is browning too quickly. Repeat with the remaining dough.

Stack the finished breads under a towel to keep them warm.

Techniques
Kneading by hand
Stages of fermentation
Shaping

Harcha MOROCCO

Mini Semolina Flatbreads

————

Makes about 20 *harcha*

Active time: 25 minutes
Blooming yeast: 10 minutes
Proofing: 30 minutes
Cooking: 4 minutes per batch

Ingredients

1⅓ cups (11.25 oz./320 g) lukewarm water

3½ tsp (0.4 oz./11 g) active dry yeast

2 cups (9 oz./250 g) all-purpose or bread flour (T55–T65)

1½ cups (9 oz./250 g) semolina flour + 2 tbsp for rolling out the dough + more for sprinkling

1 tsp (0.2 oz./5 g) salt

Equipment

2-in. (5-cm) round cookie cutter

Combine the lukewarm water and yeast in a bowl and set aside for 10 minutes, until foamy.

Pour the yeast mixture into the bowl of a stand mixer fitted with the dough hook, then add the flours and salt. Knead for 5 minutes on speed 2, until smooth and elastic.

Scatter the 2 tbsp semolina flour over your work surface. Turn the dough out onto the semolina, then flour your hands and use to flatten the dough to a thickness of ½ in. (1 cm).

Using the cookie cutter, cut out about twenty disks of dough. Place on a baking sheet lined with parchment paper, sprinkle with a little more semolina flour, and let rise in a warm place for 30 minutes, until visibly risen (proofing*).

Set an ungreased, heavy-bottomed skillet over medium heat. Cook the breads for about 2 minutes on each side, until cooked and lightly golden.

Transfer the finished breads to a rack, or stack them under a towel.

Serve warm or at room temperature.

Techniques
Kneading by hand or with a mixer
Stages of fermentation

Tortillas MEXICO

___

Makes 5–6 tortillas

Active time: 10 minutes

Resting: 1 hour

Cooking: 6 minutes per tortilla

Ingredients

¾ cup + 2 tbsp (3.5 oz./100 g) *masa harina* (nixtamalized corn flour)

1 pinch salt

¾ cup (6.25 oz./180 g) water

Equipment (optional)

Tortilla press

Combine the *masa harina* and salt in a mixing bowl. Make a well in the center and gradually pour in the water, mixing with your fingertips until the dough is pliable and no longer sticky (add a little more *masa harina* or water if the dough seems too wet or dry).

Shape the dough into a ball, cover, and let rest at room temperature for 1 hour (resting*).

Transfer the dough to a floured work surface and divide it into five to six equal pieces. Shape each into a round about the size of a golf ball. Working with one piece of dough at a time, place between two sheets of medium-to-heavy plastic (such as a freezer bag cut open along the sides).

Place in the tortilla press, if you have one, and press to form a thin tortilla. Alternatively, flatten the dough using a heavy Dutch oven or skillet.

Set an ungreased, heavy-bottomed skillet over medium to medium-high heat. Cook one tortilla at a time for 2–3 minutes on the first side, until it is charred in places and the edges begin to curl up. Flip it over and cook for 2–3 minutes on the second side.

Stack the finished tortillas under a towel to keep them warm and soft until serving.

Techniques

Kneading by hand

Shaping

Obi non CENTRAL ASIA

Central Asian Flatbread

————

Makes 4 obi non

Active time: 20 minutes
Blooming yeast: 20–30 minutes
Bulk fermentation: 2 hours
Proofing: 1 hour
Cooking: 8–10 minutes

Ingredients

3½ tbsp (1¾ oz./50 g) water
0.5 oz. (15 g) fresh yeast
1¼ tsp (0.2 oz./5 g) sugar
Scant 1½ tsp (0.25 oz./7 g) salt
Scant 1 cup (7.75 oz./220 g) lukewarm water
1 cup + 2 tbsp (5 oz./150 g) bread flour (T65)
1⅓ cups (7 oz./200 g) pastry flour (T45)
1 egg yolk, lightly beaten
3 tbsp (1 oz./30 g) sesame and/or nigella seeds

Place the 3½ tbsp (1¾ oz./50 g) water in a bowl and stir in the yeast and sugar to dissolve. Let sit at room temperature for 20–30 minutes.

Place the salt, lukewarm water, bread flour, pastry flour, and yeast mixture in the bowl of a stand mixer fitted with the dough hook. Knead for 10 minutes on speed 1 until smooth and elastic.

Shape the dough into a ball, return it to the bowl, and cover. Let the dough rise in a warm place for 2 hours until doubled in volume. Fold the dough once every 30 minutes (bulk fermentation*).

Divide the dough into four equal pieces. Shape each piece into a ball and flatten it with the palm of your hand to form disks with a diameter of about 5 in. (12 cm). Place on a baking sheet lined with parchment paper.

Using a *chekich* (bread stamp), cookie cutter, or fork, make patterns or indentations in the center of each disk. Cover and let rise for 1 hour (proofing*).

Toward the end of the rising time, preheat the oven to 480°F (250°C/ Gas Mark 9).

When the dough passes the poke test*, brush it with the egg yolk and sprinkle with seeds. Bake for 8–10 minutes, until golden.

Let cool on a rack.

Techniques
Kneading by hand or with a mixer
Stages of fermentation
Shaping
Decorative finishes

Ablos WEST AFRICA

West African Steamed Bread

Makes 8–10 *ablos*
(also known as *abolos*)

Active time: 15 minutes
Bulk fermentation: 4 hours
Cooking: 12–15 minutes

Ingredients

Scant ½ cup (2 oz./60 g) cornmeal
2 cups (1 lb. 2 oz./500 g) water
Scant 1½ cups (7 oz./200 g) rice flour
⅔ cup (3.5 oz./100 g) cornstarch
3½ tsp (0.4 oz./11 g) active dry yeast
2 tbsp lukewarm water
¼ cup (1.75 oz./50 g) sugar
1 tsp (0.2 oz./5 g) salt
Neutral oil, for the pan(s)

Equipment

Steamer pot, steamer basket,
or *couscoussier*
6–8 individual muffin-size baking pans,
or a 6–8 cup muffin pan that fits in your
steamer

Combine the cornmeal and water in a saucepan. Cook over medium heat, stirring often, until the mixture boils and thickens. Transfer to a large mixing bowl and let cool completely.

When the cornmeal is completely cool, gradually stir in the rice flour and cornstarch until smooth.

Dissolve the yeast in the 2 tbsp lukewarm water. Stir into the dough mixture, then stir in the sugar and salt until well combined—the mixture should have the consistency of a thick batter.

Cover the bowl and let the mixture rise in a warm place (77°F–80°F/25°C–27°C) for about 4 hours, until small bubbles form on the surface (bulk fermentation*).

To cook the *ablos*, put water in the steamer and bring to a boil. Grease the baking pans with oil, then fill them three-quarters full with the *ablo* mixture.

Steam for 12–15 minutes, until the *ablos* are firm and a knife inserted into the center comes out clean.

Turn out of the pans and serve warm with a dish that has plenty of sauce for sopping up.

Techniques
Stages of fermentation
Baking with steam

Dada Zahra

—

"I grew up in a family that didn't buy bread at the souk; my mother considered it shameful to eat anything other than our traditional bread. I started cooking when I was seven years old. I lived in the countryside around Agadir [in Morocco], where women's work includes a variety of tasks besides cooking, like caring for livestock and chopping wood. Women make bread every day according to their families' needs. This inheritance was passed down from my grandmother to my mother, who taught me. It's difficult work. I had to get up very early in the morning to fetch wood in the forest with my donkey. Then I had to preheat the oven at least three hours before baking the bread. When I had mastered this task, I became a perfect housewife, and was able to marry when I was thirteen.

"What I particularly love about this bread is the flavor, which is truly unique. I also like the way it is cooked using the natural materials of wood, stone, and clay. It reminds me of the carefree life I led in my little village, which I remember fondly. I forget all my troubles when I'm making this bread, and I feel independent and strong. It's also a cornerstone of my culture. By preparing it, I directly participate in preserving my family's heritage, which deserves to be passed down to future generations. I am very proud to prepare this bread for tourists staying at the hotel. All my work and weariness count for something if they appreciate it. That makes me very happy and is my motivation to continue making it."

Two French women, Hélène Larochette and her daughter Suzy, opened La Maison Arabe in Marrakech, Morocco, in 1946. Their restaurant quickly became an institution, bringing delight to locals and visiting celebrities alike, before the Italian Fabrizio Ruspoli turned it into a lovely guesthouse in the 1990s. At the time, there was no chef in the kitchen. Meals were prepared by dadas, women hailing mostly from sub-Saharan Africa and descendants of the sultans' slaves. They are the guardians of a culinary tradition infused with a variety of influences and passed down from mother to daughter through skillful gestures and observation. A chef now delights guests at the Maison Arabe, but still under the watchful eye of the *dadas*, like Zahra, who is in charge of making the bread.

www.lamaisonarabe.com

Tafarnout MOROCCO

Moroccan Flatbread
Recipe by Dada Zahra

Makes 2–3 *tafarnout*

Active time: 15 minutes
Bulk fermentation: 1 hour
Proofing: 30 minutes
Cooking: 15 minutes

Ingredients

1½ cups (9 oz./250 g) superfine semolina flour + more for dusting

4 cups + 2 tbsp (1 lb. 2 oz./500 g) bread or white whole wheat flour (T65–T80)

1 tsp (0.2 oz./5 g) salt

1 tsp instant yeast

2 cups (1 lb. 2 oz./500 g) water

For serving

Extra-virgin olive oil, honey, or a tagine of your choice

Equipment

Wood-fired oven or grill with a lid (optional)

1 generous handful of small stones; if you are using a grill, they should be large enough not to fall through the grates (optional)

Bread peel

Combine the semolina and bread flour in a large, shallow bowl (or a *gasaâ*). Make a well in the center and add the salt and yeast. Pour in half of the water and mix with your hands until combined. Add the remaining water a little at a time until a dough forms. Knead in the bowl until the dough is smooth, elastic, and no longer sticky. Cover with a towel and let rise for 1 hour in a draft-free place, until doubled in volume (bulk fermentation*).

Meanwhile, if you have a wood-fired oven, preheat it. Alternatively, preheat a grill that has a lid to high heat, or preheat a conventional oven to the maximum temperature.

Scatter the stones across the floor of the wood-fired oven or the grates of the grill, or place them on a rimmed baking sheet in the conventional oven. Let the stones heat up.

When the dough has risen, dust your work surface with superfine semolina flour. Wet your hands with water or grease them with vegetable oil and divide the dough into 2–3 pieces, each about the size of a large fist. Place on the work surface and, using the palm of your hand, flatten the dough into circles with a diameter of about 8 in. (20 cm) and about ¼ in. (5 mm) thick. Transfer to a baking sheet dusted with semolina flour and dust the tops of the breads with semolina flour, too. Let rise for 30 minutes (proofing*).

When the dough passes the poke test*, transfer the rounds one at a time to the peel, either floured or wet with water, then invert onto the hot stones. If you are using a conventional oven, set the heat to 500°F (260°C/Gas Mark 10).

Bake for 15 minutes, until the bread is golden, crisp, and charred in places. Remove the bread from the oven or grill and carefully remove any stones that have stuck to it. Work in batches if necessary.

 GOOD TO KNOW
This bread can be served hot with extra-virgin olive oil, honey, or a tagine of your choice.

Techniques
Kneading by hand or with a mixer
Stages of fermentation

Apollonia Poilâne
—

"When my grandfather, Pierre Poilâne, opened his bakery in Paris after traveling around France, he eschewed popular practices of the time and developed an entire philosophy around bread based on his reflections about the bread we eat.

"Bread should delight the body and the mind, for a well-nourished body sets the mind free. Bread is a basic food, but not a simple food—it is essential. Bread is a crossroads, where grains and fermentation intersect, and time is a key factor.

"I'm proud to have had the grandfather and father that I had, and it was always clear that I would take over from my father. I realize this now, looking back. Their ability to think critically is one of the key ingredients they have passed on to me—it is my *levain de vie*. This pride has also shaped my perspective on my craft, which consists of transforming grain into handcrafted bread, cookies, and pastries. Each product has its own distinctive feature and flavor.

"At Poilâne, we demonstrate everything that can be done with a piece of bread, the most basic being to spread it with butter—like this recipe, which is both a snub and a nod to my father, who liked to say, 'bread alone is enough.' The raw butter we use—called Beurre de Madame—has its own story to tell. Olivier Roellinger called me one day to ask for my help in saving a traditional breed of Breton cow, the Froment [meaning 'wheat'] du Léon, which gets its name from its wheat-colored coat. [It used to be called '*vache de Madame*,' or 'Madame's cow,' and the name lives on in the butter.] Its butter is fine and rich in beta-carotene—perfect on a slice of *pain au levain*."

Apollonia Poilâne is the third-generation owner of her family's bakery. Her grandfather, Pierre, set up shop in 1932 at 8 Rue du Cherche-Midi in the heart of the Saint-Germain-des-Prés neighborhood in Paris, where he made bread as he imagined it: generous loaves, using stone-ground flour, natural levain fermentation, and a wood-fired oven. Pierre's son Lionel was also drawn to bread and took over his father's bakery in the early 1970s. He grew the company considerably while preserving the traditional bread-making method.

When Pierre and his wife tragically died in 2002, his daughter Apollonia took the reins. She embraces the philosophy of her father and grandfather: favor quality over quantity. Poilâne bread is always handmade using levain and still baked in a wood-fired oven. Apollonia has also opened new bakery locations and developed new breads, along with a collection of *sablés* (shortbread biscuits) made with rye, buckwheat, oat, corn, and other flours.

www.poilane.com

Sandwich au pain Rustic French Bread Sandwich

Recipe by Apollonia Poilâne

———

Makes 1 sandwich

Active time: 10 minutes

Cooking: 3 minutes

Ingredients

1 large, thin slice sourdough *miche*, preferably pain Poilâne (see La Bonne Idée)

2 thin slices sourdough rye sandwich bread with raisins, preferably Poilâne

2 tsp–1 tbsp (10–20 g) salted artisan butter, preferably raw, at room temperature (see La Bonne Idée)

Cut the slice of sourdough *miche* in half crosswise. Lightly toast each half on one side only, so that one side is lightly crisp and the other remains tender.

Spread the toasted side of both pieces with the butter.

Working quickly, top the buttered sides of the bread with the two slices of rye bread (trim the rye bread if necessary).

Cover with the second piece of sourdough bread, toasted- and buttered-side down.

Press down gently to allow the flavors of the butter to seep into the bread and to let the residual heat from the toasting process diffuse throughout the sandwich.

Serve the sandwich while it is still slightly warm.

LA BONNE IDÉE

The Pain Poilâne *miche* has a diameter of about 12 in. (30 cm), so the slices are quite big. If your bread is smaller, you may need to use two slices.

We like to use Beurre de Madame, an artisanal raw milk butter from Froment du Léon cows in Brittany (see p. 349).

If you like, replace the butter on one or both of the sourdough bread halves with fork-mashed avocado, cheese, or a vegetable puree.

Croque Monsieur

Makes 4 sandwiches

Active time: 30 minutes

Cooking: 10 minutes

Ingredients

Béchamel

2 tbsp. (30 g) butter

3 tbsp (1 oz./30 g) flour

1¼ cups (300 ml) whole milk

Salt and freshly ground pepper

Ground nutmeg

Assembly

8 slices *pain de mie* (see recipe p. 222)

5.25 oz. (150 g) Comté or Emmental cheese, freshly grated

2 relatively thick slices ham, halved

Prepare the béchamel: Melt the butter in a saucepan over low heat. Add the flour and cook for a few minutes, stirring nonstop, without letting the mixture brown. Gradually pour in the milk, whisking constantly to avoid lumps. Cook, stirring nonstop, until the béchamel begins to bubble and thicken. When it is thick and creamy, remove it from the heat and season with salt, pepper, and nutmeg to taste. Pour into a bowl, press plastic wrap over the surface, and let cool completely before using.

Assemble and bake the croque monsieurs: Preheat the oven to 350°F (180°C/Gas Mark 4) and line a baking sheet with parchment paper.

Divide two-thirds of the béchamel between the eight slices of *pain de mie* and spread into an even layer. Sprinkle with grated cheese, saving some for the tops of the sandwiches. Place four of the slices on the prepared baking sheet, béchamel-side up. Cover each slice on the baking sheet with a half-slice of ham. Top with the remaining *pain de mie*, béchamel-side down. Press down firmly with the palm of your hand.

Cover the croque monsieurs with the remaining béchamel and grated cheese. Bake for about 10 minutes, until golden.

Serve hot or warm with green salad on the side.

San Francisco Clam Chowder

Serves 4

Active time: 30 minutes
Soaking: 1 hour
Cooking: 33–35 minutes

Ingredients

2¼ lb. (1 kg) fresh clams and/or cockles
2 cups (500 ml) fish stock
1 cup (250 ml) white wine
1 onion
2 medium potatoes
(such as Yukon gold or red-skinned)
2 small carrots
1 stalk celery
3 tbsp. (50 g) butter
4 × 6–8-in. (15–20-cm) round boules
of *tourte de meule* (see recipe p. 206)
2½ tbsp (1 oz./25 g) all-purpose flour
2 cups (500 ml) whole milk
¾ cup (200 ml) heavy cream
6 slices bacon
Apple cider vinegar
Salt and freshly ground pepper

Let the clams soak in a bowl of salted water for 1 hour, swishing them around often. Rinse well.

Combine the fish stock and white wine in a stockpot and bring to a boil over high heat. Add the clams and cook for 3–5 minutes, until opened.

Remove the clams with a skimmer and remove and discard the shells when they are cool enough to handle. Discard any unopened clams. Chop the clams into small pieces and set aside.

Strain the clam broth into a bowl through a fine-mesh sieve lined with cheesecloth.

Peel and rinse the onion, potatoes, carrots, and celery and cut them into small dice.

Melt half of the butter in a deep skillet or sauté pan over medium heat and add the vegetables. Sauté for 5 minutes, until softened. Add the strained clam broth and cook over low heat for 20 minutes, until the potatoes are tender.

While the vegetables cook, prepare the bread bowls. Cut off the tops of the boules and scoop out the insides, taking care not to break through the crust (save the insides for another recipe—see La Bonne Idée).

In a large, heavy-bottomed saucepan, melt the remaining butter over low heat. Add the flour and cook for a few minutes, stirring nonstop, without letting the mixture brown. Gradually pour in the milk and cream, whisking constantly to avoid lumps. Cook, stirring nonstop, until the sauce begins to bubble and thicken. When it is thick and creamy, stir in the vegetables and broth. Season with salt and pepper to taste and keep warm.

Cut the bacon into thin strips and cook in a skillet until golden and crisp. Stir into the chowder.

Right before serving, stir the clams into the chowder. Add a drizzle of vinegar. If necessary, gently reheat the chowder, without letting it boil.

Pour the chowder into the bread bowls and serve right away.

LA BONNE IDÉE
You can use the bread you've scooped out to make pudding (see recipe p. 433) or meatloaf (see recipe p. 408).

Pain surprise

Surprise Bread

Makes 1 surprise bread

Active time: 30 minutes
Bulk fermentation: 1½ hours
Proofing: 1–1½ hours
Cooking: 30–40 minutes

Ingredients

Bread

Scant ½ cup (3.5 oz./100 g) water

0.35 oz. (10 g) fresh yeast

5⅔ cups (1 lb. 8 oz./700 g) bread flour (T65)

5 tsp (0.75 oz./20 g) sugar

2¾ tsp (0.5 oz./14 g) salt

1⅔ cups (14 oz./400 g) whole milk

1.75 oz. (50 g) refreshed levain

Scant 1 tbsp (0.5 oz./14 g) butter, at room temperature + 1 tbsp (0.5 oz./15 g) for the pan

Fillings

Your finger sandwich fillings of choice (see La Bonne Idée)

Equipment

1 deep 6-in. (16-cm) round cake pan with a removable bottom

Techniques

Refreshing levain
Kneading by hand or with a mixer
Stages of fermentation
Folding

Prepare the bread: Place the water and yeast in the bowl of a stand mixer fitted with the paddle attachment and stir or swish to dissolve the yeast. Add the flour, sugar, salt, milk, and levain. Knead for 5 minutes on speed 1, followed by 3–4 minutes on speed 2, until the dough is smooth and elastic and pulls away from the sides of the bowl. With the mixer running on speed 1, incorporate the scant 1 tbsp (0.5 oz./14 g) butter.

Cover the bowl and let rise in a warm place for 1½ hours. Fold the dough once or twice during the rise time (bulk fermentation*).

Turn the dough out onto a floured work surface and shape it into a ball.

Thoroughly grease the cake pan with the 1 tbsp (0.5 oz./15 g) butter and place the dough in the pan, seam side down. Let rise in a warm place for 1–1½ hours (proofing*). Toward the end of the rising time, preheat the oven to 400°F (200°C/Gas Mark 6).

When the dough passes the poke test*, bake the bread for 30–40 minutes. Turn the bread out of the pan and let cool completely on a rack before cutting.

Assemble the surprise bread: To cut out the center of the bread, stand it up on its base and insert a knife, blade parallel to your work surface, into the side, ½ in. (1 cm) up from the base. Carefully work the knife around the loaf until you have made a clean cut halfway round. Repeat from the other side of the bread until you've cut completely through. Reserve the slice you cut off for another use, and flip the bread over so the cut side is uppermost.

Insert your knife vertically into the crumb, ½ in. (1 cm) in from the crust. Cut around the inside of the crust, leaving a ½-in. (1-cm) border all the way around. Carefully remove the bread core and cut it crosswise into rounds with a thickness of standard sandwich bread.

Top half of the rounds with your fillings of choice and cover with the remaining rounds. Cut each sandwich into 8 equal pieces and arrange inside the hollowed-out bread. Keep in the refrigerator until serving.

LA BONNE IDÉE

The filling possibilities are infinite, so feel free to play around. Here are some favorites.

Savory fillings: smoked salmon/cream cheese, goat cheese/cucumber, artichoke spread/cured ham, tapenade/crushed hazelnuts, mayonnaise/grated hard-boiled egg, etc.

Sweet fillings: raspberry jam, lemon curd, *gianduja* (chocolate-hazelnut paste), etc.

Pain hérisson au fromage fondant

Hedgehog Bread with Melted Cheese

———

Makes 1 hedgehog bread

Active time: 10 minutes
Cooking: 15–20 minutes

Ingredients

1 large round loaf of bread (such as *tourte de meule*—see recipe p. 206)

7 oz. (200 g) good melting cheese (raclette, Comté, Maroilles, etc.)

1 bunch fresh chives

1–2 tbsp (20–30 g) butter, melted

Preheat the oven to 400°F (200°C/Gas Mark 6) and line a baking sheet with parchment paper.

Cut a crisscross pattern into the top of the bread—cut deeply, but not all the way to the base.

Cut the cheese lengthwise into slices and tuck into the cuts on the bread, distributing cheese evenly throughout. Roughly chop several chives and sprinkle between the squares.

Brush the top and sides of the bread with the melted butter and bake for 15–20 minutes, until the cheese is melted.

Sprinkle with a few more roughly chopped chives and serve hot.

Sandwich club

Club Sandwich

_____

Makes 4 sandwiches

Active time: 15 minutes
Cooking: 10 minutes

Ingredients

Yogurt sauce

1 bunch fresh chives
Juice of 1 lemon
1 cup (9 oz./250 g) plain yogurt
Salt and freshly ground pepper

Sandwiches

8 leaves lettuce
1 medium carrot
1 stalk celery
4 hard-boiled eggs
Vegetable oil
16 slices bacon
12 large slices *pain de mie*
(see recipe p. 222)

Prepare the yogurt sauce: Wash and dry the chives and chop them finely. Place in a bowl with the lemon juice and yogurt and stir to blend. Season with salt and pepper, then chill in the refrigerator while you prepare the other components.

Prepare the sandwiches: Thoroughly wash and dry the lettuce and shred it. Peel, rinse, and julienne the carrot and celery. Set aside.

Peel the hard-boiled eggs and slice them crosswise into rounds.

Drizzle a little vegetable oil into a skillet and place over medium heat. Add the bacon and cook it until crisp. Place on a paper towel-lined plate lined to drain.

Stir together the yogurt sauce, carrot, and celery in a bowl until well combined.

Toast the bread.

Assemble the sandwiches: You'll need three slices of *pain de mie* per sandwich. For each sandwich, scatter lettuce over the first slice and arrange hard-boiled egg rounds over the lettuce. Cover with a second slice of bread. Top with four slices of bacon and a layer of yogurt sauce. Finish with a third slice of bread.

Cut each sandwich diagonally into quarters and secure with cocktail sticks. Serve right away.

Welsh Rarebit

Makes 2 sandwiches

Active time: 15 minutes

Cooking: 8 minutes

Ingredients

10.5 oz. (300 g) farmhouse Cheddar, at room temperature (remove from fridge 2–3 hours ahead of time)

2 thick slices day-old bread of your choice

⅔ cup (150 ml) pale ale or craft beer

½ tsp Dijon or grain mustard (or more to taste)

2 eggs (optional)

Salt and freshly ground pepper

Cut or grate the Cheddar into small pieces.

Toast the bread and place each slice in an oven-safe serving dish.

Preheat the broiler.

Pour a little beer into a heavy-bottomed saucepan and warm over low heat. Add the cheese and cook, stirring with a wooden spoon, until melted. Stir in the mustard. Still stirring, gradually pour in as much of the remaining beer as you need to obtain a thick, smooth sauce that coats the back of the spoon. Season to taste with salt and pepper and remove from the heat.

Immediately pour the sauce over the toasted bread and place under the broiler until bubbly and golden, watching closely to avoid burning.

If you'll be serving the rarebit with eggs, fry them to your liking.

Serve right away (topped with the optional fried eggs).

LA BONNE IDÉE

If you'd like to make your Welsh rarebit with ham, top the toast with a slice of ham before pouring the Cheddar sauce over it.

You can also drizzle a little Worcestershire sauce over the melted cheese while the rarebit is still hot.

For a complete meal, serve Welsh rarebit with fries and a green salad on the side.

Fondue savoyarde

Traditional Savoyard Fondue

———

Serves 4

Active time: 15 minutes
Cooking: 10 minutes

Ingredients

2 stale baguettes (see recipe p. 219)
7 oz. (200 g) Appenzeller
7 oz. (200 g) Beaufort
7 oz. (200 g) Swiss Gruyère
7 oz. (200 g) Comté
2 cloves garlic, peeled and halved
Scant ½ cup (100 ml) dry white wine
1 tsp baking soda
1 whole nutmeg

Equipment

Fondue pot and fondue forks

Remove the rinds from the cheeses; discard. Grate or cut cheese into small pieces.

Rub the inside of the fondue pot with the garlic and discard. Pour in the wine and warm over moderate heat.

Stir in the cheese, baking soda, and nutmeg using a wooden spoon. Cook, stirring, just until the cheese has melted and the fondue is creamy and smooth.

Cut the bread into bite-sized cubes. Serve right away with the bread on the side for dipping.

Pan bagnat
Provençal Picnic Sandwich

Makes 2 sandwiches

Active time: 30 minutes
Bulk fermentation: 1–2 hours
Proofing: 30 minutes
Cooking: 15 minutes
Chilling: 1 hour

Ingredients
Bread
⅔ cup (5.25 oz./150 g) water
1 tsp salt
2 tbsp sugar
2 cups (9 oz./250 g) all-purpose flour
0.35 oz. (10 g) fresh yeast
1 tbsp + 1 tsp (0.75 oz./20 g) butter, at room temperature, or 1½ tbsp (0.75 oz./20 g) extra-virgin olive oil

Assembly
1–2 fresh tomatoes
1 bunch scallions and/or radishes
1 green pepper (optional)
2 hard-boiled eggs
1 clove garlic, peeled and halved
¾ cup + 1 tbsp (200 ml) extra-virgin olive oil
Scant ½ cup (100 ml) balsamic vinegar
Cooked baby fava beans and/or artichoke hearts
Tuna or anchovies packed in oil, drained
Black olives, pitted
A few small leaves fresh basil
Salt and freshly ground pepper

Prepare the bread: Place the water, salt, sugar, and flour in the bowl of a stand mixer fitted with the dough hook. Crumble in the fresh yeast. Knead for 3 minutes on speed 1, followed by 4–6 minutes on speed 2. Halfway through the 4–6 minutes, add the butter or olive oil with the mixer running.

Shape the dough into a ball and place it in a lightly oiled or flour-dusted bowl. Cover the bowl and let the dough rise for 1–2 hours, until doubled in volume. Fold the dough twice during the rise time: once after 30 minutes, and once after 1 hour (bulk fermentation*).

Turn the dough out onto a floured work surface. Gently fold it and divide it into two equal pieces.

Using the palm of your hand or a rolling pin, gently flatten each piece of dough into a round with a thickness of 1¼–1½ in. (3–4 cm).

Place on a baking sheet lined with parchment paper, cover, and let rise for 30 minutes (proofing*).

Meanwhile, preheat the oven to 400°F (200°C/Gas Mark 6).

When the dough passes the poke test*, bake the bread for 15 minutes—it should remain pale, so do not let it brown.

Let the bread cool completely on a rack.

Assemble the *pan bagnat*: To prepare the fillings, wash and thinly slice the tomatoes, scallions and/or radishes, and green peppers, if using. Peel and thinly slice the hard-boiled eggs.

Cut each round of bread in half crosswise. Remove a little of the crumb to make room for the filling and rub the insides with the garlic clove. Generously drizzle with the olive oil, then drizzle with balsamic vinegar to taste. Season with salt and pepper and pile your fillings of choice over the bottom halves of bread.

Cover with the top halves, wrap tightly in aluminum foil or plastic wrap, and chill in the refrigerator for 1 hour to allow the flavors to meld before serving.

Techniques
Stages of fermentation
Folding

Lobster Rolls

Makes 6 rolls

Active time: 45 minutes
Blooming yeast: 10 minutes
Bulk fermentation: 1½ hours
Proofing: 1 hour
Cooking: 15 minutes

Ingredients

Buns

1 cup (9 oz./250 g) lukewarm whole milk + more for glazing

0.43 oz. (12 g) fresh yeast

3¼ cups (14 oz./400 g) flour

1 egg

5 tsp (0.75 oz./20 g) sugar

1½ tsp (0.25 oz./8 g) salt

3 tbsp (1.5 oz./40 g) butter, at room temperature + more for the pan

Lobster salad

1 lb. (450 g) cooked lobster meat, cut into big pieces

3 tbsp mayonnaise

1 stalk celery

1 tbsp finely chopped fresh chives

1 tsp finely chopped fresh tarragon

1 tsp lemon juice

1 pinch cayenne pepper

Salt and freshly ground pepper

Assembly

Generous 1 tbsp (20 g) butter, at room temperature

Mayonnaise

A few leaves lettuce

Finely chopped fresh chives and a few tarragon leaves, for garnish

Prepare the buns: Pour the milk into a bowl and crumble in the fresh yeast. Stir to dissolve and let sit for 10 minutes.

Place the flour, egg, sugar, and salt in the bowl of a stand mixer fitted with the dough hook. Mix for 3 minutes on speed 1, until well blended. Add the milk-yeast mixture and knead for 3 minutes on speed 2. Add the butter and knead for 5 minutes on speed 3. Cover the bowl and let the dough rise for 1½ hours. Fold the dough once after 1 hour (bulk fermentation*).

Turn the dough out onto a floured work surface. Divide it into six equal pieces weighing about 4.25 oz. (120 g) each. Shape each piece into an elongated roll and place in an 8 × 10-in. (20 × 25-cm) rectangular pan lightly greased with butter. Leaving a little space between the rolls—they should have enough room to expand, but should be close enough to fuse together during baking. Let rise for 1 hour (proofing*).

Toward the end of the rising time, place a rack at the lowest oven position and place another rack directly above it. Place an empty heavy-duty baking sheet, oven-safe skillet, or drip pan on the lower rack and preheat the oven to 350°F (180°C/Gas Mark 4). Bring 1 cup (250 ml) of water to a simmer.

When the dough passes the poke test*, brush the buns with a little milk. Place in the oven, then carefully pour the simmering water into the baking sheet, skillet, or drip pan to create steam and quickly close the oven door. Bake for 15 minutes, until golden.

Let the buns cool completely on a rack.

While the buns cool, prepare the lobster salad: Finely chop the celery. Stir together the lobster meat, mayonnaise, celery, chives, tarragon, lemon juice, and cayenne pepper in a bowl until well blended. Season with salt and pepper, then cover and chill in the refrigerator until assembly.

Assemble the rolls: Separate the buns and spread the flat sides with butter. Toast until golden on both sides in a nonstick skillet over medium heat.

Cut the buns down the middle, without cutting all the way through. Spread the insides with a thin layer of mayonnaise and line with a piece of lettuce. Fill with lobster salad and garnish with finely chopped chives and tarragon leaves.

Serve right away.

Techniques
Kneading by hand or with a mixer
Stages of fermentation
Folding
Shaping

Pan con tomate

Spanish Tapas

——————

Makes 12 tapas

Active time: 10 minutes

Ingredients

2 ripe, juicy tomatoes

About 12 small slices day-old bread (such as baguette—see recipe p. 219)

2 cloves garlic, peeled and halved

Extra-virgin olive oil

Fleur de sel

Freshly ground pepper

Wash and dry the tomatoes and cut them in half crosswise. Lightly toast the slices of bread.

Rub the bread with the cut side of the garlic, then rub it with the tomato halves, cut-side down. Press down firmly to help release the juices and some of the pulp.

Drizzle generously with olive oil, sprinkle with *fleur de sel*, and add a few grinds of fresh pepper.

Serve right away.

Egg Boats

Serves 4

Active time: 10 minutes
Cooking: 10–15 minutes

Ingredients

4 bread rolls—such as small baguettes (see recipe p. 219) or *banh mi* baguettes (see recipe p. 375)

4 eggs

2.75 oz. (80 g) grated cheese (Emmental, Comté, Cheddar, etc.)

4 tbsp (1.75 oz./50 g) crème fraîche

8 cherry tomatoes, halved or quartered

A few small leaves basil

Salt and freshly ground pepper

Preheat the oven to 350°F (180°C/Gas Mark 4) and line a baking sheet with parchment paper.

Cut a hole into the top of each roll and scoop out some of the crumb to make a "boat" for the eggs. Carefully crack the eggs directly into the holes (one egg per roll). Top each egg with 1 tbsp crème fraîche, 2 halved or quartered cherry tomatoes, and 1 basil leaf. Season with salt and pepper and sprinkle generously with grated cheese.

Bake for 10–15 minutes, until the egg is cooked to your liking.

Garnish with a little more fresh basil and serve right away.

Banh mi

Vietnamese-Style Baguette

Serves 4

Active time: 1 hour
Autolyse: 30 minutes
Bulk fermentation: 1½ hours
Resting: 30 minutes
Proofing: 1 hour
Cooking: 20 minutes

Ingredients

Banh mi baguettes

2¾ cups (12.5 oz./350 g) bread flour (T65)
¾ cup + 1 tbsp (7 oz./200 g) water
0.35 oz. (10 g) fresh yeast
2½ tsp (0.35 oz./10 g) sugar
1 tsp (0.25 oz./6 g) salt
3 tbsp (1.75 oz./50 g) butter, at room temperature

Filling

⅓ cup (2.5 oz./75 g) white vinegar
Generous ⅓ cup (2.5 oz./75 g) sugar
1 carrot, peeled and julienned
1 cucumber
4 scallions
1 small red chili pepper
1 bunch fresh cilantro
1 oz. (30 g) liver pâté, or 2 tbsp (1 oz./30 g) mayonnaise
1 cooked chicken breast, shredded
3 tbsp fried onions or shallots

Equipment

Paline (baguette transfer peel)

Techniques

Kneading by hand or with a mixer
Stages of fermentation
Folding
Shaping
Scoring
Using a baking stone

Prepare the *banh mi* baguettes: Place the flour and water in the bowl of a stand mixer fitted with the dough hook. Crumble in the fresh yeast. Mix for 3 minutes on speed 1, until well blended. Cover the bowl and let rest for 30 minutes (autolyse*). Add the sugar and salt and knead on speed 2 for 4–6 minutes. Add the butter halfway through with the mixer running.

Shape the dough into a ball and place it in a lightly oiled or flour-dusted bowl. Cover and let the dough rise for 1½ hours, until doubled in volume. Fold the dough once every 30 minutes (bulk fermentation*). Turn out onto a floured work surface and divide it into four equal pieces using a bench scraper. Quickly shape each piece into a rough oval, cover with a towel, and let rest at room temperature for 30 minutes (resting*).

Shape each piece of dough into a small baguette and place on an inverted baking sheet lined with parchment paper. Cover the dough with a towel and let rise at room temperature for 1 hour (proofing*). Toward the end of the rising time, place a rack at the lowest oven position and place another rack directly above it. Place an empty heavy-duty baking sheet, oven-safe skillet, or drip pan on the lower rack, and a baking stone or heavy-duty baking sheet on the upper rack, and preheat the oven to 475°F (245°C/ Gas Mark 9). Bring 1 cup (250 ml) of water to a simmer.

At the end of the proofing time, place the baking sheet with the baguettes on it in the refrigerator for 10 minutes to firm up the dough.

When the dough passes the poke test*, using a lame, quickly score each baguette down the center lengthwise. Roll the baguettes onto the *paline* and carefully transfer to the baking stone or sheet in the oven. Carefully pour the simmering water into the baking sheet, skillet, or drip pan to create steam and quickly close the oven door.

Bake for 20 minutes, until the baguettes are golden. Let cool completely on a rack.

Prepare the filling: To make quick-pickled carrots, combine the vinegar and sugar in a saucepan and bring to a boil, stirring to dissolve the sugar. Place the julienned carrots in a heat-resistant bowl. Pour the hot vinegar-sugar mixture over the carrots and let cool completely. Drain well before using.

Peel and seed the cucumber and cut it into matchsticks. Wash and dry the scallions and chili pepper and slice them thinly. Wash and dry the cilantro and chop roughly.

Assemble the *banh mi*: Slice the baguettes open lengthwise, without cutting all the way through. Spread the insides with pâté or mayonnaise and fill with chicken, pickled carrots, cucumber, chili pepper, and cilantro. Sprinkle with fried onions or shallots.

Serve right away.

Laura Zavan

—

"Bread plays an important role in Italy, as it does in all Mediterranean countries. You can't eat cheese or charcuterie without it, or soak up the sauce after a meal of pasta or stew. Italy is among the countries with the most variety, uses, and traditions surrounding bread. I love all the different kinds of small loaves (*mantovani, rosetta, montasù,* etc.) known as panini, which also means 'stuffed bread.' Bakers and restaurateurs are increasingly focused on the quality of bread, and in the last few years, we've seen the emergence of well-crafted, levain-based breads [*lievito madre* is the typical levain used in Italy], which are made with excellent flours.

"The most famous bread, *il pane di Altamura,* is from Altamura, a village in Puglia. This country bread has been granted Protected Designation of Origin status within Europe. Tuscan bread, called *sciapo* (literally 'bland') is unusual: this large loaf of white bread contains no salt, which makes it perfect for pairing with salty charcuterie. As for pizza and focaccia, that's a whole other story...

"In Italy, we reuse bread a lot, especially to make bread crumbs, which are sprinkled over pasta dishes instead of Parmesan in the south, or used to make stuffing and meatballs.

"*Sopa coada* literally means 'brooded soup,' because it simmers away on the wood stove. It's like lasagna, but made with slices of bread. A similar dish dates back to the Renaissance. It appears that the recipe was given to a Venetian cook by a Sardinian soldier in the late nineteenth century, and became a traditional dish in my hometown, Treviso, where there used to be many pigeon houses [dovecotes]. The dish was rediscovered in the 1960s."

Laura Zavan, originally from Treviso, Italy, has lived in Paris for over twenty years. She shares her expertise and passion for Italian cuisine through her recipes, books, and events. From Venice to Paris, through encounters and experiences, she has developed invaluable expertise in the art of selecting and celebrating quality Italian products. She is the author of a dozen successful books on Italian cuisine, including *Dolce: 80 Authentic Italian Sweet Treats, Cakes, and Desserts*[1] and *Venice: Cult Recipes.*[2]

www.laurazavan.com

1. Murdoch Books, 2016.
2. Murdoch Books, 2014.

Sopa coada Bread "Lasagna" with Pigeon and Parmesan
Recipe by Laura Zavan

Serves 6

Active time: 1 hour
Cooking: 5½ hours over 2 days

Ingredients

Stock

1 onion

1 carrot

1 stalk celery

1 lb. 2 oz. (500 g) boneless beef short ribs (*plat de côte*)

1 chicken carcass, blanched, or 2 chicken legs

2½ qt. (2.5 liters) water

Salt

Bread layer

1 lb. 2 oz. (500 g) dense, unsliced *pain de mie*, preferably day-old (see recipe p. 222)

Pigeon layer

1 onion

1 carrot

1 stalk celery

Extra-virgin olive oil

3 pigeons (squab), quartered and livers reserved (or use quail, guinea fowl, or Cornish game hen)

1 cup (250 ml) dry white wine

Assembly

4 tbsp (2 oz./60 g) butter + more for the baking dish

3.5 oz. (100 g) Parmesan, freshly grated

Salt and freshly ground pepper

Equipment

Lasagna pan

LA BONNE IDÉE

This dish is even better on the following day. Gently reheat it in a low oven and serve as indicated.

If you like, top each serving with pan-seared radicchio or endive.

The day before cooking, prepare the stock: Peel and dice onion and carrot, then dice the celery. Place in a stockpot with the beef and chicken. Cover with the water and bring to a boil. Season with salt, then reduce the heat and let simmer for 2 hours, skimming occasionally to remove any foam that rises to the surface. Let cool completely, then strain, cover, and refrigerate overnight.

On the same day, prepare the bread layer: Remove the crust from the bread (save for another recipe such as croutons p. 199), then cut the bread into ¾-in. (1.5-cm) thick slices. Let the bread dry out in the open air overnight, or, if it is fresh, dry it out in a low oven the on day you assemble the *sopa coada* (traditional recipes call for pan-frying the bread, rather than drying it out).

The next day, prepare the pigeon layer: Remove the stock from the refrigerator and gently reheat it to liquefy. Peel the onion, carrot, and celery and chop them finely.

Drizzle a little olive oil into a large sauté pan or stockpot and set over medium-high heat. Add the vegetables and sauté until softened and lightly browned. Add the pigeons and brown them lightly on all sides. Pour in the wine and cook until evaporated, then add two ladlefuls of stock and bring to a boil. Reduce the heat to low, cover, and let simmer for about 30 minutes, until the pigeon is completely tender. About 5 minutes before the end of the cooking time, add the pigeon livers to the pan.

When the pigeon is done, remove it from the sauté pan. When it's cool enough to handle, remove the bones and add them to the remaining stock. Detach and discard the skin, then cut the pigeon meat into strips and place in a large mixing bowl. Cut the livers in half and place in the bowl with the pigeon meat. Add the vegetables and pan juices and stir to blend.

Assemble and bake the *sopa coada*: Preheat the oven to 200°F (100°C/Gas Mark ¼) and grease a 8 × 12-in. (20 × 30-cm) lasagna pan with butter. Spread a little butter over both sides of each dried bread slice.

Line the base of the lasagna pan with a layer of bread. Sprinkle with Parmesan and top with half of the pigeon-vegetable mixture. Ladle a little stock over the first layer to moisten, then repeat the layers until you've used up all of the ingredients, finishing with bread—you should have three layers of bread and two layers of meat, but this will depend on the size of your pan. Pour in enough stock to cover the bread, then generously sprinkle the top with Parmesan.

Place in the oven and bake for 2 hours, adding stock from time to time so that the bread remains moist. Cook until golden on top, like a lasagna. Serve with a small bowl of stock on the side, or ladle a little stock over the base of each plate.

Florent Ladeyn

"It all started with my father, who made bread and brioche on Sundays at the inn. He would have me taste the yeast and say, 'Here, it's good for your hair!' I'll always remember the taste of raw dough.

"He taught me how to make bread that you don't find anymore. My father began working as a baker's apprentice at the age of thirteen. He was the eldest in a large family and he had to get a job. It was bread made without consideration for the living, natural world, or levain." Florent found another way.

"I started making bread because it was the only thing we weren't making ourselves at the restaurant, and not a single baker could guarantee that they were using local flour. I make everything with local products, so I can't buy vegetables and greens from Dries Delanote[1] and then use enriched flours. For example, I work with flour from the Duneleet farm in Leffrinckoucke, which is gradually shifting to heritage wheat varieties, like Blanc de Flandre.

"We don't make bread; we make *our* bread, and we have just one recipe for large levain-based loaves. We don't pretend to be bakers. We also make *faluche*s for breakfast at the hotel.

"*Flamiche* is sort of like the pizza of the north; it has the same origin story as *faluche* and *fouée*. In the past, bakers would save a little dough from the previous day's batch to verify the oven temperature. The dough was placed just inside the oven, while the wood blazed on the oven floor; when the dough was cooked, they knew they could spread the wood out to bake the day's batch of bread. The name '*flamiche*' comes from *flamme*, the French word for 'flame,' and *miche*, the French word for 'loaf.' Another theory claims that it comes from the English word 'Flemish,' because the English very much enjoyed the bread the Flemish ate with toppings. But no one really agrees."

Florent grew up in Flanders, in his family's inn, L'Auberge du Vert Mont, in Boeschèpe, France. He became a cook so he could remain in the home and in the region that he is so strongly attached to. Instead of training in prestigious restaurants, he freely draws inspiration from his native terroir and offers hyperlocal cuisine (he only makes exceptions for wine and beer made by his friends). After taking over the inn (which has since earned a Michelin star) in 2005, he opened a Flemish restaurant, Bloempot, in Lille, with his childhood friend, Kevin Rolland. In 2019 the two men, along with Florent's cousin, Clément Dubrulle, the chef at Vert Mont, opened Bierbuik, also in Lille, a new kind of café-cum-brewpub, where they also brew their own beer using local products.

www.vertmont.fr | www.bierbuik.fr | www.bloempot.fr

1. Organic farm Le Monde des mille couleurs, in Ypres (Belgium).

Flamiche à la tomme et au yaourt fermier

Tomme and Artisanal Yogurt Flamiches

Recipe by Florent Ladeyn

___

Makes 4 *flamiches*

Active time: 15 minutes + 10 minutes
Bulk fermentation:
2 hours + 24–48 hours
Cooking: 10 minutes

Ingredients

Dough
1½ tbsp (0.75 oz./22 g) salt
3 cups + 2 tbsp (27.5 oz./780 g) water
Scant 4½ cups (1 lb. 2 oz./500 g) light whole wheat flour (T110)
3⅔ cups (16.25 oz./460 g) bread flour (T65)
Scant ¾ cup (2.5 oz./75 g) rye flour
3.75 oz. (110 g) refreshed rye levain
6.5 oz. (185 g) refreshed stiff levain

Flamiches
3.5 oz. (100 g) cow's milk tomme cheese
⅔ cup (5.25 oz./150 g) artisanal plain whole-milk yogurt
Rapeseed or olive oil, for drizzling
1 handful fresh herbs and edible flowers (oxalis, fava bean flowers, chive blossoms, etc.)

Prepare the dough: Place the salt, water, flours, and levains, in that order, in the bowl of a stand mixer fitted with the dough hook. Knead for 3 minutes on speed 1, followed by 3–5 minutes on speed 2, until the dough is smooth and elastic. Cover the bowl and let the dough rise for 2 hours. Fold the dough once, after 1 hour. Cover tightly and let rest in the refrigerator for 24–48 hours (bulk fermentation*).

Prepare the *flamiches*: When the dough is ready, preheat the oven to 410°F (210°C/Gas Mark 6). Grate the tomme on the large holes of a box grater and set aside.

Weigh out 1 lb. 2 oz. (500 g) of the dough (use the rest to make a loaf of bread). Place on a lightly floured work surface and cut into four equal pieces using a bench scraper. Shape each piece into a loose ball and flatten to a thickness of ½ in. (1 cm) using the heel of your hand or a rolling pin.

Place on a baking sheet, either nonstick or lined with parchment paper. Top each *flamiche* with a generous spoonful of yogurt and spread into an even layer.

Bake for 5 minutes, then scatter the grated tomme over the *flamiches* and return to the oven for an additional 5 minutes, until the cheese is melted and golden.

Remove from the oven and let sit for 5 minutes.

Drizzle each *flamiche* with a little the oil and scatter the herbs and flowers over the top. Serve warm.

LA BONNE IDÉE
These *flamiches* are also excellent baked in a wood-fired oven, or on a well-heated baking stone on a grill.

Techniques
Refreshing levain
Kneading with a mixer or by hand
Folding
Stages of fermentation
Shaping small balls of dough

Margherita Pizza

Makes 2 pizzas

Active time: 15 minutes
Bulk fermentation: 2 hours
Proofing: 1 hour
Cooking: 8–10 minutes per pizza

Ingredients

Pizza dough

1¼ cups (10.5 oz./300 g) water
2 tsp (0.35 oz./10 g) salt
3¾ tsp (0.5 oz./15 g) sugar
4 cups + 2 tbsp (1 lb. 2 oz./500 g) bread flour (T65)
0.35 oz. (10 g) fresh yeast, or 3.5 oz. (100 g) refreshed levain + 0.2 oz. (5 g) fresh yeast (see Good to Know)
¼ cup (1.75 oz./50 g) extra-virgin olive oil

Toppings

Generous 2 cups (1 lb. 2 oz./500 g) tomato sauce or pizza sauce (preferably homemade)
1 lb. 2 oz. (500 g) buffalo mozzarella
A few leaves fresh basil
Extra-virgin olive oil

Prepare the pizza dough: Place the water, salt, sugar, flour, and yeast in the bowl of a stand mixer fitted with the dough hook. Knead for 5 minutes on speed 1, followed by 5–6 minutes on speed 2. Two minutes before the end of the kneading time, drizzle in the olive oil with the mixer running. Continue kneading until smooth.

Shape the dough into a ball and place it in a lightly oiled bowl. Cover the bowl and let the dough rise for 2 hours. Fold the dough once, after 1 hour (bulk fermentation*).

Turn the dough out onto a floured work surface and divide it into two equal pieces using a bench scraper. Roll out or stretch each piece of dough, without tearing it, to the dimensions of two 10 × 14-in./25 × 35-cm baking sheets. Line the baking sheets with parchment paper and carefully transfer the dough onto the paper. Cover loosely and let rise for 1 hour, until slightly puffed (proofing*).

Top and bake the pizzas: Preheat the oven to 500°F (260°C/Gas Mark 10).

Spread the tomato sauce over the dough in an even layer, then slice the mozzarella and scatter it over the sauce.

Bake each pizza for 8–10 minutes, until the crust is golden and crisp.

Scatter the basil leaves over the top, drizzle with a little olive oil, and serve right away.

GOOD TO KNOW

You can make this pizza dough with 100 percent levain. Replace the 0.35 oz. (10 g) fresh yeast with 5.25 oz. (150 g) levain and let the dough bulk ferment in the refrigerator for 18–48 hours before using.

Techniques
Refreshing levain
Kneading with a mixer or by hand
Stages of fermentation
Folding

Flammenküche

Alsatian Pizza

————

Serves 2

Active time: 30 minutes
Resting: 20 minutes
Cooking: 10 minutes

Ingredients

3 yellow onions

5.25 oz. (150 g) smoked bacon

9 oz. (250 g) pizza dough (see recipe p. 384) or bread dough—*tourte de meule* (see recipe p. 206) or baguette (see recipe p. 219)—after bulk fermentation

Scant ½ cup (3.5 oz./100 g) fromage blanc

Scant ½ cup (3.5 oz./100 g) crème fraîche

Salt and freshly ground pepper

Ground nutmeg

Preheat the oven to 450°F (240°C/Gas Mark 8).

Turn the dough out onto a floured work surface, shape it into a ball, and let it rest for 20 minutes (resting*).

Meanwhile, peel the onions and slice them very thinly. Cut the bacon into thin strips (see La Bonne Idée).

In a bowl, stir together the fromage blanc and crème fraîche until smooth. Season to taste with salt, pepper, and nutmeg.

Place the dough on a baking sheet, either nonstick or lined with parchment paper. Using your fingertips or a rolling pin, press or roll the dough out into as thin a circle as possible.

Spread the cheese mixture over the dough in an even layer, then scatter the onions and bacon over the cheese.

Bake the *flammenküche* for 10 minutes, without letting it brown.

Serve warm or at room temperature.

LA BONNE IDÉE

If your onion and bacon slices are a little too thick, you can sauté them together in a skillet for 5 minutes to soften and cook them a bit before adding them to the *flammenküche*. Let cool completely on a plate lined with paper towel to absorb excess grease before using.

Pissaladière

Serves 4

Active time: 30 minutes
Resting: 20 minutes
Cooking: 15–20 minutes

Ingredients

1¾ lb. (800 g) onions
2 cloves garlic
2 sprigs thyme
4 tbsp extra-virgin olive oil, divided
1 tbsp sugar
14 oz. (400 g) pizza dough (see recipe
p. 384) or bread dough—*tourte de meule*
(see recipe p. 206) or baguette (see
recipe p. 219)—after bulk fermentation
1.75 oz. (50 g) anchovy fillets, marinated
or packed in oil
1 handful black olives
Salt and freshly ground pepper

Peel the onions and slice them thinly. Peel the garlic cloves and crush them using a garlic press. Wash and dry the thyme sprigs well and remove the leaves. Discard the stems.

Heat 3 tbsp of the olive oil in a large sauté pan over low heat. Add the onions, garlic, and thyme and stir until well blended. Stir in the sugar, then season with salt and pepper.

Cover and cook for 20–30 minutes, stirring often with a wooden spoon, until the onions are meltingly tender but still pale. Near the end of the cooking time, remove the lid to allow any excess liquid to cook off. Remove from the heat and let cool.

Place a rack in the center of the oven and preheat the oven to 450°F (240°C/Gas Mark 8).

Meanwhile, turn the dough out onto a floured work surface, shape it into a ball, and let it rest for 20 minutes (resting*).

Roll or stretch the dough to fit a 10 × 14-in./24 × 35-cm baking sheet, either nonstick or lined with parchment paper. Scatter the onions over the dough, then drain the anchovies and arrange them over the onions. Sprinkle with black olives and drizzle with the remaining olive oil.

Bake for 15–20 minutes, until lightly golden.

Serve warm or at room temperature.

Grissini

Italian-Style Breadsticks

————

Makes about 20 grissini

Active time: 10 minutes
Bulk fermentation: 1 hour
Cooking: 10–15 minutes

Ingredients

1 cup (9 oz./250 g) water

0.5 oz. (15 g) fresh yeast

4 cups + 2 tbsp (1 lb. 2 oz./500 g) bread flour (T65)

2 tsp (0.35 oz./10 g) salt

Scant ⅓ cup (2.5 oz./70 g) extra-virgin olive oil + more for baking

Your choice of flavorings (sesame seeds, poppy seeds, herbes de Provence, *fleur de sel*, etc.)

Place the water in the bowl of the stand mixer fitted with the dough hook. Crumble in the fresh yeast and stir or swish to dissolve. Add the flour and salt and knead for 4 minutes on speed 1, followed by 5 minutes on speed 2. Toward the end of the kneading time, drizzle in the olive oil with the mixer running.

Shape the dough into a ball and place it in a lightly oiled bowl. Cover the bowl and let the dough rise for 1 hour, until almost doubled in size. Fold the dough once, after 30 minutes (bulk fermentation*).

Preheat the oven to 450°F (230°C/Gas Mark 8) and line a baking sheet with parchment paper.

Turn the dough out onto a floured work surface. Using your fingertips, press the dough into a rectangle, about 8 in. (20 cm) long and ½ in. (1 cm) thick. Cut the dough lengthwise into strips, ½–¾ in. (1–2 cm) thick, using a bench scraper or pizza cutter.

Shape the strips as you wish: you can roll them under your hands to make them long and thin, hold them on either end and twist them, or roll them up to make them thicker. As you shape the strips, place them on the prepared baking sheet.

Brush the grissini with a little olive oil and sprinkle with your flavoring of choice.

Bake for 10–15 minutes, until deeply golden.

Slide the grissini onto a rack with the parchment paper underneath and let cool completely.

Techniques
Kneading with a mixer or by hand
Stages of fermentation
Folding
Decorative finishes

Farine de blé ancien
MOULIN
A VENT LAN
Céréales du Sud
MEULE
DE
PIERRE
TURE BIOL

Julien Duboué

—

"Bread is a major component of each meal, each day, and each week.

"In my restaurants, I have always paid careful attention to the quality of the bread served. For a long time, I bought bread from Jean-Luc Poujauran, who, like me, is from Landes, in southwest France.

"I started making bread when I opened Corn'R, my restaurant where corn was the star ingredient. I tested seventeen *taloa* recipes before finding one I liked. Then I opened B.O.U.L.O.M, my 'bakery where you can eat.' I wanted to cook using a bread oven and showcase the French baking heritage. I will never forget the sight of my mother and my grandmother carrying large dishes to the local baker to be cooked in his oven. Watching all this dough ferment each day in the bakery gives me ideas for enormous sandwiches, bread-topped casseroles, aged sausages, and *pâté en croûte*.

"I apply the same ethical standards to the flour we use as I do to all my other products. I trust local producers, and I've even begun growing wheat myself. We began with fifty acres (twenty hectares) in southwest France, where we planted twenty-seven wheat varieties. Today we harvest one ton of wheat derived from more than two hundred varieties. We are trying to grow the business with the farmers who support our projects. It makes for a wonderful story, but it's also quite natural—when I was young, I saw my parents trading seeds. Now we do the same with our wheat."

Originally from Landes, France, Julien Duboué moved to Paris in 2001 to train with Alain Dutournier at the Carré des Feuillants, then at the Hotel George V, and then to New York to train with Daniel Boulud. He opened his first restaurant, Afaria, in Paris, then Dans les Landes in 2010. In 2014 he opened A Noste, which combines a friendly, festive space for tapas and a more refined dining area. Committed to championing products from his native region, he opened Corn'R in October 2016 in partnership with the Maison de la Nouvelle Aquitaine. In April 2018, he started B.O.U.L.O.M, an acronym for the French phrase *"boulangerie où l'on mange"* (a bakery where you can eat). There, a traditional boulangerie-patisserie opens onto a large dining area with all-you-can-eat buffets. His newest project, launched in 2019, is La Dalle at La Défense, a restaurant offering high-quality street food.

www.julienduboue.com

Cabillaud en croûte de pain, jus vert, noisettes

Cod en Croûte with Green Jus and Hazelnuts

Recipe from the B.O.U.L.O.M. restaurant

———

Serves 6

Active time: 30 minutes
Resting: 20 minutes
Proofing: 30 minutes
Cooking: 20–25 minutes

Ingredients

Green jus

2 sheets gelatin
3.5 oz. (100 g) parsley
3.5 oz. (100 g) New Zealand or regular spinach
1 clove garlic, blanched
1 tsp (5 g) salt
¾ tsp (2 g) hot chili powder
1 tsp (10 g) extra-virgin olive oil
¾ cup + 1 tbsp (7 oz./200 g) water

Cod en croûte

1 lb. 2 oz. (500 g) bread dough—
tourte de meule (see recipe p. 206)
or baguette (see recipe p. 219)—after
bulk fermentation
1 boneless, skinless cod fillet, 1¾–2¼ lb.
(800 g–1 kg)
1 tbsp (1 oz./30 g) roughly chopped
hazelnuts

Equipment

Food processor or blender

Prepare the green jus: Soak the gelatin in a bowl of cold water until softened.

Wash and dry the parsley and spinach, removing any thick stalks, then place in the bowl of the food processor with the garlic, salt, chili powder, olive oil, and water. Pulse until smooth.

Transfer the jus to a saucepan and gently warm over low heat. Squeeze the gelatin to remove excess water and stir it into the jus to dissolve.

Let cool slightly, then chill in the refrigerator until using.

Prepare the cod en croûte: Turn the dough out onto a floured work surface and divide it into two equal pieces. Cover and let rest for 20 minutes (resting*).

Cut the cod into two thin fillets and season with salt and pepper.

Roll out each piece of dough until it is ½ in./1 cm thick and slightly larger than the fish—it should be big enough to allow for a ½-in./1-cm border all the way around.

Place one of the rolled-out pieces of dough on a baking sheet lined with parchment paper. Place one of the cod fillets on the dough, centering it well. Top with the green jus and sprinkle with the hazelnuts. Place the second cod fillet over the green jus layer.

Brush the edges of the dough with water and cover with the second piece of dough. Press down around the edges to seal the dough well, so that no air can get through.

Let rise in a warm place for 30 minutes, until visibly puffed (proofing*).

Meanwhile, preheat the oven to 515°F (270°C/Gas Mark 10).

Bake the cod en croûte for 20–25 minutes, until the crust is crisp and deeply golden.

Serve warm.

Technique
Stages of fermentation

Sonia Ezgulian

——

"My Armenian grandmother taught me how to cook refined, Eastern cuisine. My other grandmother was from Auvergne, and her cooking was more austere and economical. On her farm, there was a large table with a drawer at the end that she would open after every meal and sweep bread crumbs into. When the drawer was full, she used them in cooking—to thicken soup, for example.

"When I opened my restaurant, I thought back to that zero-waste lesson, and I told myself that I would have to be creative to avoid throwing out food. My father supplied me with vegetables from his garden. I appreciated the effort it took, and out of respect, I began cooking with every part of the vegetable. I used everything, from the greens to the skins, but nothing was disguised. Instead I created something refined with them. People were often surprised—zero-waste cuisine was pretty avant-garde in the 1990s!

"Restaurants also throw out a lot of bread. I was lucky to have a cook on my team who made wonderful bread. Then I found an old recipe for *tarte au pain*, from Lyon. The original version is quite heavy, so I made it lighter and gave it a little zing by adding citrus zest, dried fruits, and spices. Now I make it with bread crumbs that I keep in a jar. It turns out differently each time and tells the story of the bread crumbs and the loaves of breads they represent. It's a recipe that requires patience, because the jar has to be full to make it. It restores the meaning of time."

Sonia Ezgulian worked as a journalist for *Paris Match* for ten years before opening the restaurant Oxalis in Lyon, France, with her husband Emmanuel Auger, which they ran for seven years.

Today she focuses her time on food writing and consulting for restaurateurs and the food industry.

www.soniaezgulian.com

Tarte aux miettes de pain Bread Crumb Tart
Recipe by Sonia Ezgulian

Makes 1 tart

Active time: 15 minutes
Chilling: 1 hour
Cooking: 30 minutes

Ingredients

Pistachio crust

1 cup (4.25 oz./125 g) all-purpose flour
⅓ cup (1.5 oz./40 g) confectioners' sugar
1 pinch salt
1 tbsp sugar
1 tbsp (2.25 oz./65 g) butter, diced, at room temperature
Scant ⅓ cup (1.5 oz./40 g) shelled pistachios, preferably Iranian, roughly chopped
1 egg

Breadcrumb filling

5.25 oz. (150 g) dry stale bread
1 cup (250 ml) whole milk
¼ cup + 2½ tbsp (2.75 oz./80 g) sugar
Scant ½ cup (1.5 oz./40 g) ground almonds
1 egg, separated
Zest of 2 lemons, preferably organic
Confectioners' sugar, for dusting

Equipment

10-in. (26-cm) tart pan

Prepare the pistachio crust: Combine the flour and confectioners' sugar in a bowl, then sift them together onto a work surface. Make a well in the center and add the salt, sugar, butter, and pistachios. Combine the ingredients with your fingertips until the mixture resembles coarse sand.

Make another well, add the egg, and work it into the dough with the heel of your hand until well combined and smooth.

Place the dough between two sheets of parchment paper and roll it into a circle slightly larger than the tart pan. Without removing the parchment paper, fit the dough into the pan. Chill in the refrigerator for 1 hour.

Prepare the breadcrumb filling: Preheat the oven to 350°F (180°C/Gas Mark 4).

Soak the bread in the milk for 15 minutes.

Meanwhile, combine the sugar and ground almonds in a large mixing bowl. Stir in the egg yolks and lemon zest until well combined. Break up the soaked bread into crumb-size pieces, add to the bowl, and stir until well combined.

Whisk the egg whites until they hold firm peaks and fold them into the filling mixture.

Assemble and bake the tart: Peel the top layer of parchment paper off the crust and pour in the filling. Spread into an even layer.

Bake for 30 minutes, until set and lightly golden.

Serve warm or at room temperature, dusted with confectioners' sugar.

Soupe à l'oignon et croûtons gratinés

Onion Soup with Cheese Croutons

Serves 4

Active time: 20 minutes
Cooking: 1 hour 50 minutes

Ingredients

Chicken stock

1 chicken carcass and giblets

2 qt. (2 liters) water

1 onion

1 whole clove

1 carrot

1 stalk celery

1 leek

1 tbsp coarse sea salt, preferably gray sea salt

5 peppercorns

Onion soup

1 tbsp (2 oz./60 g) salted butter

14 oz. (400 g) onions, thinly sliced

1 pinch *quatre-épices* spice mix (or allspice, ground mixed spice, or pumpkin pie spice)

1 tbsp (0.35 oz./10 g) flour

Salt and freshly ground pepper

Croutons

1 thin baguette (see recipe p. 219)

3.5 oz. (100 g) Emmental cheese, grated

Equipment

4 oven-safe ceramic soup dishes or bowls

Large Dutch oven or saucepan

Prepare the chicken stock (can be made 1 day ahead): Place the chicken carcass and giblets in a large stockpot. Cover with the water and bring to a boil, then lower the heat and let simmer for 15 minutes, skimming off any foam that rises to the surface.

Meanwhile, peel and rinse the onion and stick the whole clove into it. Peel and wash the carrot, celery, and leek and cut them into small pieces.

Add the vegetables, salt, and peppercorns to the pot with the chicken carcass and return to a simmer. Let simmer for 1 hour.

Strain the stock. If you'll be using it right away, return it to the stockpot and keep it hot. Otherwise, let it cool, transfer to an airtight container, and refrigerate overnight. The following day, spoon off the fat that has accumulated on the surface before using.

Prepare the onion soup: Melt the butter in a large Dutch oven or saucepan over medium heat. When it begins to foam, add the onion and cook until softened and lightly golden, but not browned, stirring often (about 10 minutes).

Reduce the heat to low and stir in the *quatre-épices* and flour. Add the stock. Season with salt and pepper to taste, cover, and let simmer for 20 minutes, stirring occasionally.

Meanwhile, prepare the croutons: Cut the baguette into thin slices—you should have enough to cover each bowl of soup. Toast the slices until golden and crisp.

Assemble and serve the soup: Right before serving the soup, place the oven rack about 6 in. (15 cm) from the broiler and preheat the broiler. Ladle the soup into the ceramic soup dishes or bowls and top with the toasted croutons, overlapping them slightly. Sprinkle with the grated cheese.

Place under the broiler for about 3 minutes, until the cheese is melted and lightly browned. Serve right away.

Panzanella

___

Serves 4

Active time: 20 minutes

Chilling: 1–3 hours

Ingredients

½ cup (125 ml) water

2 tbsp white balsamic vinegar

9 oz. (250 g) stale *pain de campagne*
(see recipe p. 250)

4 very ripe tomatoes

1 small cucumber

1 red onion

2 tbsp extra-virgin olive oil

1 handful small basil leaves

Salt and freshly ground pepper

Combine the water and vinegar in a bowl.

Slice the bread, lay it flat in a baking dish, and pour the water-vinegar mixture over it. Let the bread soak until it is softened but not soggy, then drain and squeeze it to remove excess liquid. Cut it into small pieces and set aside.

Wash the tomatoes and cucumber and peel the red onion. Cut the tomatoes and cucumber into small pieces and slice the onion thinly. Place in a serving bowl, drizzle with the olive oil, and season with salt and pepper. Stir gently. Add the bread and gently toss to combine. Scatter the basil leaves over the top.

Chill in the refrigerator for 1–3 hours to allow the flavors to meld before serving.

Lingot auvergnat

Savory Auvergne Loaf Cake

——————

Serves 4

Active time: 20 minutes
Soaking: 15 minutes
Cooking: 40 minutes

Ingredients

Butter, for the pan

7 oz. (200 g) stale bread

1¼ cups (300 ml) whole milk

2 eggs, beaten

3 tbsp (1 oz./30 g) flour

1.75 oz. (50 g) grated cheese, such as
Gruyère

3.5 oz. (100 g) diced cured ham,
or smoked bacon cut into small pieces
and fried until crisp

Several sprigs fresh herbs (parsley,
chives, etc.)

Salt and freshly ground pepper

Equipment

8–8½-in. (20–22-cm) loaf pan or covered
terrine dish

Preheat the oven to 400°F (200°C/Gas Mark 6) and grease the pan with butter.

Break up the bread into small pieces and place it in a large mixing bowl. Add the milk and let soak for about 15 minutes, until the bread is softened. Add the eggs, flour, cheese, and ham or bacon and stir to combine. Roughly chop the herbs and stir them in. Season with salt and pepper.

Pour the batter into the prepared pan and cover tightly with aluminum foil (or the terrine lid).

Bake for 40 minutes, until a knife inserted into the center comes out clean.

As soon as you remove the cake from the oven, run a knife around the edge of the pan to release the cake from the sides. Let the cake cool completely in the pan.

Turn the cake out onto a serving dish, or serve it directly from the pan.

LA BONNE IDÉE

You can serve this savory cake warm with tomato sauce, or chill it and cut into cubes for an aperitif or picnic and serve with a spicy sauce for dipping.

Kvass, boisson au pain

Fermented Bread Drink

———

Makes 4½ cups (1 liter)

Active time: 15 minutes
Soaking/resting:
5 hours + overnight + 3 days
Cooking: 5 minutes

Ingredients

2 qt. (2 liters) water
12.5 oz. (350 g) dry stale rye bread
3½ tsp (0.4 oz./11 g) active dry yeast
½ cup (2.75 oz./80 g) muscovado
or brown sugar
Zest of ½ lemon, preferably organic
¾-in. (2-cm) piece fresh ginger
3 raisins

Equipment

2-pint (1-litre) glass bottle with a flip-top
metal clasp

Bring the water to a boil in a large stockpot. Remove from the heat and immediately add the bread. Cover with a towel and let sit at room temperature for 5 hours.

Strain through a fine-mesh sieve into a large mixing bowl, pressing down on the bread to release as much liquid as possible. Save the bread for another recipe (such as bread pudding, see p. 433).

Add the yeast, sugar, and lemon zest. Peel the ginger and grate it into the bowl. Cover with a towel and let sit at room temperature overnight.

The next day, strain the liquid through a fine-mesh sieve lined with cheesecloth. Transfer to the bottle with a flip-top metal clasp (these bottles hold up well to the significant pressure that builds during fermentation). Add the raisins and close the bottle with care, ensuring it is well sealed.

Let ferment in the refrigerator for 3 days before serving.

Meatloaf

Serves 8

Active time: 20 minutes
Soaking: 10 minutes
Cooking: 45–50 minutes

Ingredients
Meatloaf
Vegetable oil
1 onion, peeled and finely chopped
1 tsp dried thyme
5.25 oz. (150 g) dry bread
Scant ½ cup (100 ml) whole milk
Scant ½ cup (100 ml) beef or chicken stock
2 eggs, beaten
1¾ lb. (800 g) ground beef
2 tbsp Worcestershire sauce
Salt and freshly ground pepper
Glaze
Scant ⅔ cup (5.25 oz./150 g) ketchup
1 tbsp yellow mustard
1 tbsp brown sugar

Equipment
11-in. (28-cm) loaf pan

Prepare the meatloaf: Preheat the oven to 350°F (180°C/Gas Mark 4) and line the loaf pan with parchment paper.

Drizzle a little vegetable oil into a large skillet and add the onion and thyme. Sauté over medium heat until the onion is softened and lightly golden, stirring often. Remove from the heat and let cool.

Break up the bread into small pieces and place in a large mixing bowl. Add the milk and stock. Let soak for about 10 minutes to soften the bread.

Add the onion and eggs and stir to combine.

Place the ground beef in a separate large mixing bowl and gradually incorporate the bread mixture with your hands until well combined and moist. Add the Worcestershire sauce and season with salt and pepper. Transfer to the prepared loaf pan and pat down into an even layer.

Prepare the glaze: Whisk together the ketchup, mustard, and brown sugar in a bowl. Brush some of the glaze over the meatloaf in an even layer, reserving the rest.

Bake the meatloaf: Bake for 30 minutes, then remove from the oven and brush with the remaining glaze. Return to the oven for 15–20 minutes, until nicely browned.

Let cool 10–15 minutes before slicing and serving.

LA BONNE IDÉE
Serve thickly sliced with barbecue sauce on the side.

You can swap out the ground beef for ground chicken and serve the meatloaf chilled with an herb mayonnaise.

Mfouar

Stale Bread Couscous

Serves 6

Active time: 15 minutes
Cooking: 3 minutes

Ingredients
2 tsp (0.2 oz./5 g) paprika
¾ cup + 1 tbsp (200 ml) olive oil
2¼ lb. (1 kg) stale bread
1 tsp (0.2 oz./5 g) salt
2 tsp (0.2 oz./5 g) ground cumin
4 cloves garlic, peeled and crushed with a garlic press

Equipment
Couscoussier (or see La Bonne Idée)
Food processor
Spray bottle

Place the paprika in a small bowl and cover with the olive oil.

Remove the crust from the bread (save crusts for another recipe such as croutons, see p. 199), then pulse the bread in the bowl of a food processor to make small couscous-like crumbs. You can pass through a large-hole strainer into a large mixing bowl, or break up any large crumbs by hand. Spritz crumbs with a little water to moisten slightly.

Add the salt and cumin, then stir the paprika and olive oil together and pour into the bowl. Spritz with a little more water and stir with a wooden spoon until well blended.

Scatter the crushed garlic cloves across the top of the *couscoussier* (the steamer part) and cover with the bread mixture. Set aside.

Fill the base of the *couscoussier* halfway with water and bring it to a simmer. Place the steamer part on top and cover with the lid. When steam begins to escape from under the lid, wait 3 minutes, then remove from the heat.

Pour the "couscous" into a shallow serving dish and toss to distribute the garlic.

Serve with a tagine, such as chickpea and vegetable, or another favorite couscous accompaniment.

LA BONNE IDÉE
If you do not have a *couscoussier*, use a colander that fits snugly over a stockpot. Depending on the size of the holes, you may want to line the colander with cheesecloth to prevent the bread from falling through.

Frites de pain

Bread Fries

Serves 2

Active time: 10 minutes
Cooking: 3–5 minutes

Ingredients

About 10 slices stale rustic bread,
¾-in. (1-cm) thick—such as
tourte de meule (see recipe p. 206)
or *pain de campagne* (see recipe p. 250)

Scant ½ cup (100 ml) milk

1 egg, beaten

Salt

Oil, for frying

For serving

Herb mayonnaise

Equipment (optional)

Deep fryer

Instant-read thermometer

Remove the crust from the slices of bread (save crusts for another recipe, such as croutons p. 199). Cut the bread into fry-shaped sticks, ¾ in. (1 cm) thick.

If the bread is not very dry, preheat the oven to 400°F (200°C/Gas Mark 6) and spread the bread "fries" across a baking sheet. Bake for about 5 minutes to dry them out.

When you are ready to proceed, place the milk in one shallow bowl and the egg in another. If you do not have a deep fryer, pour vegetable oil into a deep skillet or Dutch oven to a depth of about 2 in. (5 cm). Heat the oil to 320°F (160°C).

Dip the bread fries in the milk to moisten, then dip them in the egg. Let the excess egg drip off, then carefully immerse the fries in the hot oil. Cook, turning often, until deeply golden all over, about 3–5 minutes.

Remove from the oil with a skimmer (preferably a spider skimmer) and place on a paper towel-lined plate.

Sprinkle with salt and serve right away with herb mayonnaise on the side.

LA BONNE IDÉE
Make a cone out of parchment paper for serving your bread fries.

Charlotte Desombre and Amandine Delafon

—

"We met at university in Lille, twenty years ago. We wanted to start a business together. We shared the same interest in recycling, so we quickly turned our attention to food waste, especially bread, which represents 14 percent of all food waste in France.

"We discovered Babylone, a beer brewed by Brussels Beer Project using unsold bread. We both like beer, so last year we created the Cocomiette brand, in order to 'do our part,' like Coco the hummingbird, who appears on our labels [representing the story of the tiny creature which in legend 'did what it could' to help put out a forest fire by bringing water, a drop at a time, from a nearby stream.]

"We work with Nathalie Munsch, a freelance brewer, who helps us develop our recipes. Thirty percent of the malted grains usually used to make beer are replaced by unused bread, which creates a two-fold environmental benefit: it gives bread a second life and limits grain consumption. We collect unsold products from Boulangerie Pani in Grenoble, which supplies bread for institutional catering and uses French flours with no added improvers. The beer is then brewed at the Brasserie Artisanale du Val d'Ainan, a craft brewery in Saint-Geoire-en-Valdaine, in Isère, France. We have plans to reproduce this local, collaborative cycle in the Île-de-France region in order to limit our carbon footprint, while creating an ecosystem made up of bakers, brewers, and distributors."

After studying business and earning a master's degree in intellectual property, Amandine Delafon worked in publishing in London, then in hospitality in Florence. In 2012, she joined Sport dans la Ville, an association that works to provide employment opportunities through athletics in France, as manager of the Grenoble branch. In 2017 she created Ronalpia, an incubator for social entrepreneurs in Grenoble, and mentored several entrepreneurs for two years. This kindled her desire to become an entrepreneur while contributing to environmental sustainability.

Charlotte Desombre also studied business, before moving to Hong Kong to work for L'Oréal. In 2012, she made a big change and joined the team that would go on to create the Île-de-France branch of Sport dans la Ville as director of partnerships and events. Charlotte had dreamed of starting her own company for twenty years. Following many discussions about their desire to "do their part," the two friends decided to create Cocomiette. They currently offer three beers made with bread: a red ale, a lager, and a white beer.

www.cocomiette.com

Bière au pain Bread Beer
Recipe by Nathalie Munsch

_____

Makes 5 gallons (20 liters)

Fermentation time: 3 weeks
Brewing: about 5 hours
Bottling: about 2½ hours
Total time: 5 weeks

Ingredients

2¼ lb. (1 kg) stale bread
8 gallons (30 liters) water, divided
3 kg crushed malted barley
(see Good to Know)
2 oz. (60 g) hops
(see Good to Know)
Spices or herbs of your choice (optional)
1 packet (0.4 oz./11.5 g) dry brewing
yeast (see Good to Know)
Vodka or sanitizer, for the airlock

Priming solution

4½ cups (1 liter) of water
Scant ⅔ cup (4.25 oz./120 g) sugar

Equipment

A small grain mill for crushing your malts
if they are whole
Brew kettle or pot with a capacity of at
least 13 gallons (50 liters) with a false
bottom and spigot
Instant-read thermometer
5-gallon (20-liter) pot
6.5-gallon (25-liter) plastic fermentation
bucket with airlock
Immersion wort chiller, sanitized
30 × 25-oz. (750-ml) beer bottles
30 bottle caps
Bottle capper

Prepare to brew the beer: Scrupulously sanitize all of your equipment (see Good to Know).

Grind the stale bread to make fine breadcrumbs. Spread the crumbs out on a baking sheet and place in an oven at 120°F (50°C) for 1–2 hours until completely dry.

Make the mash: Add 4 gallons (15 liters) of water to the brew kettle and heat it to 162°F (72°C). Remove from the heat and energetically stir in the crushed malted barley and breadcrumbs, then cover and let rest for 1 hour.

Meanwhile, add 4 gallons (15 liters) water to the 5-gallon (20-liter) pot and heat to 176°F (80°C). Maintain the temperature.

Place the fermentation bucket under the spigot on the kettle and open it to allow the wort (the liquid produced by the mashing process) to drain into the bucket (the false bottom will catch the grains). While the wort is draining, gradually and carefully pour the 4 gallons (15 liters) of 176°F (80°C) water into the kettle over the mash, without stirring.

You should end up with about 6.5 gallons (25 liters) of wort in the fermentation bucket. If you have a bit more wort than this and your fermentation bucket is full, you can put the excess in the 5-gallon (20-liter) pot.

Remove the breadcrumbs and spent grain (also known as brewers' grains) from the base of the kettle (see La Bonne Idée). Clean the kettle well and pour in the wort from the fermentation bucket. Bring the wort to a vigorous boil, then add 0.35 oz. (10 g) of the hops and let boil for 1 hour.

Meanwhile, sanitize the fermentation bucket.

Remove the kettle from the heat, add the remaining hops, and let steep for 15 minutes. If you'd like to add spices or herbs, do so now. Transfer the wort to the fermentation bucket through the spigot.

Attach one end of the immersion wort chiller to your water source, and direct the other end into a drain (ensure it will stay firmly in place, as the water that comes out will be very hot). Immerse the chiller in the wort and turn on the cold water. Continue running the water until the wort has cooled to 68°F (20°C). This quick cooling process is essential to avoid the danger zone for bacterial growth.

When your future beer has reached the correct temperature, add the yeast and close the fermentation bucket. Put a little vodka or sanitizer in the airlock, which enables the CO_2 produced during the fermentation process to escape without exposing the beer to open air.

Place the fermentation bucket in a room with an ambient temperature of between 68°F–77°F (20°C–25°C). Let ferment for 2 weeks.

Transfer the bucket to an even cooler place, preferably a cool basement or the refrigerator, and let sit for 1 additional week to give any particles in suspension more time to settle to the bottom.

When you are ready to bottle the beer, sanitize your brew kettle well to use it as a bottling bucket.

Prepare the priming solution: Bring the 4½ cups (1 liter) of water to a boil and add the scant ⅔ cup (4.25 oz./120 g) sugar to make a syrup. Cook, stirring often, until the sugar has dissolved, then remove from the heat and let cool completely.

Meanwhile, slowly pour the contents of the fermentation bucket into the sanitized brew kettle, taking care not to pour in the sediment at the bottom. Stir in the cooled priming solution until well combined, then fill and cap the bottles.

Store the bottles in an upright position for 10 days at an ambient temperature of around 77°F (25°C). This gives the yeast time to process the priming sugar and produce carbonation. Transfer the bottles to a cooler place, such as a cool basement or refrigerator, and let sit for an additional week before enjoying.

GOOD TO KNOW

There is an immense variety of malts, hops, brewing yeasts, and other beer-making ingredients on the market, and the types you use will significantly influence the character of your beer. The extent to which your malted barley is roasted, for instance, determines the color, flavor, and aroma of your beer. Hops, like spices, add a range of flavors (grassy, fruity, herbal, bitter, etc.), depending on the variety. And the type of yeast you use will determine whether your beer is an ale or a lager. We encourage you to experiment with different types and combinations to find your favorite blends, and be sure to keep a record of your brews to adjust for future batches.

Many professional and amateur brewers offer tips and explanations online.

Look for specialized brewing equipment and ingredients at your local homebrew supply shop or online.

You could use the brew-in-a-bag (BIAB) method to simplify the all-grain brewing process.

If you crush your own malt, crush it roughly—you are aiming to break the grains in two. Make sure that you do not grind the malt to a flour. If the grains are too fine, they could clog the false bottom in the kettle.

It is essential to sanitize all equipment with care, not only for the best possible results, but also to avoid the risk of contamination and foodborne illness.

Don't despair if your first batch isn't a success. As is the case with bread making, preparing fermented beverages is a delicate art, and it can take you several tries before you're happy with the results. And remember, it's only by brewing that you become a good brewer.

LA BONNE IDÉE

Spent grain makes excellent feed for livestock like cows and chickens. You can also compost it if you do not have animals to feed.

François Daubinet
—

"When I started working at Fauchon in 2017, I wanted to make simpler, healthier pastry, based on taste as well as aesthetics. The idea for a bread-based recipe came to me when a culinary festival asked me to design a master class.

"Bread, with its different textures and unique taste, has always been a great source of inspiration. Back when I was head pastry chef at Taillevent, I proposed a dessert built around toast, in the form of ice cream accompanied by vanilla custard. It was a great success. Crust, like a favorite outfit, is an expression of individuality: thick or thin, light or dark, crunchy or crispy, a unique crust is what defines bread. All you have to do is break a loaf open, hearing the cracking of the outer layer under the pressure of the knife or a twist of the hand, before you share it.

"I created the '*mie-chou*' based on this sensory emotion, using flours from Roland Feuillas, which have been ground from heritage grains. Symbolically, this dessert represents a loaf of bread with a cream center infused with toast, as well as an almond praline and a crust of toasted bread. The familiar gesture of a baker sprinkling flour over a loaf is applied to the choux pastry to make an even more authentic creation."

Only in his early thirties, François Daubinet already has a long career behind him. After eight years of pastry training with the Compagnons du Devoir, he joined the ranks at prestigious establishments in New York, then in France, including the Hôtel de Crillon, the Plaza Athénée, and Taillevent, and contributed his expertise to the Michalak MasterClass [started by pastry chef Christophe Michalak]. In 2017 he took over the reins at Fauchon in Paris as executive pastry chef. He embodies a new generation of chefs and draws his inspiration from the contemporary zeitgeist.

www.fauchon.com

Mie chou Toast-Infused Cream Choux Puffs

Recipe by François Daubinet

———

Makes 20 choux puffs

Active time: 1 hour
Cooking: 1 hour
Infusing: 1 hour
Chilling: Overnight

Ingredients

Toast-infused cream

4 cups (1 liter) UHT heavy cream (at least 35% milkfat)

9 oz. (250 g) toasted bread

½ Madagascar vanilla bean, split lengthwise

1 tbsp (10 g) brown sugar

¾ tsp (3 g) pectin X58 (in specialty shops and online)

1 egg yolk

1 tsp (3 g) gelatin powder dissolved in 1 tbsp (15 g) water (0.7 oz./18 g total weight)

Choux puffs

Scant ¾ cup (6 oz./170 g) water

Scant ¾ cup (6 oz./170 g) UHT whole milk

1 stick + 4 tbsp (6 oz./170 g) butter

1¼ tsp (6 g) sugar

¾ tsp (4 g) salt

1⅓ cups (6 oz./170 g) Kamut (Khorasan) flour, sifted

1⅓ cups (11 oz./310 g) lightly beaten egg (about 6 eggs)

Rice flour, for dusting

Almond-toast praline filling

Scant 1 cup (5.25 oz./150 g) raw almonds

2.75 oz. (80 g) bread, cut into pieces

Scant ⅓ cup (2.5 oz./70 g) water

¾ cup + 1½ tbsp (6 oz./170 g) sugar

1½ tbsp (1 oz./30 g) glucose syrup

Scant ¼ tsp (1 g) fleur de sel

Equipment

Immersion blender

Pastry bag fitted with a ½- or ¾-in. (1- or 1.5-cm) plain tip + 2 pastry bags fitted with ⅛-in. (3-mm) plain tips

Instant-read thermometer

Food processor

The day before baking, prepare the toast-infused cream: Warm the heavy cream in a saucepan over low heat. Remove from the heat and add the bread, broken into pieces. Scrape in the vanilla seeds, add the bean, and let infuse for 1 hour. Strain through a fine-mesh sieve into a bowl, pressing down to extract as much liquid as possible.

Measure or weigh out 2 cups (1 lb. 2 oz./500 g) of the infused cream and place in a saucepan. Warm over low heat. Combine the brown sugar and pectin in a bowl, add to the cream, and bring to a boil. Remove from the heat and add the egg yolk and gelatin-water mixture. Mix with the immersion blender until smooth. Let cool, then cover with plastic wrap, and chill in the refrigerator overnight.

The next day, prepare the choux puffs: Preheat the oven to 315°F (155°C/Gas Mark 2) and line a baking sheet with parchment paper. Combine the water, milk, butter, sugar, and salt in a saucepan. Bring to a simmer, stirring to dissolve the sugar. Remove from the heat and add the Kamut flour all at once. Stir vigorously until the dough forms a ball and pulls away from the sides of the pan. Return to low heat for several seconds, stirring nonstop, to dry the pastry out.

Transfer to the bowl of a stand mixer fitted with the paddle attachment. With the mixer running on low speed, gradually add the egg, beating between each addition until thoroughly incorporated. Stop adding egg when the pastry is shiny, smooth, and thick, but still pipeable. Spoon the pastry into the pastry bag with the ½- or ¾-in. (1- or 1.5-cm) plain tip and pipe out puffs weighing about 1.5 oz. (40 g) each onto the prepared baking sheet. Dust with the rice flour and bake for about 1 hour, until puffed and lightly golden. Transfer to a rack and let cool completely.

Prepare the almond-toast praline filling: Preheat the oven to 325°F (165°C/Gas Mark 3). Spread the almonds across a baking sheet and toast them for 20 minutes. Remove and place in a heat-resistant mixing bowl.

Increase the oven temperature to 400°F (200°C/Gas Mark 6). Spread the bread across the baking sheet and toast, turning if necessary, until deeply browned. Add to the bowl with the almonds.

In a saucepan, heat the water, sugar, and glucose syrup to 347°F (175°C). Add the *fleur de sel* and pour over the almonds and bread. Stir to combine and let cool completely. Process it to a smooth paste using the food processor.

Fill the puffs: Transfer the toast-infused cream and almond-toast praline filling to the two separate pastry bags fitted with ⅛-in. (3-mm) plain tips. Make a hole in the base of each choux puff with the tip of a paring knife. Fill each puff two-thirds full with the toast-infused cream and fill the remaining third with the praline filling. Chill the puffs in the refrigerator until serving.

Kouign-amann

———

Makes 1 large *kouign-amann*

Active time: 1 hour
Chilling: 30 minutes
Proofing: 1 hour
Cooking: 30–40 minutes

Ingredients

4 tbsp + 1 tsp (2.25 oz./65 g) butter, well chilled + 4 tbsp (2 oz./60 g) butter, softened

9 oz. (250 g) well-chilled baguette dough (see recipe p. 219), after bulk fermentation

½ cup (3.5 oz./100 g) sugar

¾ tsp (4 g) *fleur de sel*

Equipment

6–7-in. (15–18-cm) round cake pan

Place the 4 tbsp + 1 tsp (2.25 oz./65 g) well-chilled butter between two sheets of parchment paper and pat or roll it into a 6-in. (15-cm) square. Chill in the refrigerator until firm but still pliable before using.

When you are ready to proceed, roll the baguette dough into a 10-in. (25-cm) square on a flour-dusted work surface.

Place the butter in the center of the dough square diagonally, so that each corner of the butter faces a side of the dough. Fold in each corner of the dough toward the center and lightly pinch the seams together, completely enclosing the butter.

Roll the dough into a rectangle three times as long as it is wide, with a short end facing you. Fold the dough in three, like a business letter—this is known as a single turn. Rotate the dough 90° clockwise, so that the seam is facing right, like a book. Give the dough one more single turn in the same direction, lightly flouring the dough and work surface as needed to prevent sticking. After the second turn, cover the dough and chill in the refrigerator for 30 minutes.

Roll the dough into a 10-in. (25-cm) square, dusting with flour as needed. Gently spread three-quarters of the softened butter over the square, then sprinkle with about two-thirds of the sugar and half of the *fleur de sel*. Fold the corners of the dough in to meet in the center and lightly pinch the seams together.

Break half of the remaining butter into small pieces and scatter over the point where the four corners of the dough meet in the center. Sprinkle with half of the remaining sugar and the remaining *fleur de sel*. Shape the dough into a ball with the seam side down.

Line the cake pan with parchment paper and place the dough in the center, seam-side down. Flatten the dough to a thickness of 1–1½ in. (3–4 cm) using the palm of your hand. Gently spread the remaining butter over the top and sprinkle with the remaining sugar. Let rise in a warm place for 1 hour (about 77°F/25°C), until puffed and slightly risen (proofing*).

Toward the end of the rising time, preheat the oven to 350°F (180°C/Gas Mark 4).

Place the cake pan on a baking sheet to catch any butter that drips out and bake for 30–40 minutes, until caramelized and golden.

Let the *kouign-amann* cool slightly in the pan, then turn it out and remove the parchment paper.

Serve warm.

Technique
Stages of fermentation

Glace au pain grillé

Toast Ice Cream

———

Serves 6

Active time: 15 minutes
Soaking: 1 hour
Chilling: At least 2 hours
Cooking: 5 minutes

Ingredients

Toast ice cream

4 cups (1 liter) whole milk
4–5 slices stale bread
5 egg yolks
2½ tbsp (1 oz./30 g) sugar
1 tbsp honey

Bread *tuiles*

A few slices *pain de mie*
(see recipe p. 222)
2 tbsp (1 oz./30 g) salted butter, melted
2½ tbsp (1 oz./30 g) sugar

Equipment

Ice cream maker

Prepare the toast ice cream: Pour the milk into a large mixing bowl.

Toast the slices of bread until deeply golden—stop just short of burning them. Immerse in the milk and let soak for at least 1 hour.

Strain the milk through a fine-mesh sieve into a large saucepan, discarding the bread, and bring to a simmer over low heat.

Whisk together the egg yolks, sugar, and honey in a mixing bowl until pale and thick. Gradually pour in one-third of the hot milk, whisking nonstop. Return to the saucepan and whisk to blend.

Cook over low heat, stirring nonstop with a flexible spatula, until the custard thickens. When it coats the back of the spatula, remove the saucepan from the heat. Pour into an airtight container, let cool slightly, then cover and chill in the refrigerator for at least 2 hours, or until cold.

Churn the chilled custard in the ice cream maker according to the manufacturer's instructions. Transfer ice cream to an airtight container and keep in the freezer until using.

Prepare the bread *tuiles*: Preheat the oven to 350°F (180°C/Gas Mark 4).

Remove the crust from the bread slices (save for another recipe, such as croutons p. 199). Using a rolling pin, flatten the slices until quite thin, then brush them with the melted butter. Place on a baking sheet, either nonstick or lined with parchment paper, and sprinkle with the sugar. Toast in the oven for 10 minutes, until browned around the edges.

Transfer the *tuiles* to a rack and let them cool completely so that they are crisp before serving.

Serve scoops of the toast ice cream with bread *tuiles* on the side.

Pain perdu gourmand

Decadent French Toast

_____

Serves 4

Active time: 10 minutes
Cooking: 25–30 minutes

Ingredients

4 eggs

Scant ½ cup (100 ml) whole milk

Scant ½ cup (100 ml) cream

Scant 2 tsp (7.5 g) vanilla sugar

1 tsp rum and/or ½ tsp ground cinnamon (optional)

4 thick slices stale *pain de campagne* (see recipe p. 250) or *pain de mie* (see recipe p. 222)

2 tbsp (25 g) butter

2 tsp muscovado sugar

For serving

Confectioners' sugar, for dusting

Fresh berries

Crème fraîche or whipped cream

Place a rack in the center of the oven and preheat the oven to 480°F (250°C/Gas Mark 9). If you do not have a nonstick baking sheet, line a baking sheet with parchment paper.

Whisk together the eggs, milk, cream, and vanilla sugar in a dish you can dip the bread in. Whisk in the rum and/or cinnamon, if you wish.

Soak the slices of bread on both sides in the egg mixture until saturated. Place on the nonstick or parchment-lined baking sheet.

Bake for 20–25 minutes, until cooked through and lightly golden.

Right before serving, melt the butter in a skillet. Sprinkle the French toast slices with the muscovado sugar and cook on both sides in the skillet until golden and crisp.

Dust with confectioners' sugar and serve with fresh berries and a dollop of crème fraîche or whipped cream.

Charlotte aux pommes à l'ancienne

Old-Fashioned Apple Charlotte

————

Serves 6

Active time: 40 minutes
Chilling: 30 minutes
Cooking: 40 minutes

Ingredients

10 firm baking apples, such as King of the Pippins (Reine de Reinettes) or Bramleys

5 tbsp (2.5 oz./75 g) unsalted or salted butter, divided

4 tbsp (1.75 oz./50 g) muscovado or brown sugar

2 tbsp apricot jam

Juice of 1 lemon

1 vanilla bean, split lengthwise, + ½ tsp ground cinnamon, or 3½ tbsp (50 ml) Calvados

15–20 thin slices *pain de mie* (see recipe p. 222)

Confectioners' sugar, for dusting

Equipment

8-in. (20-cm) charlotte pan

To prepare the apple filling, chill a baking sheet in the refrigerator. Peel and core the apples and remove any remaining seeds, then chop them roughly.

Melt 3 tbsp (1.75 oz./50 g) of the butter in a skillet over medium heat. Add the apples and sauté until they begin to brown around the edges, then add the sugar, lemon juice, and your flavoring of choice (the vanilla bean and cinnamon or the Calvados).

Cover, reduce the heat to low, and let simmer, stirring often, until the apples are completely tender. Remove the lid and continue cooking until the excess liquid has evaporated.

Stir in the apricot jam, then remove from the heat and spread the apples across the chilled baking sheet. Press plastic wrap over the surface and chill in the refrigerator for 3 minutes.

Meanwhile, preheat the oven to 350°F (180°C/Gas Mark 4).

Remove the crust from the bread slices (save for another recipe, such as croutons p. 199, or use for to make breadcrumbs). Cut each slice in half vertically to line the sides and then again into triangles for the top.

Melt the remaining butter in a small saucepan or skillet and remove from the heat. Briefly dip the bread in the butter, letting the excess drip off. Line the base and sides of the charlotte pan with the butter-dipped bread pieces, overlapping them slightly.

Add half of the apple filling to the pan and cover it with a layer of butter-dipped bread pieces. Top with the remaining apple filling, then dip the remaining bread in the melted butter and completely cover the apples.

Bake for about 40 minutes, until deeply golden.

Let cool for several minutes, then run a knife around the edge to release the charlotte from the sides of the pan while it is still warm. Carefully invert onto a serving plate, but do not remove the pan until right before serving.

Serve at room temperature or chilled.

LA BONNE IDÉE
This charlotte is divine with crème anglaise drizzled over the top.

Bread Pudding

Serves 6

Active time: 30 minutes
Soaking: 1 hour
Cooking: 40 minutes

Ingredients

1 lb. 2 oz. (500 g) stale bread, broken into pieces
4 cups (1 liter) whole milk + more if necessary
¾ cup + 1 tbsp (200 ml) amber rum
⅓ cup (1.75 oz./50 g) raisins
Butter, for the pan
½ cup (3.5 oz./100 g) sugar
3 eggs, beaten
½ tsp (3 g) ground cinnamon
1–2 tsp all-purpose flour, if necessary
Confectioners' sugar, for dusting

Equipment

Oven-safe Pyrex bowl or medium loaf pan with a 1½-qt. (1.4-liter) capacity

Place the bread in a large bowl and pour in the milk—the bread should be completely covered. Let soak until the bread is fully saturated and soft (about 1 hour).

Meanwhile, warm the rum and pour it over the raisins in a bowl. Let soak until the raisins are softened and plump.

Preheat the oven to 350°F (180°C/Gas Mark 4) and generously grease the Pyrex bowl or loaf pan with butter.

Roughly mash the bread in the milk using a fork, then add the sugar, eggs, and cinnamon. Drain the rum-soaked raisins and add them to the bowl. Stir until well combined. The batter should be semi-thick—neither runny nor dense. If necessary, add 1–2 tsp flour or a little more milk.

Pour the batter into the prepared dish and bake for 40 minutes, or until a knife inserted into the center comes out clean.

As soon as you remove the pudding from the oven, run a spatula or knife around the edge to release the pudding from the bowl. Let the pudding cool slightly or completely in the dish before turning it out onto a serving plate.

Dust with confectioners' sugar and serve warm, at room temperature, or chilled.

LA BONNE IDÉE
You can swap out the raisins for pitted prunes or very thinly sliced apples.

Soupe au lait et au pain

Sweet Bread and Milk Soup

_____

Serves 4

Active time: 10 minutes
Cooking: 8 minutes

Ingredients

4 thick slices bread of your choice

1 tbsp (20 g) salted butter

¼ cup + 2½ tbsp (2.75 oz./80 g) sugar, cane if possible, divided

2 tbsp roughly chopped toasted hazelnuts

4 cups (1 liter) whole milk

4 pinches freshly grated Tonka bean, or use a vanilla pod, seeds scraped, if not available

Cut the bread into cubes.

In a nonstick skillet, melt the butter over medium heat. Add the bread and sprinkle with 3½ tbsp (1.5 oz./40 g) of the sugar. Add the hazelnuts and cook for 5 minutes until the bread is golden and crisp all over. Remove from the heat.

Combine the milk, remaining sugar, and Tonka bean (or vanilla seeds) in a saucepan. Bring to a boil, stirring to dissolve the sugar.

Divide the hot milk between four soup bowls and add the hazelnuts and toasted bread. Serve right away.

LA BONNE IDÉE

To make this soup even more decadent, melt 5.25 oz. (150 g) of a good dark chocolate (the darker the better) in the hot milk.

Bread and Butter Pudding

Serves 4

Active time: 15 minutes
Cooking: 30–40 minutes

Ingredients

6 tbsp (3 oz./90 g) butter, divided

7 oz. (200 g) blueberries, blackberries, or raspberries

1 cup (250 ml) whole milk

Finely grated zest of 1 lemon, preferably organic

2 tbsp orange flower water

3 eggs

⅓ cup (2.75 oz./75 g) sugar, divided

6 large slices *pain de mie* (see recipe p. 222)

Equipment

8½ in. × 5½-in. (22 × 14-cm) baking dish

Preheat the oven to 350°F (180°C/Gas Mark 4) and grease the baking dish with 1 tbsp (20 g) of the butter. Wash the berries and pat them dry.

Combine the milk, lemon zest, and orange flower water in a saucepan and bring to a boil.

In a bowl, whisk together the eggs and ¼ cup (1.75 oz./50 g) of the sugar.

Melt the remaining butter in a small saucepan or in the microwave. Cut each slice in half and brush generously with the melted butter. Arrange the slices in the prepared dish, making an attractive pattern. Scatter the fruit between the slices, then pour in the milk, followed by the egg-sugar mixture. Sprinkle with the remaining sugar and bake for 30–40 minutes, until the custard is set and the bread is deeply golden.

Serve warm or at room temperature.

LA BONNE IDÉE

To boost the color, texture, and flavor of this bread pudding, sprinkle it with roughly chopped pistachios.

Jessica
Préalpato
—

"Bread represents my childhood; my father was a baker. He had his own style of bread with a distinctly colored crust and a pretty sour levain. I was immersed in the world of bread. What I love most of all is the feel of dough and the scent of the bakery, which remind me of being a child.

"This dessert came to me following a meeting with a supplier who invited us to taste everything a beehive can produce, including pollen and wax cells filled with honey. The chef at the Plaza Athénée, Romain Meder, wanted to create little appetizers using honey that would be served to clients upon their arrival. I was intrigued by the idea of opening a meal with something sweet. Monsieur Ducasse [chef Alain Ducasse] came up with the tartine, then our head baker Guillaume Cabrol spent a lot of time developing a recipe for beeswax bread, something dense and without too many holes that could work with a spread.

"Within the Naturalness concept we've developed at the Plaza, the finished plate showcases our suppliers' superb produce. Clients are forced out of their comfort zone at times, so I also try to include a hint of indulgence, like this *tartine*. What I mean by indulgent is something comforting—it's what puts you back on familiar ground or brings a pleasant memory to mind. For me, that would be the bread my father made."

After studying literature, Jessica Préalpato made a career shift to pastry, a profession she shares with her father and brother. The young woman from Landes, France, trained with Philippe Labbé, Philippe Etchebest, and Frédéric Vardon. In 2015, she joined the team at the Plaza Athénée in Paris, where she expresses Alain Ducasse's Naturalness concept with low-sugar, ingredient-forward desserts that demonstrate her perfect mastery of sour and bitter flavors. In 2019, The World's 50 Best Restaurants organization awarded her the title of World's Best Pastry Chef.

Restaurant Alain Ducasse at the Plaza Athénée:
www.alainducasse-plazaathenee.com

Tartine de pain à la cire, rayon de miel émulsionné, pollen frais

Beeswax Bread Tartines with Honeycomb Spread and Fresh Pollen

Recipe by Jessica Préalpato

———

Makes 10 tartines

Active time: 30 minutes
Bulk fermentation: 12 hours
Proofing: 4 hours
Cooking: 30 minutes

Ingredients

Beeswax bread

3¼ cups (14 oz./400 g) bread flour (T65)

¾ cup + 2 tbsp (3.5 oz./100 g) stoneground white whole wheat or light whole wheat flour (T80–T110)

1.75 oz. (50 g) *pâte fermentée* (see Good to Know), or 1.75 oz. (50 g) refreshed levain

0.2 oz. (5 g) barley malt syrup (optional)

1 tsp (0.2 oz./5 g) salt

1.5 oz. (40 g) food-grade beeswax, cut into pieces

1 cup (9 oz./250 g) water at 39.2°F (4°C) + a scant ½ cup (3.5 oz./100 g) room-temperature water

Honeycomb spread

7 oz. (200 g) honeycomb, or a scant ⅓ cup (3.5 oz./100 g) honey + 3.5 oz. (100 g) food-grade beeswax

Assembly

½ tsp (3 g) fresh rock rose (*Cistus ladanifer*) bee pollen granules, or use a locally produced pollen

½ tsp (3 g) fresh spring bee pollen granules

Equipment

Rectangular cake frame or a nonstick lasagna pan

Pacojet, Thermomix, or another high-speed blender

Immersion blender

Techniques

Refreshing levain
Stages of fermentation

A day before baking, prepare the beeswax bread: Place all of the ingredients for the bread except for the beeswax and water in the bowl of a stand mixer fitted with the dough hook. Place the beeswax and water in a microwave-safe bowl (it will be very difficult to clean, so disposable is best). Heat for 2 minutes on high, or until melted. Alternatively, melt in a bowl set over a saucepan of barely simmering water (bain-marie). Pour the melted wax mixture into the bowl of the stand mixer with the rest of the ingredients. Knead for 3 minutes on speed 1, followed by 9 minutes on speed 2.

If you are using a cake frame, place it on a 14 × 10-in. (36 × 26-cm) baking sheet, either nonstick or lined with parchment paper. Place the dough inside the frame or lasagna pan and spread to a thickness of 1¼ in. (3 cm). Cover tightly and let rest in the refrigerator for 12 hours (bulk fermentation*).

The next day, remove the dough from the refrigerator and let it rise for 4 hours at 75°F/24°C (proofing*).

Toward the end of the rising time, preheat the oven to 450°F (240°C/Gas Mark 8). Bake for 10 minutes, then turn the oven off and let the bread continue to bake, without opening the oven door, for an additional 10 minutes. Turn the oven on again, set to 450°F (240°C/Gas Mark 8), and prop the door ajar. Let the bread bake for another 10 minutes.

Carefully remove the cake frame, or turn the bread out of the pan. Place the bread on a rack to cool.

Prepare the honeycomb spread: If you are using honeycomb, freeze it and then process it until completely smooth using a Pacojet, Thermomix, or high-speed blender (if you are using a Pacojet, you can freeze the honeycomb directly in the beaker according to the manufacturer's instructions and "pacotize" it once frozen). If you are using honey and beeswax, melt them together in the microwave or over a bain-marie, then emulsify well with the immersion blender.

Assemble the tartines: Right before serving, cut the beeswax bread into very thin slices and toast under the broiler, keeping a close eye on the color. Spread each slice with a thin layer of honeycomb spread, sprinkle with fresh pollen, and serve right away.

 GOOD TO KNOW

Pâte fermentée is a small amount of bread dough reserved from a loaf before baking (see p. 138). For this recipe, set aside a little bread dough from another bread in this book.

INDEX

SELECTED BIBLIOGRAPHY

Bertinet, Richard. *Crumb: Show the Dough Who's Boss.* London: Kyle Books, 2019.

———. *Crust: From Sourdough, Spelt and Rye Bread to Ciabatta, Bagels and Brioche.* London: Kyle Books, 2019.

———. *Dough: Simple Contemporary Bread.* London: Kyle Cathie Limited, 2005.

Collaert, Jean-Claude. *Céréales: La Plus Grande Saga que le Monde Ait Vécue.* Paris: Rue de l'Echiquier, 2013.

de Tonnac, Jean-Philippe, ed. *Dictionnaire Universel du Pain.* Paris: Robert Laffont, 2010.

Ford, Bryan. *New World Sourdough: Artisan Techniques for Creative Homemade Fermented Breads.* Beverly: Quarry Books, 2020.

Forkish, Ken. *Flour, Water, Salt, Yeast: The Fundamentals of Artisan Bread and Pizza.* Berkeley: Ten Speed Press, 2012.

Gaudry, François-Régis. *Let's Eat France!* New York: Artisan, 2018.

Ginsberg, Stanley. *The Rye Baker: Classic Breads from Europe and America.* New York: W.W. Norton & Company, 2016.

Hadjiandreou, Emmanuel. *How to Make Sourdough: 45 Recipes for Great-Tasting Sourdough Breads that Are Good for You, Too.* London: Ryland Peters & Small, 2016.

———. *How to Make Bread: Step-by-Step Recipes for Yeasted Breads, Sourdoughs, Soda Breads, and Pastries.* London: Ryland Peters & Small, 2011.

Kimbell, Vanessa. *The Sourdough School: The Ground-Breaking Guide to Making Gut-Friendly Bread.* London: Kyle Cathie Limited, 2018.

Lahey, Jim. *My Bread: The Revolutionary No-Work, No-Knead Method.* New York: W.W. Norton & Company, 2009.

Myhrvold, Nathan, and Francisco Migoya. *Modernist Bread.* Bellevue: The Cooking Lab, 2017.

Poilâne, Apollonia. *Poilâne: The Secrets of the World-Famous Bread Bakery.* Boston: Rux Martin/Houghton Mifflin Harcourt, 2019.

Poilâne, Lionel. *Guide de l'Amateur de Pain.* Paris: Robert Laffont, 1989.

Quinn, Bob, and Liz Carlisle. *Grain By Grain: A Quest to Revive Ancient Wheat, Rural Jobs, and Healthy Food.* Washington, D.C.: Island Press, 2019.

Robertson, Chad. *Tartine Bread.* San Francisco: Chronicle Books, 2010.

ACKNOWLEDGMENTS

The author would like to thank:
Roland Feuillas, for his friendship and for his love of bread, which never fails to inspire me.
Olivier Vandromme, who kindly accepted the role of technical adviser.
Alex Croquet, my baker "*co-pain*" in Lille.
Valérie Lhomme and Bérengère Abraham—my two essential companions on this baking adventure—for the photography and photo styling respectively, as well as Alice Licata, who assisted them so efficiently.
Ryma Bouzid, who came to us with this project.
Esterelle Payany, who played the intermediary and opened a few doors at Flammarion.
All the bakers, pastry makers, chefs, and brewers who kindly shared their vision of bread, as well as their recipes, for this book.
Dr. Anthony Fardet, for reviewing the sections on nutrition with a wise and benevolent eye.
Véronique Delaporte, my best reader and friend.
Jean-Baptiste Cokelaer, mushroom expert.
Victor, Louise, and Adèle, to whom I hope I have passed down a love of good bread.
Hugues, for his unconditional support and willingness to sample my baking experiments.

The photographer would like to thank:
Marie-Laure Fréchet, with whom it is always a great pleasure to work and share ideas.
Bérengère Abraham, for her talent and constant friendship.
Alice Licata, for her invaluable help.
Ryma Bouzid, for being so attentive.

Supplies
Thank you to Margot Lhomme, Christiane Perrochon, and Jérôme Hirson, for their beautiful ceramic ware. Thank you to KitchenAid and Émile Henry.

Follow the author on **Instagram @mlfrechet**